D1175426

# NATO'S EMPTY VICTORY

# NATO'S EMPTY VICTORY

## A Postmortem on the Balkan War

edited by Ted Galen Carpenter

CATO INSTITUTE
Washington, D.C.

**Library of Congress Cataloging-in-Publication Data**

NATO's empty victory : a postmortem on the Balkan War / edited by
Ted Galen Carpenter.
   p. cm.
Includes bibliographical references and index.
ISBN 1-882577-85-X -- ISBN 1-882577-86-8
  1. Kosovo (Serbia)--History--Civil War, 1998---Participation, Foreign.
2. North Atlantic Treaty Organization--Yugoslavia--Kosovo (Serbia)
3. United States--Foreign relations--Yugoslavia. 4. Yugoslavia--Foreign
relations--United States. 5. Intervention (International law)
I. Carpenter, Ted Galen.

DR2087 .N38 2000
949.71--dc21                                                         99-054830

Printed in the United States of America.

CATO INSTITUTE
1000 Massachusetts Ave., N.W.
Washington, D.C. 20001

# Contents

# Acknowledgments

I owe a debt of gratitude to numerous people who helped make the publication of *NATO's Empty Victory* a reality. Edward H. Crane and William A. Niskanen, respectively president and chairman of the Cato Institute, have provided consistent support for Cato's foreign policy program in general and for work on Washington's Balkan policy in particular. David Boaz, Cato's executive vice president, reviewed the manuscript and offered a variety of helpful suggestions. David Lampo, the Institute's director of publications, helped keep me on schedule with periodic—and occasionally insistent—reminders of deadlines. Emily Smith labored long and hard to incorporate the revisions made by the authors. Eric Wang helped speed the editorial process by locating sometimes elusive sources. Marian Council designed a book jacket that is both appealing and provocative.

My copyeditor, Elizabeth W. Kaplan, did an excellent job of improving the manuscript and preparing it for publication. This is the sixth book project on which we have collaborated, and it has been a pleasure working with such a consummate professional on each occasion. As usual, she has gone beyond the duties normally expected of a copyeditor and provided incisive stylistic and substantive critiques of the manuscript.

A special debt of gratitude is owed to my colleague Gary Dempsey, one of the brightest stars in a new generation of experts on Balkan issues. Not only is he the author of one of the chapters and coauthor of another, but he helped facilitate publication in innumerable ways. Without his extensive assistance, it would have been impossible to publish the book in such a timely fashion.

Finally, I want to thank the various authors for their cooperation and enthusiasm. It has been a pleasure to work with them, and I believe that our collective endeavor has produced a book that identifies the real causes and consequences of NATO's war in the Balkans. The analyses contained in the book will help debunk the rapidly emerging myth that NATO achieved a great and lasting victory in that conflict.

# Introduction: A Great Victory?

*Ted Galen Carpenter*

Almost as soon as the bombs stopped falling on Yugoslavia, the Clinton administration and the other NATO governments proclaimed that the alliance had scored a great victory. They emphasized that Yugoslavia's president, Slobodan Milosevic, had capitulated to their demands for a NATO-led peacekeeping force in Kosovo and that the Albanian Kosovar refugees would be able to return to their homes. According to proponents of the war, NATO had waged a successful campaign to prevent genocide; had enhanced its credibility as an effective institution for preserving peace, stability, and justice in post–Cold War Europe; and had struck fear in the hearts of would-be aggressors around the world.

In the narrowest sense (Belgrade ultimately capitulated and the refugees returned to Kosovo), it is possible for U.S. and West European officials to "spin" the NATO bombing campaign as a victory. But all policies must be judged in their total context, and on that basis the outcome is far less impressive. Indeed, the results to date appear to be just shy of a full-blown policy fiasco. The spectacle of Albanian Kosovars attacking peacekeepers who attempt to block them from cleansing Kosovo of its remaining Serbian inhabitants (as well as Gypsies and all other non-Albanians) is only the most visible and potent symbol of an intervention that went tragically wrong.

The entire policy was ill-conceived from the outset. Although NATO leaders are loath to concede the point, there is little question that the air war lasted far longer and proved considerably more difficult than they had anticipated. As Christopher Layne shows in Chapter 1, Secretary of State Madeleine Albright and other policymakers assumed that Milosevic would either respond to NATO's ultimatum and sign the Rambouillet peace accord at the 11th hour or would do so after a brief "demonstration" bombing campaign lasting a few days. That was a grave miscalculation. The actual result

1

was an enormously destructive air war that lasted 78 days. Moreover, the war ended only when the alliance agreed to dilute the Rambouillet diktat in several respects—including explicitly acknowledging that Kosovo would remain part of Serbia and giving up the demand that NATO forces have free movement throughout all of Yugoslavia.

NATO's intransigent, confrontational negotiating stance at Rambouillet raises questions about whether the alliance was sincere about wanting a peaceful resolution to the Kosovo dispute. In Chapter 2, James George Jatras argues that NATO policy was based on a simplistic and unfair interpretation of the problems in Kosovo. Alliance leaders, especially Secretary Albright, openly sympathized with the Albanian Kosovars and placed all the blame for a complex dispute at Belgrade's door. The NATO governments seemed oblivious to the terrorist roots and other unsavory aspects of the Kosovo Liberation Army, the fact that the KLA was waging an armed insurgency against the Yugoslav government, and the probable destabilizing consequences throughout the region of the KLA's goal of creating a Greater Albania.

Doug Bandow points out in Chapter 3 that NATO was more than a trifle hypocritical in arguing that the situation in Kosovo constituted genocide and that the alliance could not stand by and let such an offense to humanity go unchallenged. During the 12 months before the NATO bombing campaign commenced, some 2,000 people—a quarter of whom were Serbs—had been killed in Kosovo. That total did not place the Kosovo struggle in even the top dozen conflicts that erupted in the world in the 1990s. Bandow observes that more people were killed in one month in Sierra Leone than perished in Kosovo during an entire year and that nearly as many died in one weekend of fighting between government and rebel forces in Sri Lanka as did during that year in Kosovo.

Closer to home, NATO has remained on the sidelines while more than 70,000 civilians have been killed in the bloody civil war that has engulfed Algeria since 1992. Worst of all, Bandow contends, is NATO's double standard of tolerating ethnic cleansing and other atrocities committed by one of the alliance's own members, Turkey. Turkish forces invaded Cyprus in 1974, occupied nearly 40 percent of the country, expelled more than 165,000 Greek Cypriots, created an ethnically pure puppet state in northern Cyprus, and brought in nearly 100,000 colonists from Turkey. In addition to its outrageous behavior in Cyprus, the Turkish government has waged a brutal war against a Kurdish secessionist rebellion in southeastern Turkey— committing many of the same offenses that NATO found intolerable when committed by Serbian forces in Kosovo. Yet the alliance not only did not threaten to take military action against Ankara, it allowed Turkey to take part in the military campaign against Serbia.

The results of the conflict could hardly have been what alliance leaders had in mind. In Chapter 4 Layne documents the extent of the tragedy for Serbian civilians and Albanian Kosovars alike. As the war went on, the list of bombing targets in Serbia and its sister republic Montenegro expanded to include such things as highway bridges and the electric power grid. The destruction of such targets had an adverse impact that was at least as great on civilians as on the Yugoslav military. There were also a distressing number of mistaken strikes by NATO aircraft, leading to the deaths of several hundred civilians. Worried about continuing public opposition to the war in some NATO countries (especially Greece, Italy, and the United States) that might be exacerbated if pilots were lost in combat, most of the bombing was conducted from elevations above 15,000 feet—increasing the likelihood of unintended civilian casualties.

Perhaps the most damning evidence that alliance officials miscalculated at Rambouillet was that there was so little preparation for the flood of refugees from Kosovo. Various Balkan experts had predicted for months that Belgrade would likely respond to any NATO military coercion by intensifying its offensive against the KLA and seeking to expel much of the Albanian population from Kosovo. That is precisely what happened, yet the alliance was so unprepared for that widely predicted response that it failed to have adequate quantities of tents, food, and medical supplies on hand to deal with a refugee crisis. There is little doubt that, at least in the short term, NATO's decision to launch a military campaign to help the Albanian Kosovars had exactly the opposite effect, turning an already bad situation into a humanitarian crisis.

Gary Dempsey notes in Chapter 5 that the intervention also had a deleterious impact on neighboring countries in the Balkans. All nations in the region suffered a blow to their economies as the conflict caused tourism to decline, disrupted normal trade routes, and frightened away investors. For example, air strikes destroyed several bridges over the Danube River, dumping wreckage into

3

southeastern Europe's longest and most important waterway and closing it to commerce. Indeed, with the NATO powers maintaining economic sanctions against Belgrade even after the war, there is little prospect that all of the bridges will be rebuilt and the river reopened to commerce anytime soon. Since many of the southeast European states had been economic laggards throughout the post–Cold War period, the last thing they needed was the turmoil caused by NATO's war.

In addition to the adverse economic impact, Dempsey contends that the intervention deepened dangerous social and ethnic divisions in neighboring countries, especially Macedonia. By strengthening the position of the KLA, NATO may have boosted the prospects of those who seek to create a Greater Albania—the principal nightmare of the governments of both Macedonia and Greece.

The disruptive effects of the war were not confined to the Balkans. As I point out in Chapter 6, the NATO intervention badly damaged the West's relations with both Russia and China. Pro-democratic Russian political leaders and intellectuals warn that there is now a large reservoir of genuine anti-Western (especially anti-American) sentiment in their country. There is little doubt that widespread Russian anger at the war—and at Russia's shabby treatment after the conflict when, despite Moscow's successful mediation efforts to help end the fighting, NATO refused to give Russia a peacekeeping zone in Kosovo—has significantly strengthened communist and ultranationalist political elements. The premature and unauthorized entry of Russian troops into Kosovo, and the resulting face-off between Russian and British forces at Pristina airport, was an apt symbol of the deterioration of relations between NATO and Russia.

As if alienating Russia were not a high enough price to pay for the Balkan war, the West also managed to antagonize China. The (apparently accidental) bombing of the Chinese embassy in Belgrade triggered a spasm of violently anti-American demonstrations in cities throughout China. It also intensified already substantial suspicions on the part of Beijing that the United States and its allies were embarked on a policy of global hegemony and that the West might someday seek to apply the Kosovo model (a dictated peace accord backed by the threat of military force) to the problems of Taiwan and Tibet. Anger at perceived Western arrogance has led to a sharp increase in strategic cooperation between Russia and China—perhaps even the initial phase of a Moscow-Beijing axis. If that occurs, the United States and the rest of NATO will have paid a very high price indeed for the "victory" in the Balkans.

Stanley Kober documents two other unfortunate consequences of the Balkan war in Chapters 7 and 8. The president's decision to authorize NATO to launch attacks on Yugoslavia without congressional approval was an astoundingly brazen example of the imperial presidency in action. Yet liberals who had denounced presidential wars in the past were strangely silent about that aspect of the Balkan intervention and did little to reassert the already frayed and tattered congressional war power. Indeed, most of them endorsed the administration's policy. Kober argues that such a precedent will make presidential usurpation of the war power even more likely in the future, contrary to the explicit intentions of the architects of the Constitution, who never wanted just one person to make the momentous decision to take the Republic into war. Kober also believes that Clinton's decision sets a dangerous example of uncontrolled executive power for countries around the world that look to the United States as a political model.

The war itself altered international perceptions of the United States and NATO in other unhealthy ways, Kober contends. Outside the roster of NATO members and other key U.S. allies (and a few European aspirants to NATO membership), global opinion was harshly critical of the bombing campaign. Opinion-forming elites in much of the world, including such key countries as India and Egypt, saw NATO's new doctrine of humanitarian intervention as little more than a facade for imperialism. The arrogance of the United States and its allies in bypassing the United Nations Security Council was especially infuriating to critics. Not only do rekindled fears of Western imperialism increase the likelihood that countries may join together to counter Washington's vast power and influence, but the growing apprehension is also impelling some of those countries to place new emphasis on acquiring credible nuclear deterrents. By mauling a small and largely defenseless Balkan country, the NATO powers may have inadvertently undermined their goal of preventing the proliferation of nuclear weapons.

The end of NATO's military campaign hardly means the end of the alliance's problems in the Balkans. To the contrary, it may be merely the start of even more frustrating and intractable troubles. Both Michael Radu in Chapter 9 and John J. Mearsheimer in Chapter

10 urge NATO leaders to begin to think outside the box on Balkan issues. Radu warns that the greatest danger to the stability of the region in the future is not Serbian expansionism but Albanian expansionism. Although partition of Kosovo and the realignment of the borders of the successor states to the defunct Yugoslav federation might create greater stability, Radu cautions that there are no easy or reliable options.

Mearsheimer argues that NATO's goal of a stable, tolerant, multiethnic Kosovo is a pipe dream. He notes that there is no instance in modern history of rival ethnic groups having waged a bloody civil war and then established a workable long-term arrangement for sharing power. The only lasting solution to the Kosovo controversy in his judgment is to partition the province. Although Belgrade would normally be expected to balk at such a proposal, Serbian leaders might ultimately accept it as part of a package deal in which the Serbian republic in Bosnia was allowed to merge with Serbia. Since Bosnia is an utterly dysfunctional Potemkin country sustained only by vast infusions of foreign aid and the presence of a large NATO peacekeeping force, partition is the only realistic option in that case as well. Mearsheimer warns that the likely alternative to a package deal based on partition and ethnic separation—however repulsive that step might be from the standpoint of Western values—is for NATO to police Kosovo and Bosnia indefinitely.

Gary Dempsey and Spiros Rizopoulos contend in Chapter 11 that the countries of southeastern Europe are ahead of the United States and the other major NATO powers in thinking about future economic, political, and security arrangements for the region. Several regional initiatives, including the establishment of the Southeast European Brigade, offer viable alternatives to making the Balkans a NATO protectorate. Dempsey and Rizopoulos note that Operation Alba—the ad hoc coalition led by Italy and Greece that intervened in Albania in 1996 when that country was convulsed by financial and political scandals and teetered on the brink of civil war—demonstrates that the Balkan countries can address troublesome security issues without NATO.

The war against Yugoslavia may have stimulated renewed interest in European-directed security institutions beyond the Balkan countries, according to Jonathan G. Clarke in Chapter 12. He notes the increasing discussions and more tangible steps to establish a common security and foreign policy—and ultimately, perhaps, a distinct

European defense identity—within the European Union. Clarke cautions, however, that rhetoric about a more active and vigorous security role for the European powers has been heard before, only to dissipate in a blizzard of worthless new acronyms and paper institutions. The real test will be whether the key EU members increase their military spending and develop the power to implement a common security and foreign policy. In addition to a more robust EU on security issues, Clarke sees the potential to invigorate the Organization for Security and Cooperation in Europe to handle future conflict-prevention missions.

I point out in Chapter 13 that, despite some intriguing hints of greater European initiative, alliance leaders seem intent on preserving a NATO-centric security policy indefinitely. The new Strategic Concept, adopted at the NATO summit meeting in April 1999, envisions the alliance routinely using its military forces in conflict-prevention and nation-building missions. Thus, the interventions in Bosnia and Kosovo are a model for NATO's primary role in the 21st century. Worst of all, there is no discernible geographic limit to such interventions. Secretary Albright has already asserted that NATO must be willing to deal with security problems from the Middle East to Central Africa. Other proponents of the "new NATO" assert that the alliance should be prepared to defend "Western interests" wherever they might be imperiled. At the April 1999 summit, alliance leaders expressed an interest in the simmering conflicts of the Caucasus region—perhaps the next arena for an intervention.

The transformation of NATO from an alliance to defend the territory of its members to an ambitious crisis-management organization has profound and disturbing implications for the United States. Although America has some important strategic and economic interests in Europe, it is not a European power and, therefore, should not have to be concerned about every adverse development on the Continent. U.S. policymakers need to discriminate between developments involving Europe's major powers—which have the potential to create a dangerous level of instability and jeopardize key American interests—and parochial quarrels and conflicts that should be left to the leading European states to resolve as they choose. NATO's metamorphosis into a crisis-intervention institution has the potential to entangle the United States in an endless array of messy, irrelevant disputes. If that is going to be the role of the new NATO, then even

7

supporters of NATO's traditional role should rethink the wisdom of America's continued membership in the alliance.

The United States and its allies technically may have achieved a military victory against Yugoslavia, but it is an empty victory. NATO's "reward" for its triumph is to become Kosovo's guardian for years and probably decades—the most thankless and pointless mission imaginable. Instead of having one Balkan protectorate (Bosnia), the alliance now has two. Indeed, one could make the argument that NATO actually has four protectorates, given the extent of its political and military presence in Macedonia and Albania.

In the course of acquiring the dubious role of baby sitter of the Balkans, NATO inflicted enormous suffering on innocent Serbian and Albanian Kosovar civilians; created serious economic and political problems for neighboring Balkan countries, thereby making additional conflicts more likely; stimulated fears throughout the world that the democratic West had embarked on a new round of imperialism under a phony banner of humanitarian intervention; further undermined a key provision of the U.S. Constitution; and badly damaged relations with two important powers, Russia and China. If those are the characteristics of a victory, one hates to contemplate the results of a policy failure.

PART I

COULD THE CONFLICT HAVE BEEN AVERTED?

# 1. Miscalculations and Blunders Lead to War

*Christopher Layne*

The Clinton administration made one miscalculation after another in dealing with the Kosovo crisis. U.S. officials and their NATO colleagues never understood the historical and emotional importance of Kosovo to the Serbian people. Those leaders seemed to believe that Belgrade's harsh repression of the ethnic Albanian secessionist movement in Kosovo merely reflected the will of President Slobodan Milosevic of Yugoslavia. The administration's foreign policy team, especially Secretary of State Madeleine Albright, mistakenly concluded that, under a threat of air strikes, the Yugoslav government would sign a dictated peace accord (the Rambouillet agreement) to be implemented by a NATO peacekeeping force in Kosovo. Administration leaders believed that, even if Milosevic initially refused to sign the Rambouillet agreement, Belgrade would relent after a brief "demonstration" bombing campaign. Those calculations proved to be disastrously wrong.

Reflecting the prevailing view within the administration on March 24—the first night of hostilities—Secretary Albright declared, "I don't see this as a long-term operation."[1] Confronted with the failure of its bombing strategy, the administration quickly changed its tune. Just 11 days after proclaiming that the campaign against Serbia would be over quickly—and confronted with the failure of the NATO bombing to achieve its expected goal of forcing Belgrade to sign the Rambouillet accords—Albright, echoing the new administration line, declared, "We never expected this to be over quickly."[2] The administration's claims that it expected the massive refugee flows that followed the start of the bombing, and that it expected the aerial campaign to be prolonged, were belied by its unpreparedness to deal with the refugees and by the hasty improvisations that marked the escalating bombardment of Yugoslavia.[3] Simply put, the

11

Clinton administration was unready to deal with the very consequences it *now* claims to have foreseen.

## Kosovo's Insurgency and the Onset of Western Meddling

History and demographics are the principal underlying causes of
the Kosovo conflict. The immediate cause of the struggle is the clash
of rival Serbian and ethnic Albanian nationalisms, which led to
a situation in which the political demands of the two sides were
irreconcilable. Constituting the overwhelming majority of the province's population, Kosovo's ethnic Albanians invoked the principle
of national self-determination and sought complete independence
from Serbia. However, because of Kosovo's historical and cultural
importance to them, Serbs view Kosovo as an integral part of their
nation, and hence they reject ethnic Albanian demands for independence and are unwilling to give up the province.

Since the beginning of the NATO air campaign, the notion has
taken hold in the West that Serbia was guilty of "unprovoked aggression" against Kosovo's ethnic Albanian population. Lost in the "perception management" waged by the administration and NATO officials in Brussels was the fact that the ethnic Albanian separatists—
through the instrument of the Kosovo Liberation Army—had been
waging an armed guerrilla insurgency to gain independence from
Belgrade.

In the early 1990s the ethnic Albanian movement was led by
Ibrahim Rugova and his League for a Democratic Kosovo. The LDK
was nonviolent (Rugova himself is a pacifist). As *The Economist*
recounts, under the LDK's leadership, "Kosovo's 2m Albanians
established a parallel state, with a parliament, president, taxation,
and an education system."[4] Without Serbian approval, the LDK
organized a 1991 referendum in which Kosovo's ethnic Albanians
overwhelmingly endorsed independence. Although, as *The Economist* noted, "Albanian leaders in Kosovo are unanimous in support
of independence," over time many ethnic Albanians became disillu-
sioned with the failure of the LDK's moderate, peaceful policy for
achieving that goal.[5] By 1996 the KLA had appeared on the scene,
and by 1998 it had become a significant political and military factor.
The KLA was committed to gaining independence for Kosovo by
waging war against the Serbian government. During the first three
months of 1998, the KLA stepped up its insurgency against Serbian

authorities in Kosovo. KLA units attacked Serbian police, waged an assassination campaign against Serbian officials in Kosovo, and attacked various government buildings and installations as well as civilian Serbs.[6]

Belgrade responded to the KLA insurgency with a brutal military crackdown on KLA strongholds in rural Kosovo. Serbian reprisals triggered a spiral of rising violence that prompted the United States, which reimposed sanctions against Belgrade, and NATO to become directly involved.[7] In early March 1998 Secretary Albright urged immediate action to punish Belgrade for its actions in Kosovo "and to encourage [the Serbian government] to finally resolve the problems in Kosovo through dialogue and reconciliation."[8] Two months later former assistant secretary of state Richard Holbrooke was sent to the Balkans in an attempt to defuse the Kosovo crisis.[9]

American efforts foundered for two reasons. First, the gap between Belgrade and Kosovo's ethnic Albanians (whose leaders were committed to separatist policies) was unbridgeable: the Albanians insisted on independence from Serbia, while Belgrade refused to relinquish its sovereignty over the province. Second, Washington's policy was undermined by a serious inconsistency: while rejecting ethnic Albanian demands for independence, the United States also opposed Yugoslavia's efforts to suppress a guerrilla insurgency on its own territory.

In June 1998 NATO conducted aerial maneuvers over Albania and Macedonia in an attempt to coerce Belgrade to desist from its counterinsurgency campaign in Kosovo. At the same time, NATO defense ministers authorized the preparation of contingency plans for both a bombing campaign against Yugoslavia and the deployment of ground troops to Kosovo.[10] By midsummer 1998 the crisis seemed to have abated, and with it the prospect of NATO intervention. During that period, Pentagon officials indicated that the United States had made it clear to the KLA that NATO would not come to its rescue. The same officials also expressed their frustration at the KLA's intransigence in diplomatic efforts to resolve the crisis.[11]

By early autumn, however, the fighting between Yugoslav and KLA forces in Kosovo had again intensified, as had calls from senior Clinton administration officials for NATO to threaten the use of force to pressure Belgrade to end its operations against the KLA.[12] In October, under threat of NATO air strikes, Belgrade agreed to

withdraw troops from Kosovo and accept an internationally moni-
tored cease-fire in the province. Three aspects of the process leading
to the October cease-fire are noteworthy. First, notwithstanding that
Yugoslavia was engaged in suppressing an insurgency by secessionist rebels on its own territory, the United States blamed Belgrade
alone for the violence in Kosovo, and NATO's military threats targeted only Yugoslavia.[13] Second, the ethnic Albanians were openly
hostile to the cease-fire because it failed to bring them closer to their
goal of independence. Third, as Yugoslav forces began withdrawing
in accordance with the cease-fire, KLA forces immediately moved
to reoccupy the territory they had lost during the Serbian offensive.[14]
The KLA also used the respite afforded by the cease-fire to reconsti-
tute its fighting power.[15]

The familiar pattern of guerrilla war soon set in: insurgent attacks
provoked Serbian reprisals, which begot more insurgent attacks and
a reintensification of the fighting. The KLA's strategy was to create
enough concern in NATO capitals about the Serbian counterinsurgency to bring about Western intervention in the war. In fact, the
U.S. intelligence community warned the administration that, in an
attempt to draw the United States and NATO into the conflict,
the KLA acted deliberately to provoke harsh Serbian reprisals.[16] By
January the Yugoslav forces had embarked upon a renewed assault
on KLA strongholds. That offensive triggered allegations that Serbian troops had massacred ethnic Albanian civilians and were engaging in ethnic cleansing. The cease-fire's unraveling heightened U.S.
and West European concerns that the fighting could lead to a humanitarian tragedy, which could spill over into Albania and Macedonia
and thereby destabilize the entire Balkan region. Those fears led to
the Rambouillet negotiations.

### The Rambouillet Negotiations: How Not to Conduct Diplomacy

At the Rambouillet meetings, the goal of the United States and
its West European allies was to gain the assent of Belgrade and the
KLA to a peace agreement for Kosovo. The proposed Rambouillet
accord would have superseded the October 1998 cease-fire agreement. The Rambouillet agreement provided for (1) the withdrawal
of most Yugoslav military and paramilitary forces from Kosovo;
(2) the restoration of Kosovo's political autonomy; (3) a three-year
transition period, at the end of which there would be a referendum

on Kosovo's future; (4) disarmament of the KLA; and (5) deployment of an armed NATO peacekeeping force in Kosovo.

After 18 days, the Rambouillet talks were at an impasse, with both Belgrade and the KLA refusing to sign the accord. The talks were thereupon adjourned for 19 days, until March 15, while the KLA emissaries returned to Kosovo for consultations with their leadership. The KLA representatives refused to sign because they did not receive an explicit guarantee that Kosovo would become independent at the end of the three-year transition period. Washington and the West Europeans had agreed only to *consider* the results of the referendum in determining Kosovo's future status. When the Rambouillet meeting reconvened, the KLA, after considerable arm-twisting by the United States, signed the proffered accord. The Yugoslavians, however, held fast in their refusal to sign, and thereupon NATO made good on its threat to bomb Yugoslavia.

Rambouillet is a textbook example of how not to practice diplomacy. The U.S. policy, charted by Secretary Albright, was fatally flawed in a number of respects: (1) it was biased; (2) it reflected an appalling ignorance of Serbia's history, nationalism, and resolve; and (3) it showed a culpable disregard for the foreseeable consequences of carrying out the alliance's military threat.

At Rambouillet the United States did not play the role of an impartial mediator attempting to bring rival parties to an agreement. Rather, the United States effectively took one side—the KLA's—in a civil war. That the United States aligned itself with the KLA against Serbia is hardly surprising. After all, in March 1998 Secretary Albright had pinned full responsibility for the unrest in Kosovo on the Belgrade government, notwithstanding that it usually requires two parties to cause an armed conflict.[17] Albright and the rest of the Clinton team seem to have overlooked the fact that in Kosovo there was an ongoing insurgency mounted by the KLA. On the eve of the Rambouillet talks, Albright declared, "If the Serbs are the cause of the breakdown, we're determined to go forward with the NATO decision to carry out air strikes."[18] At no time during the Rambouillet process did the administration threaten to take military action against the KLA if *it* caused the talks to break down. Indeed, the United States was remarkably vague about the actions it would take against the KLA under those circumstances.[19]

Once the Rambouillet talks collapsed, and the air campaign began, administration officials—including President Clinton himself—

blamed Belgrade for that outcome and claimed that the Yugoslavians failed to accept the "just peace" that was on the table.[20] That assertion hardly does justice to the facts. At Rambouillet the Yugoslavians were "negotiating" with a gun to their head. Indeed, the United States and the West Europeans were not negotiating with Belgrade at all; Belgrade was presented with an ultimatum and given the choice of signing or being bombed. That was repeatedly underscored by administration officials, including Clinton and Albright.[21]

The administration's strategy of coercing Yugoslav acquiescence to Rambouillet was knocked off the tracks by the KLA's initial refusal to sign, which, as the *New York Times* reported, "flabbergasted" the Clinton team.[22] After the Rambouillet impasse, the administration spent the better part of the recess in the talks cajoling the KLA to sign. To gain the KLA's assent, Washington used NATO's threat to bomb Serbia as a carrot. U.S. officials reminded the KLA that, unless it signed the Rambouillet pact, the alliance would be unable to carry out its threat to bomb Serbia.[23] In the end, of course, the KLA was persuaded to sign the accord, and Belgrade refused to do so.

The Yugoslavians refused to sign at Rambouillet for two reasons. First, Belgrade correctly believed that the Rambouillet settlement disproportionately favored the KLA. Although the Rambouillet plan provided that Kosovo would nominally remain part of Yugoslavia for three years, Belgrade's actual control over the province would have been reduced to a nullity. Notwithstanding that the United States and NATO did not explicitly specify Kosovo's status at the end of the plan's three-year transition period, the KLA made it quite clear what would happen: either Kosovo would become independent or the KLA would resume the war. Indeed, even as they agreed to sign the Rambouillet accord, KLA leaders expressed their intent to ignore its disarmament provisions and to keep the KLA's military capabilities intact.[24] The Yugoslavians also refused to sign because they believed that the provision requiring them to accept the presence of NATO soldiers in Kosovo (as peacekeepers) infringed on their sovereignty. Indeed, an appendix to the Rambouillet agreement would have permitted NATO to deploy its forces not only in Kosovo but anywhere on Yugoslav territory. Belgrade hardly can be condemned for balking at the prospect of such a pervasive regime of military occupation. Few, if any, governments would willingly accept such onerous terms. Specifically, Chapter 8, Annex B, Section 8 stated:

NATO personnel shall enjoy, together with their vehicles, vessels, aircraft, and equipment, free and unrestricted passage and unimpeded access *throughout the FRY* [Federal Republic of Yugoslavia] including associated airspace and territorial waters. This shall include, but not be limited to, the right of bivouac, maneuver, billet, and utilization of any areas or facilities as required for support, training, and operations.[25]

## NATO Resorts to Force

With the KLA's signature in hand, and Belgrade's refusal to agree to the Rambouillet accord, the United States and NATO proceeded to make good on their threat to bomb Yugoslavia, ostensibly to (1) compel Belgrade to reconsider its position and to accept the Rambouillet plan and (2) deter the Serbs from expelling ethnic Albanians from Kosovo. The bombing campaign was based on serious miscalculations about its effect on the Serbs and on events on the ground in Kosovo.

The available evidence indicates that the Clinton foreign policy team, especially Secretary Albright, expected that the Rambouillet process would have one of two outcomes. In all likelihood, U.S. officials believed, Belgrade ultimately would bow to American and NATO threats and sign the Rambouillet accords. But if Belgrade refused to do so, it would quickly change its mind after NATO conducted a brief "demonstration" bombing of Yugoslavia. Indeed, many U.S. and NATO policymakers apparently believed that NATO's threat to use force, or its actual use in a brief but intense bombing campaign, would be welcomed by Milosevic. The reasoning was that by submitting to superior force Milosevic could resolve the Kosovo problem on NATO's terms without damaging his domestic political position. In reaching that conclusion, U.S. officials, especially Secretary Albright, believed that precedent pointed to such an outcome. After all, according to the Clinton administration's misinterpretation of recent history in the Balkans, NATO air strikes on the Bosnian Serbs in 1995 had caused Belgrade to agree to the Dayton accords. And, in October 1998, the alliance's threat to bomb Yugoslavia apparently had persuaded Belgrade to agree to a cease-fire in Kosovo.[26]

The administration's reading of past events was flawed. In particular, Belgrade was brought to the negotiating table at Dayton, not by

NATO air strikes, but by the Croatian army's devastatingly success-ful ground offensive in the summer of 1995. The comparison with Bosnia was flawed in three additional respects. First, Dayton was possible because the Bosnian Serbs had wearied of the war. There was no corresponding Yugoslav war weariness with respect to Kosovo. Second, Belgrade and the Bosnian Serbs could accept the Dayton accords because they largely had achieved their key war aim of establishing a Serbian enclave in Bosnia. In Kosovo, prior to the bombing campaign, Belgrade had not achieved its key objectives. Finally, Washington did not understand that Kosovo was far more important to the Belgrade government, and the Serbian nation, than Bosnia and the Krajina. Hence Belgrade would fight for Kosovo.

It is evident that, in framing its Kosovo policy, the Clinton team had only the most superficial understanding of the origins of the Kosovo crisis, the complexity of the dispute, and the nature of Ser-bian nationalism. Blinkered by her obsession with viewing all inter-national crises through the lens of the "1930s analogy," Secretary Albright most egregiously failed to understand the distinctive roots of the conflict in Kosovo. For her, Milosevic was a modern-day Hitler, Yugoslavia's counterinsurgency campaign against the KLA was analogous to Nazi aggression against Czechoslovakia and Poland, and any attempt to resolve the crisis on terms Belgrade might accept was "appeasement."[27] And it was hardly reassuring to hear Clinton say, on the very eve of the bombing campaign, that he "had just been reading up on the Balkans."[28]

The result of such an accumulation of miscalculations, arrogance, and ineptitude was a tragic war that could have been averted. Good intentions alone cannot excuse the administration's bungled policy in the months leading up to the bombing campaign.

### Notes

1. "Interview with Secretary of State Madeleine Albright," *Online Newshour*, March 24, 1999. A U.S. military officer involved in the air campaign said of the Clinton administration's foreign policy team: "It was representational bombing. They didn't think it was necessary to go whole hog. They thought it would be over in a week." Quoted in Doyle McManus, "Debate Turns to Finger-Pointing on Kosovo Policy," *Los Angeles Times*, April 11, 1999, p. A1.

2. Quoted in ibid.

3. Both President Clinton and Secretary Albright denied that the United States was unprepared for the refugee problem. "President Clinton and Secretary of Defense Cohen Statement on Kosovo," White House, Office of the Press Secretary, April 5, 1999;

and "Madeleine K. Albright, Interview on *Meet the Press,* April 4, 1999," Department of State, Office of the Spokesman, April 5, 1999.

4. "The Balkans Survey," *The Economist,* January 24, 1998, p. 15.

5. Ibid.

6. On the growing insurgency in Kosovo in early 1998, see Tracy Wilkenson, "Anti-Serb Militancy on the Rise in Kosovo," *Los Angeles Times,* January 9, 1998, p. A1; Chris Hedges, "In New Balkan Tinderbox, Ethnic Albanians Rebel against Serbs," *New York Times,* March 2, 1998, p. A1; Chris Hedges, "Ravaged Kosovo Village Tells of a Nightmare of Death," *New York Times,* March 9, 1998, p. A3; Tracy Wilkenson, "Kosovo's Rebels Are Armed and Ready," *Los Angeles Times,* March 25, 1998, p. A1; and Chris Hedges, "Ranks of Albanian Rebels Increase in Kosovo," *New York Times,* April 6, 1998, p. A3.

7. Chris Hedges, "Gun Battles in Serbia Raise Fear of 'Another Bosnia,'" *New York Times,* March 6, 1998, p. A3.

8. Quoted in Steven Erlanger, "Albright Tours Europe to Whip Up Resolve to Punish Serbia," *New York Times,* March 9, 1998, p. A3.

9. Tracy Wilkenson, "In Kosovo, U.S. Envoy Hears Dire Warnings," *Los Angeles Times,* May 11, 1998.

10. John-Thor Dahlburg, "NATO Will Stage Mock Raids to Pressure Serbs," *Los Angeles Times,* June 12, 1998, p. A9; and Craig R. Whitney, "NATO to Conduct Maneuvers to Warn Off Serbs," *New York Times,* June 12, 1998, p. A1.

11. Steven Lee Myers, "NATO Threat to Intervene in Kosovo Fades," *New York Times,* July 16, 1998, p. A12.

12. Steven Lee Myers, "U.S. Urging NATO to Step Up Plans to Act against Yugoslavia," *New York Times,* September 24, 1998, p. A8; Norman Kempster and Craig Turner, "Reports of Massacres in Kosovo Spur Warnings," *Los Angeles Times,* October 1, 1998, p. A1; and Steven Erlanger, "NATO May Act against Serbs in Two Weeks," *New York Times,* October 2, 1998, p. A1.

13. John-Thor Dahlburg and James Gerstenzang, "Kosovo Agreement Could Stave Off NATO Airstrikes," *Los Angeles Times,* October 13, 1998, p. A1; and Steven Erlanger, "Clinton Presses Yugoslavs As NATO's Role Is Hailed," *New York Times,* October 14, 1998, p. A11.

14. Paul Watson, "Rebels Moving In on Kosovo As Serbian Forces Pull Back," *Los Angeles Times,* October 18, 1998, p. A1. Many Western analysts regarded the cease-fire skeptically. Noting that winter would reduce hostilities in any event, they speculated that large-scale fighting would break out again when spring brought improving weather conditions. Jane Perlez, "Kosovo's Battles Appear Headed into the Chill of Winter," *New York Times,* October 18, 1998, p. A8.

15. Steven Erlanger, "Among Rebels' Officer-Trainees, No Sign Kosovo Fighting Is Over," *New York Times,* February 18, 1999, p. A1.

16. Barton Gellman, "How We Went to War," *Washington Post,* national weekly edition, April 26, 1999, pp. 6–9.

17. See Geoffrey Blainey, *The Causes of War* (London: Macmillan, 1973), pp. 57–67.

18. Quoted in John-Thor Dahlburg and Tyler Marshall, "U.S. to Pressure Sides at Kosovo Peace Talks," *Los Angeles Times,* February 14, 1999, p. A1.

19. The United States made vague threats to withdraw its support from the KLA, and thereby make it more difficult for the KLA to obtain arms. That was essentially a hollow threat. The KLA was well financed by the ethnic Albanian diaspora in North America and Western Europe, and hence was able to purchase arms overtly,

or covertly, on the international arms market. Moreover, Albania itself was awash in weapons, many of which ended up in the KLA's hands.

20. Thomas W. Lippman and Dana Priest, "NATO Agrees to Target Belgrade; Russian Mission to Milosevic Fails; More Strikes in Kosovo Planned," *Washington Post*, March 31, 1999, p. A1; and Olivia Wood, "We Are on the Brink of Military Action; U.S. Envoy Struggles to Find Kosovo Solution," *Toronto Star*, March 23, 1999, p. A10.

21. Norman Kempster, "U.S. Presence in Kosovo Would Be Open-Ended," *Los Angeles Times,* February 17, 1999, p. A1; Paul Watson and Tyler Marshall, "U.S. Steps Up Pressure on Milosevic," *Los Angeles Times*, February 19, 1999, p. A1; and Elizabeth Becker, "No 'Stonewalling' on Kosovo Peace, Milosevic Is Told," *New York Times*, February 20, 1999, p. A1.

22. Jane Perlez, "Talks on Kosovo Break Down; Deadline Is Today," *New York Times,* February 23, 1999, p. A1.

23. Jane Perlez, "Kosovo Albanians, in Reversal, Say They Will Sign Peace Pact," *New York Times*, February 24, 1999, p. A1; Norman Kempster and John-Thor Dahlburg, "Kosovo Talks End with Only Partial Plan to Halt Revolt," *Los Angeles Times*, February 24, 1999, p. A1; Carlotta Gall, "Envoys Push for Talks As Kosovo Fights On," *New York Times*, March 6, 1999, p. A5; Philip Shenon, "U.S. Says Kosovo Rebels Are Ready to Sign Peace Pact," *New York Times*, March 9, 1999, p. A3; Carlotta Gall, "U.S. Official Sees 'Collision Course' in Kosovo," *New York Times*, March 10, 1999, p. A1; and Craig R. Whitney, "In New Talks on Kosovo, NATO's Credibility Is at Stake," *New York Times*, March 14, 1999, p. A14.

24. Erlanger, "Among Rebels' Officer-Trainees."

25. Interim Agreement for Peace and Self-Government in Kosovo (Rambouillet agreement), February 23, 1999, www.balkanaction.org/pubs/kia299.html. Emphasis added.

26. Thomas W. Lippman, "A Major Miscalculation on Milosevic's Thinking," *Washington Post*, national weekly edition, April 12, 1999, p. 16; and Elaine Sciolino and Ethan Bronner, "How a President, Distracted by Scandal, Entered Balkan War," *New York Times*, April 18, 1999, p. A1.

27. Owen Harries, "Madeleine Albright's 'Munich Mindset,'" *New York Times*, December 19, 1996, p. A29.

28. "Remarks by President Clinton to AFSCME Conference," Federal News Service, Washington, March 23, 1999.

# 2. NATO's Myths and Bogus Justifications for Intervention

*James George Jatras*

The rationale for the U.S.-led NATO intervention in Kosovo—and for assisting the Kosovo Liberation Army—was based on the worst sort of simplistic mythology. Indeed, NATO's interpretation of events in Kosovo was a stark foreign policy melodrama featuring villainous Serbs and innocent ethnic Albanians. The reality was quite different and more complex.

## NATO's Alice-in-Wonderland Interpretation

NATO's version of reality went something like this: The crisis in Kosovo is simply the latest episode in the aggressive drive by extreme Serbian nationalism, orchestrated by Yugoslav president Slobodan Milosevic, to create an ethnically pure Greater Serbian state. That aggression—first in Slovenia, then in Croatia, and then in Bosnia—finally came to Kosovo, largely because the West—notably NATO—refused to stand up to Milosevic.

Prior to 1989, the NATO mythology goes, Kosovo was at peace under a system of autonomy that allowed the ethnic Albanian majority a large degree of self-rule. That status quo was disturbed when the Serbs revoked Kosovo's autonomy and initiated an apartheid system of ethnic discrimination. After a decade of oppression by the Serbs, the ethnic Albanians of Kosovo were ultimately faced with a pre-planned program of genocide, similar to that undertaken by the Serbs in Bosnia. The rise of the KLA was an inevitable response to that threat.

This analysis does not represent the view of any Senate member or office. It reflects the author's professional judgment as a policy analyst and his personal opinion, for both of which he is solely responsible.

The United States and the international community exhausted the possibilities for a diplomatic settlement to the crisis, repeatedly offering the Serbs the opportunity to accept the Rambouillet agreement, a peaceful solution that would be fair to all parties. But while the ethnic Albanians, including the KLA, chose the path of negotiation and peace, the Serbs rejected it. Accordingly, NATO had no choice but to move ahead with a military response, namely air strikes, which in Bosnia had forced the Serbs to the peace table. The subsequent air campaign in the spring of 1999 was directed against Milosevic and his security apparatus, not against the Serbian people.

Unfortunately, as the Serbs moved ahead with their pre-planned program of genocide, the NATO air campaign could not stop the displacement of hundreds of thousands of Albanians. Nevertheless, failure to achieve NATO's overall objectives would have been completely unacceptable. International stability would be threatened, and American and NATO credibility would be destroyed if genocide were allowed in the heart of Europe at the dawn of the 21st century.

That, in a nutshell, was the case presented by U.S. and NATO officials. The trouble is that hardly any part of it is true. Some parts were skewed or exaggerated interpretations of the facts, some were outright falsehoods. However, as in Bosnia, the Clinton administration's Kosovo policy cannot be justified without recasting a frightfully complex conflict, with plenty of blame to go around, as a caricature: a morality play in which one side is completely innocent and the other entirely villainous.

## A Complex Reality

To start with, pre-1989 Kosovo was hardly the fantasyland of ethnic tolerance the pro-intervention caricature makes it out to be. The 1974 constitution imposed by communist dictator Josef Broz Tito elevated Kosovo to effective equality with the federal republics. Kosovo's Albanians exercised virtually complete control over the provincial administration. Tens, perhaps hundreds, of thousands of Serbs left during the 1970s and 1980s in the face of pervasive discrimination and the refusal of the authorities to protect them from ethnic violence. The resulting shift in the ethnic balance that accelerated during this period is the main claim ethnic Albanians now make to exclusive ownership of Kosovo. During the same period, ethnic Albanian demands mounted that the province be detached from Serbia and given republic status within the Yugoslav federation. Republic status, if granted, would, in theory, have allowed Kosovo the legal right to declare its independence from Yugoslavia.

One of the ironies of the present Kosovo crisis is that Milosevic began his rise to power in Serbia in large part because of the oppressive character of pre-1989 ethnic Albanian rule in Kosovo. At a 1987 rally he promised local Serbs, "Nobody will beat you again."[1] In short, rather than blame Milosevic for being the cause of the Kosovo crisis, it would be correct to say that intolerant ethnic Albanian nationalism in Kosovo was a springboard of Milosevic's rise to power.

Second, Kosovo's autonomy was not revoked in 1989 but downgraded—at the federal level at Milosevic's initiative—to what it had been before 1974. Many Albanians refused to accept Belgrade's reassertion of authority, and large numbers were fired from their state jobs. The resulting standoff—marked by boycotts and the creation of alternative institutions on the Albanian side and by increasingly severe police repression on the Serbian side—continued for most of the 1990s. Again, the political question in Kosovo—up until the bombing began—had always been, How much autonomy would the Kosovo Albanians settle for? When one hears now that autonomy is not enough and that only independence will suffice, one can't help but think of Turkish Kurdistan (southeastern Turkey) where not only have the Kurds never been offered any kind of autonomy but even suggesting there ought to be autonomy will land the speaker in jail. Yet the "international community" doesn't bomb Turkey because of its ill-treatment of the Kurds; to the contrary, as a NATO member, Turkey participated in bombing the Serbs.

Third, while after 1989 there was a tense standoff in Kosovo, there was not open warfare until 1997. That began, not because of any pre-planned Serbian program of ethnic cleansing, but because of the KLA's deliberate—indeed classic—strategy for turning a political confrontation into a military confrontation. Attacks directed against not only Serbian police and officials but Serbian civilians and insufficiently militant Albanians were undoubtedly, and accurately, calculated to trigger a massive and largely indiscriminate response by Serbian forces. The growing cycle of violence, in turn, further radicalized Kosovo's Albanians and led to the possibility of NATO military

23

intervention, which, given the Bosnia precedent, was the KLA's real goal, rather than any realistic expectation of victory on the battlefield. In every respect, it was a stunningly successful strategy.

Fourth, the Clinton administration's claim that NATO resorted to force only after diplomacy failed is flatly untrue. As I pointed out in a paper issued by the Republican Policy Committee in August 1998, the military planning for intervention was largely in place at that time—seven months *before* NATO's air campaign began. All that was lacking was a suitable pretext.[2] The October 1998 agreement between former U.S. assistant secretary of state Richard Holbrooke and Milosevic, to which the KLA was not a party, mandated a partial Serbian withdrawal. The KLA responded by occupying roughly half of Kosovo and cleansing dozens of villages of their Serbian inhabitants. Any reaction on the Serbian side, however, risked NATO bombing. Finally, the Rambouillet process cannot be considered a negotiation under any normal definition of the word: Lawyers at the State Department wrote a 90-page document, pushed it in front of the parties, and said: "Sign it. And if you (one of the parties) sign it and he (the other party) doesn't, we'll bomb him." And, of course, when they said that, Secretary Albright and the State Department knew that one of the parties would not, indeed, could not, sign the agreement. Why? Because—although our supposedly inquisitive news media have paid little attention to the fact—it provided for NATO occupation of not just Kosovo but all of Yugoslavia (see Chapter 1, p. 17).

I have it on good authority that one senior administration official told the media (off the record, of course) at Rambouillet: "We intentionally set the bar too high for the Serbs to comply. They need some bombing, and that's what they are going to get."[3] In short, Rambouillet was just Albright's charade to get to a bombing campaign. The big mistake of administration officials was their assumption that their splendid little war would be over in a very short time. It all happened just as they planned, except the last part: Milosevic refused to run up the white flag for a surprisingly long time.

Fifth, nobody can doubt there were atrocities committed in Kosovo by Milosevic's forces, although the extent and specifics of the reports that the media (as they did in Bosnia) treat as established fact are open to question. Agence France-Presse described those reports as "confused, contradictory, and sometimes plain wrong."[4] However, it did not appear to detract from their propaganda value that "reports coming from NATO and U.S. officials appear often as little more than regurgitation of unconfirmed information" from the KLA.[5] For example, there was the report peddled by State Department spokesman James Rubin, among others, that some 100,000 Albanian men had been herded into the Pristina sports stadium—until a reporter actually went to the stadium and found it empty.

Moreover, one should not doubt that a lot more civilians—both Serbs and Albanians—were killed by NATO than Western officials initially were willing to admit. As the war went on, the air strikes were increasingly directed against what is euphemistically called "infrastructure" (i.e., civilian) targets. Some Albanian refugees said that they were fleeing the Serbs, but others mentioned NATO's bombs. The Clinton administration has vainly tried to claim that all the bloodshed that occurred after March 24 was Milosevic's fault, insisting that the Serbian military offensive would have taken place even if NATO had not bombed. But that argument is unconvincing. After the failure of the Rambouillet talks and the breakdown of the October 1998 Milosevic-Holbrooke agreement, a Serbian offensive against the KLA may have been unavoidable—and no doubt it would have been conducted with the same light touch the Turks have used against the Kurdistan Workers Party or the Sri Lankans against the Tamil Tigers, who, like the KLA, do not play by Marquis of Queensberry rules. But a full-scale drive to push out all or most ethnic Albanians and unleash a demographic bomb against NATO staging areas in Albania and Macedonia may not have been inevitable.

Sixth, because the administration's decision to bomb turned Kosovo from a crisis into a disaster, we no longer have a Kosovo policy; we have a KLA policy. As documented in a paper released by the Republican Policy Committee on March 31, 1999,[6] the Clinton administration had elevated to virtually unchallenged status as the legitimate representative of the Kosovo Albanian people a terrorist group whose activities raise very serious questions about its criminal involvement—particularly in the drug trade—and about radical Islamic influences, including that of Osama bin Laden and the Iranians.[7] Advocates of U.S. assistance to the KLA, such as the Heritage Foundation, argued that, on the basis of the experience of aiding the mujahedin in Afghanistan, we could use our aid as leverage for "reforming" the KLA's behavior. However, I would ask what radical group of any description—in Afghanistan (where we could at least claim that the vicissitudes of the Cold War justified the risks); or the Izetbegovic regime in Bosnia; or, for that matter, the Castro regime in Cuba; or the Sandinistas in Nicaragua; or the Palestine Liberation Organization—has ever genuinely abandoned its radical birthright for a mess of American pottage.

Seventh, advocates of a cozy relationship with the KLA suggest that it be contingent on guarantees that that organization not attack civilians and not pursue objectives beyond Kosovo (i.e., a Greater Albania). Given the pre-1989 history of Kosovo and the KLA's behavior to date, the first suggestion is laughable. As for the second, one should examine a map from the Web page of the Albanian American Civic League (www.aacl.com), a pro-KLA group in the United States. That map shows the areas claimed by the KLA, including not only Kosovo but other areas of southern Serbia, parts of Montenegro and Macedonia (including their capitals), and parts of Greece. When I first saw this map—which the webmaster has made considerably harder to print since I first referenced it in the Republican Policy Committee study—it triggered a recollection of something I had seen before. It is strikingly similar to the map I have (printed by the State Department in 1947) of interim territorial arrangements during World War II under the Axis occupation. I fail to see what interest the United States has in helping to restore the Nazi-imposed borders of 1943 or how doing so would help preserve European stability.

Eighth, the Clinton administration repeatedly rebuffed attempts by the Serbian opposition to gain support against Milosevic, including a meeting between Madeleine Albright and Bishop Artemije, the Serbian Orthodox prelate of Kosovo, in which he appealed for an initiative that would have strengthened moderate forces on both sides, begun genuine negotiations (instead of the Rambouillet farce), and weakened Milosevic.[8] Predictably, that appeal fell on deaf ears. But this administration cannot say it was not warned.

Ninth, the administration's "humanitarian" justification for the war—the contention that it was about returning Albanian refugees to their homes—is rank hypocrisy. Many commentators have noted that the administration had turned a blind eye to the cleansing of hundreds of thousands of Serbs from the Krajina region of Croatia in 1995. That is not quite accurate. U.S. officials did not turn a blind eye; they assisted the Croatian army's Operation Storm. Retired U.S. military consultants provided tactical training and operational planning under the guise of "democracy training"—with the blessing of the Clinton administration. Indeed, there is evidence that U.S. assistance in the ethnic cleansing of the Krajina Serbs may have included air strikes and psychological warfare operations.[9]

Tenth, the notion that Milosevic is a dedicated nationalist bent on creating a Greater Serbia is incorrect. Milosevic—unlike the equally thuggish Franjo Tudjman, president of Croatia, and Alija Izetbegovic, leader of Bosnia's Muslim-dominated regime—is an opportunist who likely would have been more than willing to sell out Kosovo, as he did the Serbs of Krajina and the Serbian population of Bosnia, if the Clinton-Albright policy had not been so completely incompetent as to paint him into a corner where he had to stand and fight. As for the goal of Greater Serbia (as opposed to Greater Albania)—it is all in the definitions. The one consistent rule of Western policymakers in dealing with the breakup of Titoist Yugoslavia seems to be that the Serbs—the only constituent nationality that gave up its own national state to create Yugoslavia—alone have no legitimate right to political self-determination. On the one hand, Serbian minorities in the other newly independent republics were expected to accept as authoritative Tito's borders or be branded as "aggressors" for wishing to remain in the state (Yugoslavia) in which they had up until then been living. On the other hand, Kosovo, a region that was part of Serbia even before Yugoslavia was created, is up for grabs. The double standard is breathtaking.

The Clinton administration's blundering policy in the Balkans has harmed American interests and those of nearly everybody else concerned (with the notable exception of the KLA). It has harmed an unknown number of innocent civilians, both Serbian and Albanian, killed or injured by NATO's bombing; delayed prospects of political reform in Serbia that would remove Milosevic from power; harmed the U.S. security posture, as our forces around the world have been stripped down to devote resources to Kosovo; harmed the already fragile stability of neighboring states and the region as a whole; and harmed our relationship with Russia, which should be among our first priorities. Indeed, the air war seemingly gave substance to every lie the Soviet Union ever told about NATO's aggressive intentions.

The Clinton administration's incompetent policy in Kosovo has had one small benefit: it has exposed the fact that in 1998, when the

Senate gave its advice and consent to the expansion of NATO's membership, it also approved the expansion of NATO's mission. If the Clinton administration and NATO are ultimately successful in Kosovo, not only will the principle of state sovereignty in the face of an out-of-control international bureaucracy be fatally compromised, but we can also expect (and indeed some observers have already started to set out the case for) new and even more dangerous adventures of this sort elsewhere, notably in the Caucasus.[10]

For President Clinton, Secretary Albright, and their "Third Way" European cronies of the Tony Blair stripe, "winning" means, not establishing a successful overall policy toward the Balkans, but winning the propaganda war—an exercise in media spin, polls, and focus groups. As Albright suggested in 1998, the leaders of some countries, including Serbia, "try to grab the truth and leash it like a dog, ration it like bread, or mold it like clay. Their goal is to create their own myths, conceal their own blunders, direct resentments elsewhere and instill in their people a dread of change."[11] However true that description is of Slobodan Milosevic, Secretary Albright should look in the mirror. No, the war against Serbia was not about American interests but about vindicating the intelligence of Madeleine Albright and the good word of Bill Clinton. It was a war that could have been—and should have been—avoided.

### Notes

1. Quoted in Blaine Harden, "Yugoslav Area Rejects Communists; Slovenia Seeks Sovereign Independence," *Washington Post*, April 14, 1990, p. A1.

2. United States Senate Republican Policy Committee, "Bosnia II: The Clinton Administration Sets Course for NATO Intervention in Kosovo; Goals, Potential Costs, and Motives All Uncertain," August 12, 1998, rpc.senate.gov.

3. Confidential conversation with a reliable media source.

4. "Questions Mount on Accuracy of Kosovo Atrocity Reports," Agence France-Presse, March 31, 1999.

5. Ibid.

6. United States Senate Republican Policy Committee, "The Kosovo Liberation Army: Does Clinton Policy Support Group with Terror, Drug Ties? From 'Terrorists' to 'Partners,'" March 31, 1999, www.senate.gov/rpc.

7. See ibid.; "KLA Finances Fight with Heroin Sales; Terror Group Is Linked to Crime Network," *Washington Times*, May 3, 1999, p. A1; and "KLA Rebels Train in Terrorist Camps; Bin Laden Offers Financing, Too," *Washington Times*, May 4, 1999, p. A1.

8. Copy of proposal in author's possession.

9. To date, to the author's knowledge, no media have seen fit to investigate in depth indications of a direct U.S. role in not only the planning but the execution of

Operation Storm. Nevertheless, several news accounts described elements of such involvement. See "4 Navy Jets Bomb Serb Missile Sites," *Navy Times*, August 21, 1995, p. 2, describing in detail strikes the Pentagon subsequently denied, when questioned, had ever taken place; "Martic Aide Says NATO Led Croat Offensive," *Oslobodjenje* (Sarajevo), August 23, 1995, p. 4, as translated by the Foreign Broadcast Information Service, September 5, 1995, p. 46, describing panic broadcasts on Krajina Serb radio frequencies in the wake of NATO strikes; and accounts of "democracy training" as cover for strategy and tactics: Chris Black, "U.S. Veterans' Aid to Croatia Elicits Queries," *Boston Globe*, August 13, 1995, p. 12; Charlotte Eager, "Invisible United States Army Defeats Serbs," *The Observer* (UK), November 5, 1995, p. 25; Paul Harris, "Corporate Mercenaries with Links to Arms Sellers and the Pentagon Are Fulfilling United States Policy Aims by Proxy," *Scotland on Sunday* (UK), May 5, 1996 p. 15; Yves Goulet, "MPRI: Washington's Freelance Advisors," *Jane's Intelligence Review*, July 1, 1998, p. 38; and Raymond Bonner, "War Crimes Panel Finds Croat Troops 'Cleansed' the Serbs," *New York Times*, March 21, 1999, p. A1.

10. Eduard Sheverdnadze and Heydar Aliyev, former members of the Soviet Politburo and currently the presidents of the independent republics of Georgia and Azerbaijan, respectively, have each suggested that the NATO intervention in Kosovo may provide a precedent for settlement of conflicts in their countries. Georgia faces an insurgency in its northwestern Abkhazia region; oil-rich Azerbaijan has failed to crush an independence bid by the ethnic Armenian-majority region of Nagorno-Karbakh. A prospective NATO intervention in either region of the former Soviet Caucasus would be seen as a direct challenge to Russia. See "NATO's Kosovo Campaign Touches Nerve in the Caucasus," Agence France-Presse, July 6, 1999; Stephen Kinzer, "Azerbaijan Asks United States to Establish Military Base," *New York Times*, January 31, 1999, p. A1; and "Shevardnadze Sees Latest Events in Kosovo as Model for Conflict Settlement," BBC Worldwide Monitoring, June 9, 1999.

11. "Madeleine K. Albright, Remarks at the Rosalynn Carter Distinguished Lecture Series, Atlanta, Ga., December 3, 1998," U.S. Department of State, Press Office.

# 3. NATO's Hypocritical Humanitarianism

## Doug Bandow

When ethnic Albanian guerrillas originally rejected the peace settlement for Kosovo fashioned by Secretary of State Madeleine Albright, a colleague of Albright's told *Newsweek*, "She's angry at everyone—the Serbs, the Albanians and NATO."[1] Rather than question the administration's dubious handiwork, another Clinton official raged: "Here is the greatest nation on earth pleading with some nothing-balls to do something entirely in their own interest—which is to say yes to an interim agreement—and they defy us."[2]

With such hubris infecting the administration, it should come as no surprise that it so badly bungled policy toward Kosovo. The aggressive policy toward Yugoslavia championed by the Clinton administration and, in turn, NATO was flawed in both principle and practice. In particular, the administration

- illegally embarked upon war, in contravention of the U.S. Constitution, the treaty that established NATO, and the United Nations Charter;
- launched an unprovoked assault against a nation that had not threatened the United States or any U.S. ally, thereby lowering the bar against aggressive war worldwide;
- deepened European dependence on America for defense of European interests that have little relevance to America; and
- put U.S. military personnel at risk without any serious, let alone vital, American interest at stake.[3]

Any one of those failings should have been sufficient to invalidate Washington's, and NATO's, decision to inaugurate war. But none of those mistakes is quite as galling as the sanctimony with which the allies justified their aggression. NATO representatives, from President Clinton to British prime minister Tony Blair to assorted military officers and government spokesmen, asserted that their attack was based on morality, not narrow national interests.[4] The

31

war was directed against "a vicious campaign of ethnic cleansing," explained President Clinton.[5]

Much of the establishment media picked up the cry. "This was the first military conflict since the end of the Cold War fought primarily for humanitarian purposes," declared the *New York Times*.[6] *U.S. News & World Report* publisher Mortimer Zuckerman declared, "We fought not for territory but for values and moral principles."[7]

### Hypocrisy on Multiple Levels

In fact, NATO's war against Serbia illustrated the worst sort of hypocrisy for all the world to see. The assertion that the allies were forced to attack out of concern for the human rights of the Albanian Kosovars was difficult to accept, given NATO's lack of concern about far worse conflicts, not only around the world but in NATO's own backyard.

Since the early 1990s a civil war has raged in Algeria—just across the Mediterranean from several NATO countries—claiming more than 70,000 lives. Worst of all, Turkey, a NATO member, has engaged in ethnic cleansing and other atrocities in not one but two locales. "How grievous and shameful would it have been to turn aside from murder and expropriation?" asked Zuckerman.[8] The answer is, No more shameful than doing so elsewhere in the world, as the NATO countries routinely do. The war against Yugoslavia was a selective and cynical humanitarianism, based on the ethnicity of the victims, the allied status of the belligerents, and the expansiveness of media coverage.

Indeed, the war was based on a lie from the start. The allies did not exhaust their diplomatic options, as they constantly claimed. Nor did they threaten war to stop massive human rights abuses— the large-scale Serbian crackdown actually occurred in response to the NATO bombing.[9]

Rather, NATO used force to impose compliance with an international diktat to establish an unstable, jury-rigged autonomous government to be backed by a permanent foreign occupation of what is recognized internationally as indisputably Yugoslavian land. The nearly 100-page agreement presented at Rambouillet set forth a variety of complicated government institutions and convoluted enforcement processes. The plan might have represented a creative response to a law school final exam question; it did not represent the aspirations of the Albanian or the Serbian people.[10] The system would have been inherently unstable and could have been sustained only with a permanent foreign occupation. Hence the attempt to impose it by force. Were any other nation to make such a demand, Washington would consider it high hubris—and justification for war. The administration's ultimatum never had a chance. One Western diplomat expressed bewilderment at Slobodan Milosevic's refusal to sign: "He's detached from reality."[11] But NATO officials were the ones detached from reality.

Had NATO truly exhausted the diplomatic option, and not attempted to impose such an unrealistic agreement, it might have achieved its ends through negotiation. "The haunting question," as Alan Kuperman of the Brookings Institution puts it, is whether the agreement that ended the war "could have satisfied Milosevic and achieved peace at Rambouillet if only the U.S. had offered it."[12] In that case the war would have been entirely unnecessary.[13]

Even if the administration and its allies had genuinely humanitarian motives, the Kosovo war made no sense. It has often been said that the world is a dangerous place, and it certainly is. But not particularly to the United States. Most members of the industrialized West, and especially America, are not confronted with the prospect of war—unless they seek it out.

It is a tragic truism, however, that conflict wracks many other countries around the world. There have been mass murder in Burundi, Cambodia, Rwanda, Sudan, and Uganda; brutal insurgencies in Angola, the Democratic Republic of the Congo (formerly Zaire), Ethiopia, Liberia, Mozambique, Sierra Leone, and Sri Lanka; bloody wars between Armenia and Azerbaijan, Ethiopia and Eritrea, and India and Pakistan; endless civil war in Afghanistan; violent separatist campaigns in Georgia (Abkhazies and Ossetians), Indonesia (East Timorese), Iraq (Kurds), Mexico (Chiapans), Northern Ireland (Irish Catholics), Russia (Chechens), Spain (Basques), and Turkey (Kurds); and strife for various reasons in Algeria, Burma, Guatemala, India, Moldova, Tajikistan, Tibet, and elsewhere.

Then there is Kosovo. Without doubt, the situation there has been tragic for many years. Yet the one constant of guerrilla insurgencies and civil wars is their brutality—by both sides. The Serbian government has inflicted numerous civilian casualties in Kosovo, but its conduct does not exist in a vacuum. In June 1998 a U.S. diplomat in Belgrade told me, "If you're a Serb, hell yes the KLA is a terrorist organization."[14] Even ethnic Albanians admit that the KLA had targeted Serbian policemen and other government employees, Serbs viewed as abusing Kosovars, and Albanian "collaborators." Each cycle of violence has spawned another.

The resulting suffering of the Albanian Kosovars was obvious. Yet—at least until NATO intervened—the fighting in Kosovo barely rose to the status of atrocity in today's world. It certainly never constituted genocide, a term now routinely tossed around with wild abandon. An estimated 2,000 people, including Serbs, were killed in Kosovo in 1998 and the first two months of 1999. At least three times as many people died in January 1999 alone in Sierra Leone. Nearly as many people died in one three-day battle between Tamil guerrillas and the Sri Lankan government in the fall of 1998 as died in Kosovo during all of that year.

Thus, even if it might arguably have been right to intervene in those other cases on humanitarian grounds, it would not necessarily have been "right to defend the Kosovans [sic]," as author Salmon Rushdie argued.[15] By any normal standard, the suffering in Kosovo was less severe than that in many other nations around the world.

NATO continues to exaggerate the extent of Belgrade's abuses. Despite allied claims that 100,000 or more Kosovars were being massacred during the war, estimates now range between 3,000 and 10,000. That is horrid, of course, but one could find numerous African countries that have suffered that many deaths from armed conflicts.

Indeed, it is difficult to take administration, and NATO, moralizing about Kosovo seriously. Death tolls in the millions (Afghanistan, Angola, Cambodia, Sudan, Rwanda, Tibet), hundreds of thousands (Burundi, East Timor, Guatemala, Liberia, Mozambique), and tens of thousands (Algeria, Chechnya, Congo, Kashmir, Sierra Leone, Sri Lanka, Turkey) are common. The estimated death toll in Kosovo was exceeded even by the number of dead in Northern Ireland's sectarian violence.[16] Yet none of the many other victims has proved to be sufficiently "interesting" to Western leaders, as one analyst put it.[17]

Similarly, although the attack on Yugoslavia generated mass refugee flows—nearly 1 million toward the end of the war—they, too, pale in comparison with those in other conflicts. Some 7.3 million people have had to flee violent strife in Africa. Some 30,000 sought escape in Gabon from civil war in the Congo Republic in just one week in July 1999. Over the last decade hundreds of thousands of people have been displaced from such countries as Armenia, Azerbaijan, Krygyzstan, Tajikistan, and Uzbekistan. The government of Bhutan "cleansed" more than 100,000 ethnic Nepalese earlier this decade. Then there's the Middle East, with 3.6 million refugees.[18] When asked if he would devote the same attention to ensuring the return of Palestinian refugees as he had to that of Kosovar refugees, Bill Clinton could only compliment the journalist for asking a good question.[19]

Washington and other NATO governments have routinely tolerated such cases of genocide and ethnic cleansing around the globe. The West is also ever-ready to ignore brutal civil wars and counterinsurgency campaigns conducted by allies. NATO members seem to be offended only when nations deemed unfriendly to NATO's interests play by the same rules.

In 1991 the West encouraged the breakup of Yugoslavia. Then the United States and its European allies decided that Serbs were not entitled to secede from the newly minted countries of Croatia and Bosnia. In the latter a particularly bloody conflict ensued. NATO eventually used its air power to assist the Muslims in Bosnia and helped impose the bizarre Dayton accord, under which three antagonistic groups are supposed to live together in an artificial state ruled by international bureaucrats.[20] The same hypocrisy is being played out in Kosovo. Washington unreservedly supported Britain, Spain, and Turkey, for instance, in dealing forcibly with violent separatists; has placed no pressure on Macedonia to offer autonomy to its ethnic Albanians; and ignores violent campaigns to suppress sucessionist movements elsewhere around the globe. But the United States holds Serbia to a much higher standard.

## NATO's Double Standard: The Case of Turkey

It is instructive to contrast U.S. policy toward Turkey with that toward Serbia. Slobodan Milosevic is a demagogic thug, but, in fact, the behavior of his government toward Albanians looks not unlike that of Turkey, a NATO member and a favorite U.S. ally, toward the Kurds. In Turkey a full-fledged guerrilla war has raged for 14 years as the Kurds have fought for self-determination. (There is a similar conflict in Iraq, where Washington has imposed a no-fly zone to help protect Kurdish separatists.) Ankara rules the predominantly Kurdish southeastern region of the country through repression.

Although there is much to criticize about the Kurdistan Workers Party (PKK), which has killed alleged Kurdish "collaborators," including teachers, the Turkish military is worse. Human Rights Watch attributes nearly six times as many civilian casualties to the government as to the PKK.[21] Assassination, torture, and summary executions are the norm. Moreover, Turkey has often imposed upon Kurds a Hobson's choice: create Village Guards aligned with Ankara or lose their homes. The military has destroyed some 3,000 villages, using U.S.-supplied tanks and planes. As many as 2 million people have been ethnically cleansed. Some 37,000 are estimated to have died in the conflict.[22]

Turkey is a democracy that is less than democratic. Neither political freedom nor civil liberties are secure. After years of military intervention in politics, Turks can now vote again. They are unable to decide basic issues, however. The army suppresses parties and dictates policy. Moreover, according to Human Rights Watch, "Police continue to shoot and kill peaceful demonstrators."[23] To advocate education or broadcasts in the Kurdish language is to risk jail. Supporters of Kurdish autonomy face trial for treason. In March 1999 the U.S.-based Committee to Protect Journalists announced that "for the fifth consecutive year, Turkey held more journalists in prison than any other country." Most of them "are victims of the government's continued criminalization of reporting" on the conflict in Kurdistan.[24] All told, reports Human Rights Watch, there is "massive continuing abuse of human rights in Turkey."[25]

Turkey has also engaged in ethnic cleansing in Cyprus. On July 20, 1974, Ankara invaded the independent island after the so-called Greek colonels fomented a coup d'état against Cypriot president Makarios. Turkey argued, with at least plausible justification, that the Turkish minority was at risk.[26] However, despite the collapse of the coup in Cyprus (and, subsequently, the junta in Greece) and restoration of Makarios to power, Ankara staged a second, wider invasion a month later. Turkey grabbed 37 percent of the island and displaced between 165,000 (UN estimates) and 180,000 to 200,000 (Cypriot estimates) ethnic Greeks. Thousands of Cypriots were killed and thousands more remain missing (a number of the latter were apparently murdered after being captured). Those who fled lost their property. Today the city of Famagusta lies empty; a once-prosperous resort has become a ghost town.[27]

Although ethnic Turks had lived throughout the island, virtually all moved north to create the so-called Turkish Republic of Northern Cyprus, which is recognized only by Ankara. Ankara's policy of ethnic cleansing damaged the welfare of Turkish Cypriots as well as that of Greek Cypriots. The Turkish Cypriot community numbered about 124,000 in 1974 but has since dropped to between 65,000 and 80,000 because of emigration. At the same time, Turkey has moved an estimated 100,000 settlers from its Anatolian region to northern Cyprus.[28] They are among the fiercest supporters of the rabidly nationalistic government of Rauf Denktash, which has prohibited private, intercommunal meetings as well as rejected negotiations over anything except de jure independence for the TRNC. If Turkey's actions in Cyprus do not constitute ethnic cleansing, then the term has no meaning.

Yet NATO, despite its supposed commitment to humanitarian values, does nothing. The Clinton administration voices no outrage, proposes no bombing of Ankara, demands no NATO occupation to restore the rights of beleaguered Kurds and Greek Cypriots. To the contrary, Washington supplies the weapons Ankara uses to repress Kurdish separatists and apparently helped Turkey capture Kurdish rebel chief Abdullah Ocalan. The United States and the other NATO members had no problem allowing Turkey to participate in the military campaign against Serbia.

Of course, some advocates of humanitarian intervention don't care about consistency. Richard Land of the Southern Baptist Convention contends, "The inability of the United States, even as the world's only remaining superpower, to intervene effectively everywhere does not relieve us of the moral responsibility of intervening where we can make a critical difference."[29] Even if that is theoretically true, in practice the United States has the power to intervene in any conflict anywhere, even in Africa and Central Asia. If it doesn't want to go everywhere, Washington should follow some objective standards. The administration has articulated none.[30]

### Criteria for Humanitarian Crusades

In practice, the United States seems prepared to conduct armed humanitarian crusades under three conditions:

- those being killed are white Europeans,
- the perceived aggressor is not a U.S. ally, and
- there is saturation media coverage of the conflict.

Even a Kosovo hawk like *New Republic* writer Peter Beinart admits that "America's Kosovo war is unintelligible without reference to the race of the victims."[31] Moreover, Washington's allies and clients routinely get away with murder. In 1995 Croatia "cleansed" the Krajiana region of up to 300,000 ethnic Serbs (the estimates vary). The Croatian military shelled and strafed columns of Serbian refugees, who were fleeing ancestral lands, and carried out summary executions. Investigators for the Balkans war crimes tribunal concluded that the attack constituted a war crime and recommended the indictment of three Croatian army generals. Yet the U.S. government helped train the Croat military, said nothing as refugees were being murdered, and obstructed the war crimes probe.[32] The *Wall Street Journal* editorial page, which enthusiastically endorsed the war in Kosovo, even called claims that the Serbs had suffered ethnic cleansing "effrontery."[33] As noted earlier, Turkey uses American weapons to kill and displace Kurds on a massive scale and preserve the division of Cyprus. Brutality in such countries as Algeria, Indonesia, and Pakistan, all of which have been backed by Washington, is pervasive. And on it goes.

The role of the media is particularly important, and media coverage of atrocities is more than a little selective. The apparent murder of 45 Kosovars in the village of Racak received prominent (frontpage) coverage in leading newspapers around America and on television.[34] The deaths of more than 6,300 people in Sierra Leone gained a paragraph or two in the largest papers. No wonder one business manager supported the war against Serbia by observing: "All you had to do was look on TV. America should be ashamed of itself if we don't stop this brutality."[35] And what of the far worse atrocities that the television networks did not cover?

The Albanian diaspora also recognizes the importance of lobbying Congress and the administration, the kind of effort more traditionally associated with a desire for farm subsidies at home than with bombing campaigns abroad. Thus, complex foreign events, such as the killings in Racak, which appear to be the ugly but normal violence associated with insurgencies, are manipulated by domestic interests and foreign parties for political ends, in this case, U.S.-NATO intervention. Basing intervention on such factors, however, makes a mockery of the humanitarian justifications advanced by Western leaders.

The administration's unprincipled humanitarianism has adverse humanitarian consequences as well. It tends to intensify local conflicts. For instance, Kosovar leaders have long understood the importance of positive media coverage. Alush Gashi, an adviser to Ibrahim Rugova, admitted to me in June 1998 that the prospect of NATO intervention "depends on how we look on CNN. People need to see victims in their living rooms."[36] Guerrilla forces are therefore more likely to rely on terror in hopes of sparking brutal retaliation, which will, in turn, generate widespread revulsion abroad.

### The Many Victims of Humanitarian Crusading

NATO intervention in Kosovo immeasurably worsened the humanitarian situation. The alliance turned a minor tragedy into a widespread disaster, as Belgrade responded to Western aggression by killing several thousand Kosovars and turning hundreds of thousands of Kosovars into refugees. Of course, after triggering the mass refugee flows, Secretary of State Madeleine Albright and British foreign secretary Robin Cook shamelessly claimed, "We are fighting to get the refugees home, safe under our protection."[37] It was the ultimate bootstrap argument: NATO intervenes, sparking a violent Serbian crackdown, which in turn causes humanitarian chaos, which then justifies NATO intervention.

Yet so little concerned was NATO about those victims that it focused on minimizing allied casualties rather than destroying the field power of the Yugoslav military.[38] Allied bombing inflicted widespread destruction in Kosovo, as well as killing and victimizing Yugoslav civilians. As *Chicago Tribune* columnist Steve Chapman put it, NATO was winning its war against Yugoslavia's "civilian population. Women and children, the elderly and the newborn, the sick and the lame—they are no match for the most powerful military alliance in history."[39] Early in the conflict Pentagon spokesman Ken Bacon was forced to admit that it was "difficult . . . to say that we have prevented one act of brutality."[40]

Barely two months after the war ended, Albanian Kosovars had killed hundreds of Serbs, kidnapped hundreds more, and driven out nearly three-quarters of Kosovo's prewar Serbian population. Gypsies were also targeted for allegedly collaborating with Belgrade.[41] Deaths were estimated to be running about 30 a week, an annual rate almost as high as that before the allies attacked. NATO officials say there isn't much they can do—in marked contrast to the prewar argument that such atrocities against Albanian Kosovars were intolerable.[42] Yet the ethnic cleansing of Serbs and Gypsies is an abuse for which the allies are directly responsible, having forcibly seized control of the province. When the "protection" force, embarrassed at its failure, began to crack down more aggressively on the KLA, it engendered growing Albanian hostility.[43]

NATO's failure to halt the suffering in Kosovo should be no surprise. Where has previous U.S. military intervention resolved deep-seated humanitarian crises? Somalia was a disaster, reconciliation is a fantasy in Bosnia, and Haiti now enjoys a presidential instead of a military dictatorship. U.S. threats and bombs brought Kosovo no closer to having a tolerant, democratic, multiethnic society. It is far easier to loose the dogs of war than to control where they run. Wars are almost always extremely destabilizing. Not only do conflicts develop in unpredictable ways, but they typically escalate and irredeemably change the status quo. Particularly dubious is the sort of war waged by NATO, one which, in the words of columnist Robert Samuelson, "shifted almost all of the risk of American policy onto the Kosovars." In this way, he argues, Clinton "managed to make a moral crusade immoral."[44]

### Lowering the Barriers to War

Misguided humanitarian intervention risks other ill effects as well. There is much to dislike about governments' routine abuse of national sovereignty, but the alternative is almost unthinkable. If national polities sometimes run murderously out of control, a coercive global order is likely to be far more dangerous.

The bar against aggressive war offered at least one barrier to the spread of conflict. Ever since the Peace of Westphalia in 1648, military intervention across borders (with rare exceptions) has been defined as aggression. "This may not sound like a very lofty principle, but for 350 years it has been the basis of what order first Europe and then the rest of the world has known," observes columnist David

Frum.[45] That standard offered an important, however limited, way to maintain the peace.

Of course, some modern legal theorists argue that sovereignty is not absolute and that exceptions should be made for humanitarian purposes. Sen. Max Cleland (D-Ga.) contends, "We also have a humanitarian interest in preventing atrocities against civilians."[46] That is an appealing notion, but it raises serious practical issues— particularly the likelihood of spreading conflict in unpredictable ways, just as did NATO's war in Kosovo. Intervention in otherwise limited internal disputes automatically internationalizes and often expands them.

Moreover, what is the standard for making war? What justifies the extreme step of Washington's unleashing death and destruction on another people? Traditionally, it has been the existence of at least a plausible military threat to the United States. That standard was clearly inapplicable to Kosovo.

If compassion becomes an all-purpose exception to the barrier to outside intervention, where does it end? Before NATO's intervention on behalf of the Albanian Kosovar insurgents, Kosovo's civil war was among the more minor international conflagrations. Granted, Serbia's treatment of the Kosovars was atrocious. But so has been Turkey's handling of the Kurds, and the conduct of Indonesia in East Timor, as well as the behavior of two score other governments in a variety of conflicts around the globe. Is war the right remedy in all of those cases?

If Kosovo does provide an exception to the traditional rule, then the traditional rule has ceased to exist, and any state can justify intervening anywhere at any time against another country. In principle, virtually any intervention can be justified by its proponents as righting some wrong. Russia could invade the Baltic states or Ukraine in the name of protecting ethnic Russians, or Turkey to safeguard the Kurds. China and Pakistan could invade India to defend the Kashmiris. India could invade Sri Lanka to protect the minority Tamils from the Sinhalese-dominated government.

In those and innumerable other cases, the West could offer no principled objection to military incursions that previously would have been automatically condemned. Of course, the United States and its allies might quibble over whether the human rights violations in a particular case justified armed intervention. But if 2,000 dead in

Kosovo warrant war, what civil war, armed insurgency, or sectarian strife does not invite outside meddling? And NATO would have no standing to complain about ostensibly humanitarian intervention by other powers, having asserted the right to be judge and jury in Kosovo. Indeed, the allies consciously refused to go to the United Nations, the only truly international forum, since the Chinese and Russians would have blocked military action.

Furthermore, there is nothing compassionate about sending others off to fight. It's one thing to ask young men (and now young women) to risk their lives for their own political community. It is quite another thing for armchair warriors to have them die righting wrongs for other nations and peoples. However compelling may seem the humanitarian concerns, there is nothing selfless about ivory tower policymakers and commentators advocating that other people—the men and women in uniform—die in a supposedly moral cause. The U.S. government has an obligation to the members of its armed forces. Their lives shouldn't be treated as gambit pawns to be sacrificed in yet another global chess game. Real humanitarianism requires not risking their lives for purposes, however grand, unrelated to the interests of their own country.

## Conclusion

During the war President Clinton declared, "We cannot respond to such tragedies everywhere,"[47] but the "victory" over Yugoslavia seems to have emboldened him. He has since promised: "In Africa or Central Europe, we will not allow, only because of difference in ethnic background or religion or racism, people to be attacked. We will stop that."[48] So far, though, he seems no more serious about keeping this promise than about keeping the many others he has broken. In early August 1999 a bombing raid by the Sudanese military backing Congo's government reportedly killed 524 people, mostly civilians—more than 10 times the toll at Racak, which helped convince NATO to attack Yugoslavia.[49] Strangely, none of the avid humanitarian warriors—Clinton, Albright, Blair, Cook, and other advocates of NATO's crusade in the Balkans—bothered to express the outrage of the "international community," let alone propose doing something about the bloodshed.

Warmongering in the name of peace is an oxymoron. The Kosovo war has dramatically exposed humanitarian warmaking as the grossest sort of hypocrisy, a callous attempt to seize the moral high ground while cynically playing the grand game of global politics. But NATO's aggression is likely to have lasting humanitarian consequences. It was no mean achievement, but the intervention simultaneously exacerbated human rights abuses, spread the underlying conflict, encouraged similar lawlessness by other states, and lowered the barriers to aggression everywhere.

This is presumably why Owen Harries, the editor of the *National Interest*, warned, "What is wrong is not the impulse to give foreign policy a moral content, but the presumption that doing so is an uncomplicated business, one not requiring calculation and compromise but merely purity of intention."[50]

Those who have made such a calculation have ended up largely abandoning humanitarianism as a justification. German foreign minister Joschka Fischer gradually began defending the war against Yugoslavia, not as "a moral question" or "a question of human rights," but as involving "a question of the security and stability of Europe."[51] In trying to explain why NATO should intervene in Kosovo but not Rwanda, *Washington Post* columnist Richard Cohen observed: "[N]either is Rwanda in Europe. There—and not Africa— is where the United States has twice fought in this century."[52] Even more candid was French president Francois Mitterrand, who declared in 1994, "In such countries [as Rwanda], genocide is not too important."[53]

Indeed, many honest Kosovo hawks acknowledge that the policy was determined by perceived interests, not abstract morality.[54] Author David Rieff, for example, admits that the United States went to war in the Balkans for "a political reason."[55] Even the president's national security adviser, Sandy Berger, claimed that Kosovo involved tangible national interests, though the specific interests he cited seem trivial causes for going to war: bolstering NATO's credibility (which was on the line only because the administration had placed it there) and preventing the region from being destabilized by refugee flows (which were triggered by NATO's intervention).[56] So much for the principle of *humanitarian* intervention.

True humanitarianism would keep the United States out of foreign conflicts, except when, as Bill Clinton declared three decades ago, they "involve immediately the peace and freedom of the nation."[57] As Secretary of State John Quincy Adams observed last century, America should be the well-wisher of the liberty and independence of all but "need not go abroad in search of monsters to destroy." To do so, he warned, would destroy the essential values that set her apart: "The fundamental maxims of her policy would insensibly change from liberty to force. She might become dictatress of the world. She would be no longer the ruler of her own spirit."[58] Avoiding unnecessary wars is the only truly moral foreign policy.

## Notes

1. Quoted in Michael Hirsh and Mark Dennis, "Balk in the Balkans," *Newsweek*, March 8, 1999, p. 26.

2. Quoted in ibid.

3. All of these issues are dealt with extensively in this volume, as well as in other articles such as Doug Bandow, "NATO's Balkan Disaster: Wilsonian Warmongering Gone Mad," *Mediterranean Quarterly* 10, no. 3 (Summer 1999): 70–88.

4. See, for example, Jack Spencer, "Catalogue of Confusion: The Clinton Administration's War Aims in Kosovo," Heritage Foundation Backgrounder no. 1281, May 13, 1999.

5. William Jefferson Clinton, "A Just and Necessary War," *New York Times*, May 23, 1999, p. WK 17.

6. "Lessons of the Balkan War," Editorial, *New York Times*, June 17, 1999, p. A30.

7. Mortimer Zuckerman, "A Moment to Savor Victory," *U.S. News & World Report*, June 21, 1999, p. 72.

8. Ibid.

9. The chronology of events speaks for itself. See Christopher Layne, "Blunder in the Balkans: The Clinton Administration's Bungled War against Serbia," Cato Institute Policy Analysis no. 345, May 20, 1999, pp. 10–12.

10. See, for example, ibid., pp. 6–7; and Gary Dempsey, "Kosovo: More Spin Than Win," *Orange County Register*, June 13, 1999, Commentary Section, pp. 1, 5.

11. Quoted in Thomas Lippman, "Albright Misjudged Milosevic on Kosovo," *Washington Post*, April 7, 1999, p. A1.

12. Alan Kuperman, "Botched Diplomacy Led to War," Letter to the editor, *Wall Street Journal*, June 17, 1999, p. A27.

13. See, for example, Brian Mitchell, "Was Kosovo Bombing Needed?" *Investor's Business Daily*, June 15, 1999, pp. A1, A22.

14. Quoted in Doug Bandow, "Testimony before the House International Relations Committee, Hearing on the U.S. Role in Kosovo," March 10, 1999, p. 2.

15. Salmon Rushdie, "Kosovo's Cruel Realities," *Washington Post*, August 4, 1999, p. A21.

16. Obviously, many casualty estimates are suspect. But most analysts agree on the general magnitude of death tolls. See, for example, "When to Jump In: The World's Other Wars," *Time*, April 19, 1999, pp. 30–31; Vincent Browne, "When Is Slaughter of Innocents Not an Outrage?" June 16, 1999, p. 2, www.ireland.com.

17. John D. Lierman, "Guilty Silences," *The Religion & Society Report* 16, no. 6 (June 1999): 2.

18. For various estimates of the number of refugees, see Coum Lynch, "U.N. Refugee Chief Says Rich Nations Favor Kosovo over Africa in Aid," *Washington Post*, July 27, 1999, p. A20; Kenneth Roth, "Kosovars Aren't the Only Refugees," *Wall Street*

*Journal*, June 8, 1999, p. A18; Jack Redden, "Palestinians Still Searching," *Washington Times*, June 6, 1999, p. C13; George Gedda, "Concern for Kosovo Overshadows World's Other Refugees," *Washington Times*, May 23, 1999, p. C11; "Driven Out of House and Home," Editorial, *Washington Post*, May 22, 1999, p. A13; and Ian Fisher, "Help for Vast African Refugee Crisis May Suffer in Kosovo's Shadow, Aid Groups Say," *New York Times*, May 9, 1999, p. 8.

19. "Clinton to Tough Questioner: 'That's Really Good,'" Associated Press, July 1, 1999.

20. See, for example, Gary Dempsey, "Rethinking the Dayton Agreement: Bosnia Three Years Later," Cato Institute Policy Analysis no. 327, December 14, 1998.

21. Richard Boudreaux, "Ocalan's Dueling Images: Terrorist and Liberator," *Los Angeles Times*, February 24, 1999, p. A1.

22. For critical reviews of Turkey's conduct, see Department of State, *Country Reports on Human Rights Practices for 1996*, Report submitted to the Committee on Foreign Relations, U.S. Senate, and the Committee on International Relations, U.S. House of Representatives (Washington: Government Printing Office, February 1997), pp. 1153–73; *Destroying Ethnic Identity: The Kurds of Turkey, An Update* (New York: Human Rights Watch, September 1990); "Turkey: Forced Displacement of Ethnic Kurds from Southeastern Turkey," Human Rights Watch Report, October 1994; "The Kurds of Turkey: Killings, Disappearances and Torture," Human Rights Watch Report, March 1993, "Kurds Massacred: Turkish Forces Kill Scores of Peaceful Demonstrators," Human Rights Watch Report, June 1992.

23. "The Kurds of Turkey," p. 4.

24. Quoted in Norman Solomon, "American Journalists Have No Reason to Be Smug," Creators Syndicate, April 8, 1999.

25. "The Kurds of Turkey," p. 5.

26. There was much to criticize about the behavior of the ethnic Greek majority (and the government that it dominated) toward the roughly one-fifth of Cypriots who were ethnic Turks. But the coup did not directly threaten the latter, and the invasion turned out to be a prelude to partitioning the island rather than to negotiating guarantees for the Turkish minority.

27. In 1998 the European Court of Human Rights ruled that Turkey had violated the right of a Cypriot citizen, Titina Loizidou, "to the peaceful enjoyment of [her] possessions," that is, her land in the occupied zone. Louis Klarevas, "Turkey's Right-v.-Might Dilemma in Cyprus: Reviewing the Implications of *Loizidou v. Turkey*," *Mediterranean Quarterly* 10, no. 2 (Spring 1999): 97. Ankara has refused to pay the damages assessed by the court.

28. Gregory Copley, "Turkey, So Close to the Promise of Ataturk, Sees Its Strategic Options Withering," *Defense & Foreign Affairs Strategic Policy* 27, no. 7 (July 1999): 7.

29. Richard Land, "Do We Pay Now or Later?" *Light*, May–June, 1999, p. 10.

30. Not that doing so is necessarily helpful. Former representative Stephen Solarz and Brookings Institution scholar Michael O'Hanlon proposed that the United States intervene if the death rate in another country rises above America's murder rate. Michael O'Hanlon and Stephen Solarz, "Deciding When to Go," *Washington Post*, February 7, 1999, p. B1. That idea appropriately met with widespread derision, but proponents of humanitarian crusades have difficulty articulating a better criterion.

31. Peter Beinart, "War Fair," *New Republic*, May 31, 1999, p. 6. To his credit, Beinart admits that racism underlies existing policy and favors intervening in Africa as well. Leon Wieseltier of the *New Republic* says the failure to intervene in Rwanda

was a "historical dereliction of [Clinton's] duty" but nevertheless argues that the killing in Kosovo was different because "it was happening in our moral and cultural sphere . . . in our community." Quoted in Paul Starobin, "The Liberal War Hawks," *National Journal* 31, no. 20 (May 15, 1999), electronic version.

32. Raymond Bonner, "War Crimes Panel Finds Croat Troops 'Cleansed' the Serbs," *New York Times*, March 21, 1999, electronic version. The prosecutor, Louise Arbour, charged Croatia with impeding the investigation. Louise Arbour, "Request by the Prosecutor under Rule 7 BIS (B) That the President Notify the Security Council of the Failure of the Republic of Croatia to Comply with Its Obligations under Article 29," July 28, 1999, Document submitted to the International Criminal Tribunal for the Former Yugoslavia, electronic version.

33. "The Milosevic Problem," Editorial, *Wall Street Journal*, April 29, 1999, p. A26.

34. As in most guerrilla wars, it is never easy to tell apart combatants and civilians. The OSCE autopsy report was never released, and questions remain about whether the KLA turned casualties from a shoot-out into apparent massacre victims. See, for example, Ben Works, "Racak: Does the U.S. Have Credible Evidence?" *Strategic Issues Today*, January 28, 1999, electronic version; "Kosovo—When a Massacre Is Not a Massacre," *Strategic Issues Today*, January 20, 1999, electronic version.

35. Quoted in Dirk Johnson, "To Some Midwesterners, Milosevic Indictment Gives War New Meaning," *New York Times*, May 29, 1999, p. A7.

36. Quoted in Doug Bandow, "To Die for Kosovo," *American Spectator*, October 1998, p. 67.

37. Madeleine Albright and Robin Cook, "Our Campaign Is Working," *Washington Post*, May 16, 1999, p. B7. Of course, NATO's war aims were many and varied and seemed to change by the day if not the hour. See, for example, Spencer; Clinton; and Arianna Huffington, "Where's Any Sign of Outrage?" *Washington Times*, April 7, 1999, p. A16.

38. Nat Hentoff, "Morality at 15,000 Feet," *Washington Post*, June 19, 1999, p. A19.

39. Steve Chapman, "Under Fire: The Right Way to Kill Enemy Civilians," *Chicago Tribune*, May 27, 1999, electronic version. Land mines and cluster bombs continue to kill. See Carlotta Gall, "Mines and NATO Bombs Still Killing in Kosovo," *New York Times*, August 6, 1999, p. A3.

40. Quoted in Mary McGrory, "Commander in Cleats," *Washington Post*, April 1, 1999, p. A3.

41. Alas, National Security Adviser Samuel Berger had difficulty treating the ethnic cleansing of Serbs as ethnic cleansing. "Newsmaker Interview," Transcript of interview with Samuel Berger, *NewsHour with Jim Lehrer*, July 26, 1999.

42. See, for example, Steven Erlanger, "Despite the G.I.'s, Kosovo Town Is Purged of Serbs," *New York Times*, August 5, 1999, pp. A1, A3; Peter Finn, "NATO Losing Kosovo Battle," *Washington Post*, August 4, 1999, pp. A1, A18; and Tom Cohen, "Serbs Lose Faith in NATO Security," *Washington Times*, August 3, 1999, p. A12.

43. Peter Finn, "Kosovo Hostility Aimed at NATO," *Washington Post*, August 14, 1999, p. A1; and Carlotta Gall, "NATO-Led Forces Begin Crackdown on Kosovar Army," *New York Times*, August 15, 1999, p. A1.

44. Quoted in Robert Samuelson, "A War of Good Intentions," *Washington Post*, June 2, 1999, p. A21.

45. David Frum, "Westphalian Rule Can and Does Work," *National Post* (Toronto), March 27, 1999, p. B8.

46. Quoted in John Dunbar, "Showdown Intensifies; Decision to Intervene Abroad Turns Decisive," *Florida Times-Union*, March 27, 1999, p. A1.

47. Clinton.

48. "Clinton Says NATO Is Ready to Fight Repression in Europe, Africa," Agence France-Presse, June 22, 1999. Curious is the absence of Asia from his list. British prime minister Tony Blair seems to be traveling down a similar path, even though his nation possesses a much less potent military. See, for example., George Parker, "'Blair Doctrine' to Tackle Brutal Regimes," *Financial Times*, April 23, 1999, p. 2.

49. "Bombing Clouds Peace Prospects, Rebels Say," *Washington Times*, August 6, 1999, p. A13.

50. Owen Harries, "First Kosovo. Then Russia. Now China," *New York Times*, May 16, 1999, p. WK 17.

51. Quoted in Steven Mufson, "Once a Pacifist, German Official Defends War," *Washington Post*, June 11, 1999, p. A17.

52. Richard Cohen, "The Liberal Fantasy," *Washington Post*, May 14, 1999, p. A33. The *Wall Street Journal* similarly proclaimed, "No world war ever started in Rwanda." "Why Kosovo?" Editorial, *Wall Street Journal*, April 16, 1999, p. A14.

53. Quoted in Philip Gourevitch, "Comment," *New Yorker*, April 26 & May 3, 1999, p. 39.

54. Of course, the president's contention that the Balkans are the "heart of Europe" and sparked two world wars this century represents geographic ignorance (periphery of Europe is more accurate) and historical ignorance (the Balkans were irrelevant to the onset of World War II and triggered World War I only because the great powers chose to intervene in otherwise irrelevant ethnic feuds). For a general critique of the security arguments, see Benjamin Schwarz and Christopher Layne, "The Case against Intervention in Kosovo," *Nation*, April 19, 1999, pp. 11–16.

55. "US Foreign Policy," *All Things Considered*, National Public Radio, June 29, 1999, transcript, p. 3.

56. Bob Davis, "Pledging a 'Clinton Doctrine' for Foreign Policy Creates Concerns for Adversaries and Allies Alike," *Wall Street Journal*, August 6, 1999, p. A12.

57. Quoted in Harry Summers, "Forsaken Military Principles," *Washington Times*, June 1, 1999, p. A13.

58. John Quincy Adams, Address of July 4, 1821, in *The Home Book of Quotations: Classical and Modern*, 3d ed., ed. Burton Stevenson (New York: Dodd, Mead, 1937), p. 58.

PART II

THE CONSEQUENCES OF THE WAR

# 4. Collateral Damage in Yugoslavia

*Christopher Layne*

A central argument that President Clinton and his advisers invoked to justify their decision to use force against Yugoslavia was that NATO bombing was needed to prevent a Serbian military offensive in Kosovo and its concomitant "ethnic cleansing." The bombing campaign was disastrously counterproductive with regard to that goal. Indeed, it helped to cause, and greatly magnified, the human tragedy in Kosovo and throughout the rest of Yugoslavia.

## NATO's Air War Leads to Tragedy

In believing that either the mere threat of air strikes or a token bombing campaign would force Belgrade to submit quickly, the Clinton administration clearly erred. But, equally important, it failed to foresee the consequences of the initiation of the air campaign. On March 20, 1999, President Clinton said that unless Belgrade agreed to the Rambouillet accords, NATO would need to use air power to prevent what he described as Serbian atrocities against ethnic Albanians in Kosovo: "Make no mistake, if we and our allies do not have the will to act, there will be more massacres. In dealing with aggressors in the Balkans, hesitation is a license to kill. But action and resolve save lives."[1] However, when the president spoke those words, there was, in fact, no large-scale campaign being mounted against Kosovo's ethnic Albanians by the Yugoslav army. The mass expulsion of ethnic Albanians from the province, and the reports of widespread atrocities, did not occur until *after* NATO commenced its air campaign. Although *New York Times* columnist William Safire, echoing the administration and NATO, calls this a "big lie,"[2] it is quite easy to document the chronology of events (in large part by using the coverage of Safire's own newspaper).[3]

As had been widely reported, Belgrade obviously had a contingency plan to drive the ethnic Albanians out of Kosovo and had made preparations to implement that plan.[4] Planning is one thing, however; implementation is another. (NATO, for its part, began planning for possible military action against the Serbs in June 1998.) Prior to March 24, 1999, Belgrade was restrained from putting its plan into effect by the presence of European civilian monitors on the ground in Kosovo. This is not to say that there was no violence in Kosovo before the commencement of NATO's air campaign. Clearly, there was. However, the operations of the Yugoslav army up to that point were directed at rooting out the Kosovo Liberation Army from its strongholds, not at expelling ethnic Albanians en masse from Kosovo.[5] On March 20, the *New York Times* reported that there were no more than 20,000 ethnic Albanian refugees in Kosovo. Moreover, they were attempting to flee the fighting between the KLA and the Yugoslav army and were not targets of deliberate ethnic cleansing.[6]

The massive expulsion of ethnic Albanians, and the consequent humanitarian disaster, began only after NATO commenced bombing. Indeed, the Clinton foreign policy team was explicitly warned by both the Pentagon and the U.S. intelligence community that (1) Belgrade would respond to NATO air strikes by undertaking a forcible mass expulsion of Kosovo's ethnic Albanians and (2) the bombing campaign would not be able to stop the Yugoslav army from driving ethnic Albanians out of Kosovo.[7] The event that opened the door for the Yugoslav forces to move from counterinsurgency to population expulsion was the withdrawal of the monitors who had been deployed in Kosovo as part of the October 1998 cease-fire. As one monitor said just prior to the withdrawal order: "There is a lot of tension in the area. But while they [the monitors] stay where they are, things are more or less O.K."[8] The monitors were withdrawn on March 19, to ensure that they would be out of harm's way when the bombing campaign began. The administration was told by the intelligence community, and by its own diplomatic representative in Kosovo, William Walker, that withdrawal of the monitors would be taken by Belgrade as a green light to proceed to drive ethnic Albanians out of Kosovo.[9]

In the interval between withdrawal of the monitors and commencement of the air campaign, Yugoslav forces stepped up their offensive against the KLA. They still did not, however, engage in an ethnic cleansing campaign. Indeed, just two days before the alliance launched its air strikes, NATO officials were asking the KLA to desist from terrorist attacks against Serbs in Kosovo so as not to give Belgrade a pretext to engage in ethnic cleansing.[10] On the day the air campaign began, and in the days that immediately followed, ethnic Albanians in Kosovo expressed fear that the NATO action would trigger an upsurge in Serbian violence against them.[11] Those fears were justified, and on May 10 the U.S. State Department released a 30-page study titled "Erasing History: Ethnic Cleansing in Kosovo" that admitted the ethnic cleansing began *after* the bombs started falling on Yugoslavia. In fact, the study states:

> Since the withdrawal of the KVM [the Organization for Security and Cooperation in Europe's Kosovo Verification Mission] on March 19, 1999, Serbian military, paramilitary, and police forces in Kosovo have committed a wide range of war crimes, crimes against humanity, and other violations of international humanitarian and human rights law.[12]

And the study adds that by "late March 1999, Serbian forces *dramatically increased* the scope and pace of their efforts, moving away from selective targeting of towns and regions suspected of KLA sympathies toward a sustained and systematic effort to ethnically cleanse the entire province of Kosovo."[13]

The factual record is clear: not until NATO began its bombing did Belgrade's objective in Kosovo change from counterinsurgency to a campaign to expel the province's ethnic Albanians. As the great baseball manager Casey Stengel once said, "You could look it up." It was not until the air campaign had been under way for several days that the first reports of mass expulsions and atrocities began to surface.[14] It was in response to the refugee situation in Kosovo after commencement of the bombing that, on March 28, the alliance announced a purported switch in its bombing strategy: from attacks on Yugoslavia's air defenses to attacks on Yugoslav units on the ground in Kosovo to halt the expulsion of ethnic Albanians.[15]

Having contributed to the humanitarian catastrophe, the Clinton administration, notwithstanding its after-the-fact public statements to the contrary, was unprepared to deal with it.[16] If the administration and NATO *really* had anticipated that the air strikes would lead to the mass expulsion of ethnic Albanians from Kosovo, one wonders why the infrastructure was not already in place to feed, shelter, and provide medical assistance to them.

## Needless Civilian Casualties

Despite repeated U.S. and NATO pronouncements that the alliance had "no quarrel with the Serbian people," its decision to attack such targets as the Yugoslavian power grid and Serbian television clearly sent a contrary message. Indeed, by conducting a bombing campaign that it knew would cause widespread "collateral damage" (the military's Orwellian euphemism for civilian casualties), NATO hoped to cause enough terror and pain among Yugoslavia's civilian population to force Belgrade's capitulation.[17] Over the course of 11 weeks, NATO dropped more than 15,000 bombs and precision-guided munitions on Yugoslavia, releasing about 13,000 tons of explosive power. According to most estimates, those weapons killed between 1,200 and 2,000 civilians, or roughly one civilian for every 10 tons of explosives detonated.[18] That ratio is remarkably similar to that of major bombing campaigns during the Vietnam War. In the Christmas 1972 bombing around Hanoi and Haiphong Harbor, for example, 20,000 tons of explosives killed 1,600 civilians.[19]

The range of civilian targets mistakenly hit by NATO munitions was wide: from the Chinese embassy in Belgrade and a passenger train in Grdelica to an old-age home in Surdalica and an open-air market in Varvarvin.[20] In a grotesque example of Washington's spin mentality, the Clinton administration actually tried to turn such civilian casualties into a source of national pride. In fact, U.S. Secretary of Defense William Cohen told the Senate Armed Services Committee: "We go to extraordinary lengths to reduce the risk to innocent civilians. I don't think any other nation or combination of democracies would consider going through what we go through in the way of planning and training and exercising every conceivable precaution in order to reduce harming innocent civilians. And we should take great pride in that."[21] In other words, Americans should be pleased that NATO nations kill fewer innocent people than other nations do.

Finally, the Clinton administration and NATO claimed that one of the bombing campaign's objectives was to prevent "humanitarian tragedy" in Kosovo. (The administration made that claim notwithstanding that NATO military officers, in a rare moment of candor, finally admitted that the air campaign would not succeed in halting the ethnic cleansing in Kosovo.)[22] However, the alliance's concern for the plight of ethnic Albanians in Kosovo, and for limiting civilian casualties, was belied by its apparently indiscriminate use of cluster bombs in Kosovo itself. Contrary to NATO claims, it now is apparent that, in addition to Serbian actions, the bombing of Kosovo by the alliance was a major cause of the refugee outflow from that province.[23] As one American reporter on the ground in Kosovo has noted, people there, both Serbs and ethnic Albanians, "were left to wonder whether Kosovo had become a free-fire zone."[24]

Indeed, NATO's bombs accidentally killed 79 ethnic Albanian refugees on a road near Djakovica on April 14, 47 civilians on a passenger bus traveling north of Pristina on May 1, 87 refugees near the village of Korisa on May 13, and 19 inmates and guards at a Pristina jail on May 21.[25] In addition, NATO's bombs destroyed much of Kosovo's infrastructure and employment capacity. According to some estimates, reconstruction costs in the province may exceed $5 billion.[26] That's nearly five times the prewar annual gross domestic product of Kosovo, which had a population of 2.1 million and a per capita GDP of $541.[27]

## A Policy Fiasco

On March 25 President Clinton declared, "Our purpose is to prevent a humanitarian catastrophe or a wider war."[28] But NATO's air campaign clearly helped to create the very tragedy it ostensibly was intended to prevent. Policymakers are responsible for the reasonably foreseeable consequences of their actions. The Clinton administration was told that expulsion of ethnic Albanians was the likely consequence of air strikes. It elected to go ahead anyway, notwithstanding that its air power strategy was neither intended to stop, nor capable of stopping, the expulsions once they began. The Clinton administration bears a major share of the culpability for the humanitarian tragedy in Kosovo. Belgrade pulled the trigger, but by withdrawing the monitors and initiating the air strikes, the Clinton administration handed the Serbian authorities the gun.[29]

Having gone to war for the declared purposes of preventing a humanitarian disaster in Kosovo and preventing Balkan instability, the Clinton administration caused the very consequences it sought to prevent. More than 850,000 ethnic Albanians fled or were driven from Kosovo, and hundreds of thousands were internally displaced.[30] NATO also set Yugoslavia's economy back at least 10 years in the process, creating yet another failing state in the Balkans. The conflict and the resulting refugee crisis exacerbated already serious social, economic, and political tensions in neighboring Macedonia and Albania. Finally, the NATO intervention has allowed the volatile KLA—recently called "wildest of the wild cards" by a NATO insider because of the group's internal power struggles and nationalist ideology—to assert its control throughout the war-torn province.[31] That action sows the seeds of renewed tensions in Yugoslavia and throughout the Balkans.

## Notes

1. Quoted in John M. Broder, "Clinton Says Force Is Needed to Halt Kosovo Bloodshed," *New York Times*, March 20, 1999, p. A1.

2. William Safire, "Defeat's 19 Fathers," *New York Times*, April 26, 1999, p. A25. Referring to the possibility that NATO was seeking a diplomatic compromise that would fall short of victory for the alliance, Safire says, "The Big Lie undergirding the deal is already in place: that ethnic cleansing was caused by NATO bombing, not the other way around."

3. See John Kifner, "The Ravaging of Kosovo: How Serb Forces Purged One Million Albanians," *New York Times*, May 29, 1999, p. A1. As Kifner explains: "On the night of March 24, as NATO bombs began falling over Yugoslavia, Hani Hoxha said he saw black-masked Serbs swaggering through Djakovica, shooting, cutting throats and burning houses. At 3:30 in the morning, about nine miles east, a tank pulled up and parked in front of Isuf Zhenigi's farmhouse in the village of Bela Crkva. At daybreak the slaughter began there. That day, in Pec, 22 miles to the northwest, and Prizren, 15 miles southeast, Serbian forces began firing wildly and burning Albanian-owned shops. Meanwhile, in Pristina, about 44 miles to the northeast, Serbian operatives driving military jeeps and private cars set fire to Albanian-owned cafes, clinics and the printing presses of Kosova Sot, an independent Albanian newspaper. These were the opening assaults in what quickly became a drive to empty the city, the provincial and intellectual center of Kosovo."

4. R. Jeffrey Smith and William Drozdiak, "A Blueprint for War: The Serbs' Military Campaign Was Meticulously Planned Months Ago," *Washington Post*, national weekly edition, April 19, 1999, p. A6.

5. Carlotta Gall, "New Floods of Refugees Are on the Move," *New York Times*, March 20, 1999, p. A4; and Carlotta Gall, "Thousands in Kosovo Flee Serb Drive," *New York Times*, March 21, 1998, p. A10.

6. See ibid.; and Gall, "New Floods of Refugees."

7. Craig R. Whitney and Eric Schmitt, "NATO Had Signs Its Strategy Would Fail in Kosovo," *New York Times*, April 1, 1999, p. A1; and Jane Perlez, "Unpalatable U.S. Options," *New York Times*, March 23, 1999, p. A1.

8. Quoted in Gall, "New Floods of Refugees."

9. Ibid.; Whitney and Schmitt, "NATO Had Signs"; and Perlez, "Unpalatable Options."

10. Steven Erlanger, "U.S. Issues Appeal to Serbs to Halt Attack in Kosovo," *New York Times*, March 23, 1999, p. A1. On the night of March 22, the KLA apparently was responsible for several bombings of bars in Pristina that killed at least one person and wounded eight.

11. Carlotta Gall, "With Flash in Sky, Kosovars Fear Ground Fighting," *New York Times,* March 25, 1999, p. A1; and Carlotta Gall, "Ethnic Albanians Now Fear Wrath of Serbs," *New York Times,* March 26, 1999, p. A1.

12. U.S. Department of State, "Erasing History: Ethnic Cleansing in Kosovo," http://www.state.gov/www/regions/eur/rpt_9905_ethnic_ksvo_toc.html.

13. Ibid. Emphasis added.

14. Paul Watson, "Airstrikes May Be Triggering New Massacres," *Los Angeles Times,* March 27, 1999, p. A1; Jane Perlez, "White House Tells of Reports of a Forced March in Kosovo," *New York Times,* March 27, 1999, p. A1; and Jane Perlez, "U.S. Stealth Fighter Is Down in Yugoslavia As NATO Orders Attack on Serb Army Units: 'Ethnic Cleansing,'" *New York Times,* March 28, 1999, p. A1.

15. Eric Schmitt, "NATO's Claim of New Focus Is Challenged," *New York Times,* March 28, 1999, p. A1; and R. W. Apple Jr., "Bombs Fall, Goals Unmet?" *New York Times,* March 28, 1999, p. A1.

16. For the statements of President Clinton and Secretary Albright that the United States was not caught off guard by the refugee crisis, see Doyle McManus, "Debate Turns to Finger-Pointing on Kosovo Policy," *Los Angeles Times,* April 11, 1999, p. A1.

17. Michael Dobbs, "Deconstructing Yugoslavia," *Washington Post,* April 25, 1999, p. A1; and Daniel Williams, "NATO Bombs Serbia into Darkness," *Washington Post,* May 3, 1999, p. A1.

18. Fred Kaplan, "Bombs Killing More Civilians than Expected," *Boston Globe,* May 30, 1999, p. A33; Robert Fisk, "War in the Balkans: 72 Days, 1,500 Dead: Serbs Ask Why," *Independent* (London), June 4, 1999, p. 1; and Calvin Woodward, "A High Human Cost from Wars Large and Small," Associated Press, June 12, 1999.

19. Kaplan.

20. See Steven Erlanger, "NATO Bombs Reported to Kill 20 Civilians in Southern Serbia," *New York Times,* April 28, 1999, p. 14; "NATO's Other Attack Blunders Tallied," *Chicago Sun-Times,* May 23, 1999, p. 6; "The Growing List of Allied Blunders," *New York Post,* May 23, 1999, p. 2; Richard Bourdreaux, "Civilian Deaths in Airstrikes Erode NATO Credibility in the Balkans: Nine People Are Killed in Bridge Attack," *Los Angeles Times,* May 31, 1999, p. A1; Julijana Mojsilovic and Stephen Bates, "Planes Buzzed Overhead and Then Death Came: Bridge Carnage Eyewitnesses Describe the NATO Attack on Their Town," *Guardian* (London) May 31, 1999, p. 5.

21. Quoted in Julie Moffett, "Yugoslavia: U.S. Regrets Civilian Casulties," Radio Free Europe/Radio Liberty, April 16, 1999.

22. Norman Kempster, John-Thor Dahlburg, and Janet Wilson, " 'Ethnic Cleansing' Unstoppable, Top NATO Official Says," *Los Angeles Times,* May 5, 1999, p. A16.

23. Steven Erlanger, "Fleeing Kosovars Dread Danger of NATO Above and Serb Below," *New York Times,* May 4, 1999, p. A1.

24. Paul Watson, "NATO Bomb Kills 17 More Civilians," *Los Angeles Times,* May 4, 1999, p. A16. His first-hand accounts probably were decisive in forcing NATO to retract its denials (1) of bombing a refugee column near Djavocika and (2) of bombing residential areas in several towns in Kosovo. Watson's stories also documented how the use of cluster bombs caused widespread civilian casualties, especially among children playing with unexploded bomb canisters. Paul Watson, "Not So Smart Weapons Are Terrifying Civilians," *Los Angeles Times,* April 14, 1999, p. A1; Paul Watson, "Cluster Bombs May Be What Killed Refugees," *Los Angeles Times,* April 16, 1999, p. A1; and Paul Watson, "Unexploded Weapons Pose Deadly Threat on Ground," *Los Angeles Times,* April 28, 1999, p. A1. Other news reports confirmed the

tragic effects of NATO cluster bombs on innocent civilians. See Dan Eggen, "In Kosovo, Death Comes in Clusters," *Washington Post*, July 19, 1999, p. A1.

25. "NATO Today Admitted That Its Warplanes Bombed Convoy in Kosovo," Associated Press, April 15, 1999; William Goldschlag, "Bombing Kills 79: Refugees' Deaths Blamed on NATO," *New York Daily News*, May 15, 1999, p. 2; and "NATO Mistakenly Bombs Rebel Stronghold," *Seattle Times*, May 23, 1999, p. A3.

26. Charles Fleming, "Construction Firms Take Cautious Approach to Kosovo— Rebuilding the Province Won't Be a 'Bonanza,' And Funding Is Unclear," *Wall Street Journal*, June 21, 1999, p. A2.

27. Gramoz Pashko, "Kosovo: Facing Dramatic Economic Crisis," in *Kosovo: Avoiding Another Balkan War*, ed. Thanos Veremis and Evangelos Kofos (Athens: University of Athens, 1998), p. 339. Figures are based on 1990 dollars coverted into 1998 dollars by Layne.

28. Quoted in John-Thor Dahlburg and Paul Richter, "2nd Wave of Allied Firepower Pounds Yugoslavia; Serbs Continue Assaults," *Los Angeles Times*, March 26, 1999, p. A1.

29. As a West European diplomat admitted after the first four days of bombing, "We have to confront the possibility that the air campaign, by forcing the independent observers and Western journalists out of Kosovo, has given the Serbs a sense that they can do whatever they like without anyone being able to prove that they did." Quoted in Apple.

30. Serge Schmemann, "From President, Victory Speech and a Warning," *New York Times*, June 11, 1999, p. 1; and David Finkel, "Casualties of War: In the Hills, Scraping to Survive, Some Ethnic Albanians Have No Reason to Go Home," *Washington Post*, June 15, 1999, p. A1.

31. Matt Spetalnick, "NATO, KLA Sign Accord for Rebels to Disarm," Reuters, June 21, 1999. See also Marcus Gee, "The KLA Makes Its Presence Felt," *Globe and Mail* (Toronto), June 16, 1999, p. A13; Tom Walker, "Balkans War: Taming the Guerrillas," *Times* (London), June 17, 1999, p. 6; Paul Watson and Marjorie Miller, "Defying NATO, Rebels Try to Grab Government Control," *Los Angeles Times*, June 19, 1999, p. A1; and Donna Bryson, "KLA Challenges UN Authority," Associated Press, June 20, 1999.

# 5. Headaches for Neighboring Countries
## Gary Dempsey

NATO's 11-week air war is estimated to have cost the struggling economies of Yugoslavia's neighbors more than $4.2 billion.[1] The most visible losses were those associated with Albania's, Bosnia's, and Macedonia's efforts to manage the flood of refugees from Kosovo. But the bulk of economic losses resulted from the severing of transportation routes along the Danube River and over land through Yugoslavia, and the loss of the Yugoslavia market itself as a result of the war and sanctions that have yet to be lifted. As a consequence of those trade disruptions, nearly all of Yugoslavia's neighbors are expected to register export declines for 1999 (Table 5-1). Hardest hit will likely be Macedonia, which formerly shipped more than two-thirds of its exports to or through Yugoslavia, and the Serbian half of Bosnia, which saw its wartime exports to Yugoslavia fall by 75 percent.[2]

Other economic losses have resulted from reduced tourism receipts, higher prices for imported goods, and reduced product

*Table 5-1*
PROJECTED 1999 DECLINE IN EXPORTS

| Country | Decline |
| --- | --- |
| Albania | NA |
| Bosnia | 10% |
| Bulgaria | 10% |
| Croatia | 10% |
| Hungary | 1% |
| Macedonia | 15% |
| Romania | 2% |

SOURCE: Peter Bennett, "The Danube Blues: The Kosovo Conflict Exacts a High Toll on Region's Businesses," *Wall Street Journal Europe*, May 31, 1999, p. 12.
NA = not available.

*Table 5-2*
PREWAR V. POSTWAR 1999 GDP GROWTH PROJECTIONS

| Country | Prewar | Postwar | Change |
|---|---|---|---|
| Albania | 5% | 3% | −2% |
| Bosnia | 16% | 11% | −5% |
| Bulgaria | 0.5% | −1.5% | −1% |
| Croatia | 2% | 1% | −1% |
| Hungary | 4% | 3.7% | −0.3% |
| Macedonia | 5% | 0% | −5% |
| Romania | −4% | −5% | −1% |

SOURCE: Peter Bennett, "The Danube Blues: The Kosovo Conflict Exacts a High Toll on Region's Businesses," *Wall Street Journal Europe*, May 31, 1999, p. 12.

competitiveness as a consequence of having to use more costly alternate transportation routes. The various war-induced losses have already had a significant macroeconomic impact on Yugoslavia's neighbors, and economists expect that the 1999 GDP of each affected country will fall short of earlier projections of growth (Table 5-2). But the economic losses are not limited to just the immediate term. Declining asset values are expected to result from diminished consumer confidence within each country. Economists at the International Monetary Fund report: "All the countries in the vicinity of Kosovo will suffer the adverse effects of the crisis on confidence of [foreign] investors. In particular, a serious loss of foreign direct investment is projected for Albania, Macedonia, Bulgaria, and Croatia."[3] "Most countries," the IMF's economists add, "are projected to face higher borrowing costs in international capital markets and in some cases access to private financing may dry up entirely."[4]

The economic blow inflicted by NATO's air war comes at an especially precarious time. The slowing of internal and cross-border economic activity is expected to produce budgetary shortfalls within each affected country. In fact, lost tax revenues and reduced customs receipts, combined with emergency expenditures related to refugee assistance and increased border control, are expected to raise the aggregate 1999 budget gaps of Yugoslavia's neighbors to more than half a billion dollars.[5] Moreover, NATO's air war has slowed the post–Cold War recovery of Yugoslavia's neighbors even further;

## *Figure 5-1*
### 1989–98 GDP FOR SELECTED COUNTRIES IN SOUTHEASTERN EUROPE

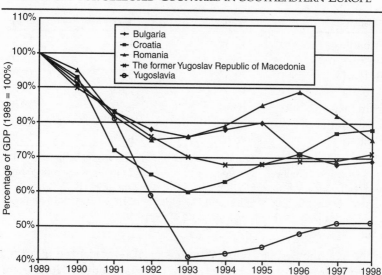

SOURCE: United Nations Economic Commission for Europe, Economic Analysis Division, "Economic Survey of Europe," no. 2 (1999), www.unece.org/ead/pub/survey.htm.

most countries have been in economic regress since 1989 (Figure 5-1), and most are still trying to overcome the effects of 1998's economic meltdown in Russia and the United Nations' embargo on Yugoslavia during the 1992–95 war in Bosnia.

Nearly all of Yugoslavia's neighbors are also already plagued by double-digit unemployment (Table 5-3), and the war's downward pressure on exports and industrial output has aggravated joblessness. Accordingly, IMF economists fear that public support for privatization and market reform will suffer as it becomes more difficult to sustain a political consensus under weaker economic conditions and higher unemployment.[6] Even more worrisome, economists at the UN's Economic Commission for Europe fear that the unemployment situation in the countries around Yugoslavia may be "reaching levels that must inevitably raise questions about the prospects for social stability."[7]

The political fallout of NATO's air war is also troubling: the governments of Albania and Macedonia now face the prospect of growing pan-Albanian nationalism in the wake of the Kosovo Liberation Army's apparent success in gaining Kosovo's de facto independence;

*Table 5-3*
1996–98 Unemployment Rates

| Country | 1996 | 1997 | 1998 |
|---------|------|------|------|
| Albania | 12.3% | 14.9% | 17.6% |
| Bosnia | N/A | 39.0% | 38.0% |
| Bulgaria | 12.5% | 13.7% | 12.2% |
| Croatia | 15.9% | 17.6% | 18.6% |
| Hungary | 10.1% | 8.9% | 8.0% |
| Macedonia | 39.8% | 42.0% | 40.0% |
| Romania | 6.6% | 8.8% | 10.3% |

Sources: United Nations Economic Commission for Europe, Economic Analysis Division, "Economic Survey of Europe," no. 2 (1999), www.unece.org/ead/pub/survey.htm; *OECD Economic Outlook: June 1999* (Paris: Organization for Economic Cooperation and Development, 1999); and "Still Nervous in Macedonia," *The Economist*, June 12, 1999, p. 44.

in Bosnia, the Serbian population has been reradicalized at a time when their government is in political crisis; and ethnic Hungarians in the Transylvania and Banat regions of Romania have taken a cue from Kosovo's separatists and are stepping up their demands for political autonomy. What follows in the remainder of this chapter is a country-by-country summary of the political and economic consequences that NATO's air war has had for Yugoslavia's neighbors.

### Albania

The primary impact of NATO's air war on the economy of Albania was the tidal wave of refugees that immediately followed the commencement of air strikes. The refugee crisis put a huge strain on Albania's already poor administrative capacity. The war also increased Albania's incremental balance of payments gap to $133 million, or 3.5 percent of GDP. The crush of refugees, combined with the loss of trade and foreign investment, is estimated to have cost Albania a total of $802 million.[8]

For Albania, the most far-reaching political consequence of NATO's air war is the de facto independence that is taking root in Kosovo and the resulting prospect of a Greater Albania. That is something the Clinton administration said NATO's bombs were meant to prevent.[9] Yet from the beginning, the KLA has made it clear that it is interested not only in independence for Kosovo but in uniting the 8 million ethnic Albanians of Albania, Kosovo, Macedonia, Greece, and Montenegro. That goal is shared by some high-profile politicians in Albania, including former president Sali Berisha. Berisha referred to the KLA insurgency in Kosovo as a "holy war," and he defines the "Albanian nation" as including not only Albania but also Kosovo and western Macedonia, both of which have large ethnic Albanian populations.[10] In 1998 Berisha gave his family farm in northern Albania to the KLA guerrillas to use as a military training ground and referred to Albania's former prime minister, Fatos Nano, as an "enemy of the Albanian nation" for failing to support the KLA.[11]

The potential for growing pan-Albanian nationalism should not be underestimated. *New York Times* reporter Chris Hedges, who spent more than a year investigating the KLA, explains that the KLA has "little sympathy with or understanding of democratic institutions" and that the KLA is "uncompromising in its quest for an independent Kosovo now and a Greater Albania later."[12] Accordingly, the Pentagon believes that even a modestly empowered KLA creates an "undesirable, but highly likely" set of circumstances inimical to Western interests, a scenario the U.S. military planners describe as "a perverse residual regional imperative that is very difficult to avoid."[13] In fact, a militant KLA determined to fashion a greater Albania, supported by patrons within Albania itself, puts the entire region at risk. Macedonia could be broken apart, drawing in Greece and Bulgaria to defend the ethnic Greeks and Bulgarians who live there. The violence could also infect northern Greece and southern Montenegro where there are significant ethnic Albanian populations. In short, NATO's air war may have simply replaced one problem—Serbian nationalism—with another problem—Albanian nationalism.

## Bosnia

NATO's air war against Yugoslavia had a substantial economic impact on Bosnia. The primary stress points were reduced exports, especially of products of heavy industries linked with Yugoslavia, and decreased foreign and domestic investment in the face of increased uncertainty. There were also costs associated with managing the influx of 30,000 refugees from Kosovo—an additional $5.5 million burden, according to Bosnia's deputy minister for civilian affairs.[14] Bosnian exports are expected to be off 10 percent in 1999, and imports are expected to decline 11 percent. In the Republika Srpska (the Serbian half of Bosnia) Deputy Prime Minister Djuradj Banjac estimates that more than $360 million was lost in trade and industrial output, and tens of thousands of employees were laid off.[15] Overall, Bosnia's 1999 GDP growth is expected to fall short of earlier projections by 5 percentage points.

Hostility toward the West has also increased in Bosnia, worsening a political situation rocked by two crises earlier in the year: the decision by the chief Western official overseeing the Dayton Peace Accord to remove from power the lawfully elected president of the Republika Srpska and the decision by a Western arbitrator not to award the strategic town of Brcko to the Bosnian Serbs. Tension among the 1 million Serbs in the Republika Srpska, who were already upset with those decisions, was increased by NATO's air strikes. In separate incidents, angry Bosnian Serbs ransacked and looted Western-occupied buildings, trashed international aid vehicles, fired a rocket-propelled grenade at a helicopter of the NATO-led force in Bosnia, lobbed grenades from cars, and launched other armed attacks.[16] At present, the three-way presidency in Bosnia does not function, the main ethnic political parties are squabbling, and the trickle of returning refugees has all but stopped.

NATO's air war has also destabilized the military balance of power that was negotiated between Yugoslavia, Croatia, and the two political units that make up Bosnia—the Muslim-Croat Federation and the Republika Srpska. Under an agreement negotiated in Vienna in 1996, the ratio of arms of the Muslim-Croat Federation and the Republika Srpska was set at 2:1, balanced by a 5:2 ratio between Yugoslavia and Croatia. But NATO's destruction of a large portion of Yugoslavia's military and industrial capacity means that the Muslim-Croat half of Bosnia and Croatia now has a significant military advantage over the Serbs in Bosnia.

## Bulgaria

The wreckage of six bridges that NATO bombs dropped into the Danube had the greatest economic impact on Bulgaria's economy, paralyzing shipping traffic along the 1,750-mile waterway that links Germany to the Black Sea.[17] Bulgarian businesses, which moved 65 percent of their exports along the Danube before the war, were forced to spend $8 million in April 1999 alone to reload their cargo onto trucks and railroad cars.[18] Bulgaria's deputy foreign minister, Alexander Bozhkov, reported that his country was losing $1.5 million a day in exports after NATO rendered the Danube impassable.[19] The Organization for Economic Cooperation and Development estimated the daily losses at slightly less, pegging them at $1.25 million.[20] Overall, Bulgarian exports dove 24 percent in the first quarter of 1999, according to a postwar assessment made by Bulgaria's National Statistics Institute.[21] And, according to Bulgaria's trade minister, the Bulgarian trade economy lost $70.7 million as a result of the war: $30.8 million in transport, $22.7 million in industry, $9.1 million in agriculture, and $8.1 million in other sectors.[22]

One company that really felt the pinch was the Bulgarian logistics company Econt Trans. It normally arranges river transport for 100,000 tons of iron ore, 20,000 tons of steel products, and 10,000 tons of chemicals from Bulgarian ports to customers in the West each year. "As you can imagine, it is difficult to arrange alternative transport for 20,000 tons of steel in a couple of days," explains one manager at the company.[23] Predictably, blocking the Danube has had a corresponding effect on the employment picture in Bulgaria. The state-owned shipping company, for example, has already laid off nearly 1,000 workers.[24]

On the political side, over 90 percent of Bulgarians opposed NATO's air war against Yugoslavia, and the percentage of Bulgarians who want their country to join NATO dropped from 60 percent before the war to barely 50 percent in May.[25] The Bulgarian government, nevertheless, officially supported NATO's air war, but it may pay a price come the next elections, or sooner.[26] Indeed, no Bulgarian government has lasted its full term since the collapse of communism in 1990. And if economic hardship sets in, it could undo the current ruling Union of Democratic Forces government in the same way it undid the Socialist government in 1997, when the economic situation floundered and inflation raged at 300 percent.

### Croatia

NATO's air strikes against Yugoslavia had a significant effect on three areas of the Croatian economy: a reduction in foreign tourism receipts, less foreign trade, and lower privatization-related foreign direct investment. The Croatian National Bank estimates that Croatia may end up losing 10 to 15 percent of its 1999 tourism receipts.[27] In an even gloomier forecast, Croatia's minister of tourism, Ivan Herak, says Croatia's tourism receipts may drop by as much as 50 percent.[28] In the beach-side city of Dubrovnik alone, cruise ship and hotel cancellations reached 9,000 per week during NATO's air war, and the manager of one of the city's luxury hotels reported that while NATO was bombing neighboring Yugoslavia only 70 of his 1,000 beds were occupied each night.[29]

The IMF worries that the war has slowed privatization and foreign investment in Croatia by creating transaction delays and lower sale prices for state-owned assets.[30] Moreover, while investors predictably avoided Croatia during NATO's air war, most have not returned now that the bombing has stopped. In fact, turnover on the Zagreb Stock Exchange has dipped to near historic lows, averaging $200,000 to $300,000 on a good day, with only a handful of most trusted issues trading.[31] Roger Monson, a strategist for the Dutch financial giant Rabobank, also fears that the devastation NATO's bombs inflicted on Yugoslavia's economy will further hamper Croatian companies that are trying to revive old business ties that existed with Serbia before the Yugoslav federation began disintegrating in 1991.[32] A notable loser, says Monson, will likely be Pliva, a Croatian pharmaceutical company that used to supply the entire former Yugoslavia.[33] Overall, the damage NATO's air war caused to Croatia's economy is expected to amount to more than $522 million in 1999, according to Croatian Reconstruction and Development Bank officials.[34] The IMF and private-sector economists expect that Croatia's 1999 economy could contract by as much as 2 percent.[35]

## Hungary

NATO's air war also took its toll on the Hungarian economy, which had only begun recovering from the financial blow it received in 1998 as a result of the economic meltdown of one of its major trading partners, Russia. The main sectors affected by NATO's campaign were shipping, exports, and tourism. Although the OECD has tried to downplay the economic impact of NATO's war on Hungary's economy, Hungary's Central Statistics Office estimates that the first 50 days of the war cost Hungary's overall economy $200 million, and GKI, a respected Hungarian research firm, estimates that Hungary's tourism sector alone could lose as much as $300 million by the end of 1999.[36]

The greatest impact on Hungary's economy resulted from NATO's blocking of the Danube. In a normal year, 10 million tons of freight travel the river through Yugoslavia, but according to Peter Balas, deputy state secretary at the Hungarian Economics Ministry, full Danube traffic is not likely to be restored until sometime in 2000.[37] One Hungarian shipping company, Manhart, saw 20 percent of its capacity stranded by the downed bridges and expects to ship half a million fewer tons of cargo in 1999 than in 1998.[38] That, say company executives, could slash Manhart's revenue by as much as a half.[39] Unfortunately, NATO blocked the Danube just as Hungary's shipping industry was beginning to recover from the long slump created by the embargoes placed on Yugoslavia during the war in Bosnia.

Hungarian producers who depend on river shipping were hard hit, too. Indeed, since it cost $100 extra per ton to ship over land, Hungary's agricultural exports to the Middle East were crippled; Hungarian farmers had no cost-efficient way to deliver $450 million worth of their summer 1999 harvest to their customary markets to the east.[40] The chief Hungarian steel company, Dunaferr, was forced to replace thousands of tons of Ukrainian and South African ore, which it was prevented from importing via the Danube.[41]

While Budapest officially supported NATO's air war and granted the alliance permission to use Hungarian airbases, Hungarian opinion polls showed that two-thirds of the public opposed launching air strikes from inside Hungary's borders, and a number of prominent Hungarian intellectuals publicly opposed the bombing campaign.[42] Many Hungarians also worried that cooperating with NATO might give a resentful Belgrade a tailor-made excuse to turn its sights some day on the 300,000 ethnic Hungarians living in Serbia's northern Vojvodina province.[43] Like Kosovo, Vojvodina enjoyed substantial autonomy until it was abolished in 1989 by the Milosevic regime. Many Hungarians also feared that NATO's bombing raids on Vojvodina's capital city, Novi Sad, would inadvertently kill ethnic Hungarian civilians.[44]

Throughout NATO's 11-week bombing campaign, Budapest's support was underwhelming, at best. Hungary provided no warplanes or munitions and made only a token contribution of a 30-member medical team.[45] What's more, Hungarian foreign minister Janos Martonyi ruled out the possibility of any Hungarian participation in a NATO land action, and he rejected the idea that Hungary should help pay for the multi-billion-dollar operation.[46] Hungary's leading opposition party, which was the architect of Hungary's membership in NATO when it was in power in 1998, was even less supportive of the operation, urging the Hungarian parliament to ban NATO air strikes from Hungarian territory altogether.[47]

## Macedonia

NATO's air war against Yugoslavia inflicted enormous costs on Macedonia's economy as a result of the disruption of trade, the influx of refugees, and the perceived increased risk of political and economic instability. The closure of the border with Yugoslavia resulted in a dramatic loss in export markets, since direct trade with and transit trade through Yugoslavia represented roughly 70 percent of Macedonian exports. As a result, Macedonia's 1999 incremental balance of payments gap is expected to rise from $38 million to $337 million, or 9.5 percent of GDP.[48] The war also forced Macedonian factories that do business with Yugoslavia—among them are some of Macedonia's largest employers—to stop or curtail production. For example, a Macedonian factory that produced parts for the Zastava car company in Yugoslavia has had to lay off 6,000 workers because Zastava's factory was destroyed by NATO bombs.[49] Macedonian trade unions, moreover, report that 40,000 Macedonian workers are on "forced leave" and that 120,000 workers have not been paid in months.[50] The economic blow could not have come at a worse time for Macedonia. The unemployment rate is already one of the highest in Europe, and after years of turbulent economic weather, the country has seen its foreign investment all but disappear. Macedonia is also expected to miss its 1999 GDP growth projection by 8 percentage points, and, as a result of lower revenues and direct refugee-related expenditures, Macedonia's 1999 budgetary deficit is expected to increase from $6 million, or 0.1 percent of GDP, to $185 million, or 4.5 percent of GDP.[51]

On the political side, the impact of NATO's air war could prove dire. Anti-NATO sentiment has risen among Macedonian Slavs, who feel that their Serb brothers have been unfairly singled out by a hypocritical NATO alliance. In fact, the day after the commencement of NATO's air strikes, there was an anti-NATO riot in the Macedonian capital, and the U.S. embassy was attacked.[52] But, even more worrisome than anti-NATO furor, Macedonia faces rising ethnic tensions. The country is already ethnically divided between Macedonian Slavs and ethnic Albanians, who make up about one-third of the population. NATO's air war has made Macedonia poorer, sharpening tensions between the ethnic groups. Macedonia's foreign minister, Alexander Dimitrov, stresses the stabilizing importance of a healthy economy, but by the end of 1999, he says, his country will have lost some $1.5 billion in war-related damages. Many factories have had to close, and privatization has all but stalled. "There may be social tension, strikes, and trouble," worries Dimitrov. "I fear inter-ethnic tension."[53] More recently, Macedonian prime minister Ljubco Georgievski has warned: "If we do not receive serious [economic] assistance . . . we'll have a serious crisis. And we should not underestimate the possibility that a social disaster would displace ethnic tolerance."[54]

## Romania

When the Danube was closed by the wreckage of bombing, 126 Romanian barges and 18 foreign barges destined for Romania, carrying 60,000 tons of merchandise, were suddenly stranded.[55] Romania's Ministry of Industry estimates that its exports to Hungary, Austria, and Germany will be off by as much as $300 million in 1999.[56] The Romanian Association of River Shipowners and Harbor Operators, which represents 92 percent of Romania's shipping capacity, estimates that nearly $90 million was lost during NATO's 11-week air campaign: shipping companies lost $63.9 million, port operators lost $11.9 million, brokers lost $4.9 million, harbor and waterway utilities lost $4.0 million, and shipbuilders lost $1.3 million. The shipping association also fears that losses will continue well into 2000.[57] Many Romanian shipping companies are also complaining that they will have to lay off workers or sell part of their fleets to make up for the losses; those companies have lodged formal protests with NATO, the European Union, the European Danube Commission, and the U.S. embassy in Bucharest.[58]

Consider the case of Navrom, the Romanian state-owned river transport company. Navrom says 167 of its 423 barges were left idle by the war and it will probably have to lay off half of its 3,000 workers as a result.[59] "The situation is not good at all," explains Sorin Rodeanu, an adviser to Navrom's general manager. May and June fell in the middle of the war, and they "are the best periods for us, because we can load the barges full. We had contracts worth $22 million up until the end of December, and if we cannot make these contracts, we will lose it all," Rodeanu says. Many of Navrom's customers were in Yugoslavia, and their facilities have been bombed. It could therefore take years before Navrom's customer base is fully restored. "And we're still in debt from the Bosnian embargo," adds Rodeanu.[60]

The economic situation in Romania has been deteriorating for years, but NATO's air war against Yugoslavia has made things worse. Romania's GDP shrank by 7.3 percent in 1998 and by 6.6 percent in 1997.[61] In 1999 it was expected to shrink by 4 percent, but the postwar projection is that it will shrink by 5 percent.[62] According to government estimates, NATO's air war cost Romania more than half a billion dollars in lost trade and higher transportation costs, and the total economic loss for Romania is expected to approach $915 million for 1999.[63] Romania's currency has also lost half its value since January 1999, and foreign direct investment dropped from $29 million a month before the war to $3 million once the war began.[64] Today, laments one financial analyst, Romania "continues to be virtually boycotted" by foreign investors.[65] As a result of those factors, Romania is closer than ever to defaulting on its foreign-debt payments.[66]

Meanwhile, unemployment in Romania is at 12 percent, but it is likely to increase in the wake of NATO's air war and if government plans for industrial restructuring are implemented. Should Romania's workers display their notorious militancy and skepticism about NATO grow, Romania's general election in 2000 could produce a government less sympathetic to economic reform and the West. Already, there are political tremors. In fact, when Romanian president Emil Constantinescu announced support for the air strikes, his popularity dropped 10 points overnight in public opinion polls.[67]

For Romania, however, the most troubling political consequence of NATO's intervention in Kosovo is the example it has set. There are 1.6 million ethnic Hungarians in Romania, and the nationalists among them now seem encouraged to push their own separatist agenda.[68] The Hungarian Democratic Union of Romania, which is in Romania's ruling coalition, sent a letter to Bill Clinton in June claiming ethnic cleansing was occurring in Romania and requesting his support for political autonomy for Romania's ethnic Hungarian population.[69] Moreover, a declaration is now being circulated among ethnic Hungarian intellectuals in Transylvania and Banat that asserts that the two regions are more advanced economically than the rest of Romania and should be granted autonomy.[70] The radical Hungarian National Front has also reiterated its calls for a "revision of the borders and a Hungarian state of the Carpathian basin."[71] If Romania's economy continues to sink and Hungary's economy improves, pressure from Romania's ethnic Hungarian population for political autonomy may reach the breaking point.[72]

## Conclusion

In any military conflict, people are killed and property is destroyed, but the complete fallout isn't always immediately apparent. That certainly is the case with NATO's air war against Yugoslavia: the economic and political consequences are still unfolding and will likely unfold into the 21st century. An added consequence that has yet to be fully appreciated is the environmental impact of NATO's air war; NATO used depleted-uranium munitions, and the bombing of oil refineries and petrochemical plants created oil slicks and toxic spills that flowed down the Danube into the Black Sea.[73]

Furthermore, in a turn of events that foreshadows the huge costs that may await Washington's future interventions, a number of Yugoslavia's neighbors that officially supported NATO's air war have announced that they will seek money from the IMF and the World Bank to cover their economic losses. Albanian officials are the most direct: "We are going to stress especially the big contribution of Albania during the crisis and, based on this, to demand from [the] international community assistance for Albania."[74] That development suggests that other countries' commitment to NATO's cause may not be as thoroughgoing as Washington proclaims. It also suggests that encouraging other countries' expectations that they will be indemnified against war-related losses is one way Washington manufactures coalitions and minimizes foreign opposition to its interventionist policies.

## Notes

1. This figure was derived by adding the various government and private-sector estimates cited for each country examined in the body of this chapter. Economists at the International Monetary Fund estimate that the economic impact of the war (excluding refugee costs) on the economies of Yugoslavia's neighbors (excluding

Hungary) will amount to from $1.1 billion to $1.7 billion in 1999. See International Monetary Fund, "The Economic Consequences of the Kosovo Crisis: An Updated Assessment," May 25, 1999, www.imf.org/external/pubs/ft/kosovo/052599.htm. The Economist Intelligence Unit, a London-based think tank, estimates that the Kosovo conflict cut $7.8 billion from the aggregate 1999 gross domestic product of Yugoslavia and its seven neighbors. See "Kosovo War to Cost Balkans Nearly USD 8 Bln in '99," *New Europe*, June 28–July 4, 1999, p. 32.

2. International Monetary Fund; "Kosovo War Costs Balkan Neighbors a Bomb," Agence France-Presse, May 29, 1999; and John Zarocostos, "Kosovo War Devastates Trade for Balkan Neighbors," *Journal of Commerce*, May 20, 1999, p. 7A

3. International Monetary Fund.

4. Ibid.

5. Ibid.

6. Ibid.

7. United Nations Economic Commission for Europe, Economic Analysis Division, "Economic Survey of Europe," no. 2 (1999), www.unece.org/ead/pub/survey.htm.

8. R. C. Longworth, "Reward Sought for Aiding West's War," *Chicago Tribune*, June 1, 1999, p. 1.

9. See Joseph Fitchett, "New Concern over a Surge in Nationalism, The Silent Issue: Greater Albania," *International Herald Tribune*, April 6, 1999, p. 1; Andrew Borowiec, "Greece Fears 'Greater Albania,'" *Washington Times*, April 15, 1999, p. A15; and Bob Shacochis, "The 'Greater' Threat in Kosovo," *Wall Street Journal*, June 15, p. A18.

10. Chris Hedges, "Kosovo Rebels and Their New Friend," *New York Times*, June 10, 1998, p. A14.

11. Ibid.

12. Chris Hedges, "Kosovo's Next Masters?" *Foreign Affairs* 78, no. 3 (May–June 1999): 24–42.

13. Quoted in Fitchett.

14. Betsy Pisik, "Bosnia's Economy Teeters with Influx of Refugees," *Washington Times*, April 22, 1999, p. A15.

15. "Bosnian Serb Economy Suffers because of NATO Raids on Yugoslavia, Deputy Premier," BBC Worldwide Monitoring, May 14, 1999.

16. Dave Carpenter, "Hostility over Bombs Chips Away at Peace for Now: Peacekeepers Keeping Lid on Tensions," *Boston Globe*, April 17, 1999, p. A11.

17. Anne Thompson, "Bombing Halts Danube Barges: Destroyed Bridges Jam River Traffic," *Arizona Republic*, April 9, 1999, p. A12.

18. Peter Bennett, "The Danube Blues: The Kosovo Conflict Exacts a High Toll on Region's Businesses," *Wall Street Journal Europe*, May 31, 1999, p. 12.

19. Richard Whittle, "Yugoslav Neighbors Feel Economic Crunch from Impassable Waterway," *Dallas Morning News*, April 23, 1999, p. A21.

20. Christopher Rhodes, "Kosovo's Neighbors Feel Economic Blow," *Wall Street Journal Europe*, May 19, 1999, p. 9.

21. "Bulgaria Trade Decrease Affects Outlook—Analysts," *New Europe*, July 19–25, 1999, p. 35.

22. "Losses of the War Amount to 136.5 Million Levs," *Novinar* (Sofia), June 9, 1999, English summary at www.us.capital.bg/bp_digest/99-23/wed.htm.

23. Quoted in Bennett.

24. Barry Shlachter. "Trade Cut Off along Danube," *Fort Worth Star-Telegram*, May 29, 1999, p. 15.

25. "NATO and Bulgaria: Brave Gamble," *The Economist*, May 29, 1999, p. 47.

26. Ibid.

27. Judith Matloff, "The War Also Batters Rest of Region: Europe's Poorest States See Trade, Investments Dive after Kosovo," *Christian Science Monitor*, April 28, 1999, p. 1.

28. *Newsline*, Radio Free Europe/Radio Liberty, April 27, 1999.

29. Bill Whitman, "In Tourist-Free Dubrovnik, More Collateral Damage," *Washington Post*, June 6, 1999, p. E2.

30. International Monetary Fund.

31. Kolumbina Bencevic, "Croatia Not Seen Luring Investors before Elections," Reuters, July 16 1999.

32. "Counting the Costs of Kosovo," CNN Financial Network, April 13, 1999, htp://cnnfn.com/worldbiz/europe/9904/13/kosovo_economy/index.htm.

33. Ibid.

34. "Kosovo Crisis Reportedly Costs Croatia 522m Dollars," BBC Worldwide Monitoring, June 8, 1999.

35. Geoffrey Smith, "Croatian Official Expects Economy to Minimize Crisis," *Wall Street Journal Europe*, June 23, 1999, p. 32.

36. Susan Milligan, "Central European Countries Find Vacationers Staying Away," *Boston Globe*, June 3, 1999, p. A30; and "Kosovo Conflict Seen Costing Hungary's Economy $200 Million," Dow Jones News Service, May 20, 1999.

37. Adam LeBor, "The Danube: Bridges over Troubled Waters," *Globe and Mail* (Toronto), April 26, 1999, p. A10.

38. John Tagliabue, "Crisis in the Balkans: Front-Line Hungary Feels Anxiety," *New York Times*, May 2, 1999, p. 16.

39. Ibid.; and Bennett.

40. Whittle.

41. "Economic Risks of Kosovo Crisis for Hungary," *News In-Depth on Emerging Markets*, May 25, 1999, www.emergingeconomies.net/kos-hungary.html.

42. Michael J. Jordan, "NATO Enlists a Reluctant Hungary into Kosovo War," *Christian Science Monitor*, June 2, 1999, p. 6; and "Orban Appeals to Parties to Put Their Interests Aside," Associated Press, May 3, 1999.

43. Tagliabue; and "Hungarian Opposition Urges Parliament to Block NATO Strikes from Hungary," Agence France-Presse, May 28, 1999.

44. Ibid.

45. George Gedda, "America's NATO Burden Too Large, Some Analysts Say," *Houston Chronicle*, April 4, 1999, p. 1; and "Hungary to Join Peacekeeping Operation 'Outside' Kosovo," BBC Worldwide Monitoring, May 30, 1999.

46. "Hungarian Minister Rules Out Involvement in Land Action in Yugoslavia," BBC Worldwide Monitoring, April 18, 1999; and "Hungarian Minister Rejects German Idea of All NATO States Sharing War Cost," BBC Worldwide Monitoring, June 1, 1999.

47. "Hungarian Opposition Urges Parliament to Block NATO Strikes from Hungary."

48. International Monetary Fund; and Elizaveta Konstantinova, "Interview (with Macedonia's Finance Minister, Boris Stojmenov): Macedonia Faces Collapse without Help," Reuters, April 28, 1999.

49. Richard Mertens, "Macedonia Taking Hits Indirectly: NATO Action Affecting Sales, Factories in Region," *Houston Chronicle*, May 19, 1999, p. 1.

50. Joe Cook, "Macedonia 'On the Brink of Economic Crisis,'" *Financial Times* (London), July 20, 1999, p. 3.

51. Bennett; and Konstantinova.

52. "Anti-NATO Protestors in Macedonia Attack Embassy," Reuters, March 25, 1999.

53. Quoted in "Still Nervous in Macedonia."

54. Quoted in Cook.

55. Thompson.

56. Whittle.

57. "Romanian Danube Shippers Claim 86m Dollars Damages due to Kosovo War," BBC Worldwide Monitoring, June 18, 1999.

58. Ibid.

59. Bennett.

60. Quoted in ibid.

61. "Romania: Casualty of War," *The Economist*, June 12, 1999. p. 68.

62. Bennett.

63. "Romania: Casualty of War."

64. Ibid.

65. Herve Richard, director for Romania at KPMG Corporate Finance, quoted in "Romania Continues to Be 'Virtually Boycotted,'" *New Europe*, August 9–15, 1999, p. 12.

66. "Romania: Casualty of War."

67. Stephen Handelman, "NATO's War Is a Threat to the Entire Region," *Toronto Star*, April 27, 1999, p. 1.

68. Ron Popeski, "Successive Cries for Autonomy in the Balkans Makes [sic]Hungarians in Romania Sitting Ducks for Separatist Forces," *New Europe*, June 28–July 4, 1999, p. 7.

69. "Romanian Premier Rejects Ethnic Hungarian Radicals' Letter to Clinton," BBC Worldwide Monitoring, June 17, 1999.

70. "Hungarian, Romanian Communities 'Equal Nations' in Transylvania, Declaration," BBC Worldwide Monitoring, June 10, 1999.

71. Quoted in "Hungarian Far-Right Leader Criticizes Reaction to Reannexation Proposal," BBC Worldwide Monitoring, June 6, 1999.

72. In a worrisome backlash, anti-Hungarian demonstrations erupted in the Transylvanian city of Cluj after a soccer match between Hungary and Romania. The mayor of the city, who is also the head of the nationalist Party of Alliance for the Romanians' Unity, rallied the crowds with anti-Hungarian comments, sparking a demonstration of several thousand people in front of the Hungarian consulate. The demonstrators shouted slogans such as "We will defend Transylvania" and "Out with the Hungarians from the country." Scattered incidents of vandalism against Hungarian properties also took place. See "Romanian Soccer Fans Hold Anti-Hungarian Demonstration after Match," BBC Worldwide Monitoring, June 6, 1999.

73. See Allen Salkin, "Radioactive Bullets Fire Up Huge Controversy," *New York Post*, May 2, 1999, p. 4; Alex Kirby, "Pentagon Confirms Depleted Uranium Use, Aftermath of a Raid: Is Depleted Uranium Adding to the Hazards?" *BBC News*, May 7, 1999, http://news.bbc.co.uk/hi/english/sci/tech/newsid_337000/337855.stm; Thomas Williams, "Europeans Decry Use of Depleted Uranium Coating on NATO

Bombs," *Hartford Courant,* May 20, 1999, p. A1; Michael Kallenback, "Conflict in the Balkans: Danube Black with Oil after Air Raids," *Daily Telegraph* (London), April 19, 1999, p. 6; and Tom Walker, "Missile Strikes Pollute Danube," *Globe and Mail* (Toronto), April 19, 1999, p. A12.

74. Albania's foreign minister, Paskal Milo, quoted in Peter Finn, "Albania Seeks Show of Western Gratitude," *Washington Post,* July 22, 1999, p. A18.

# 6. Damage to Relations with Russia and China

*Ted Galen Carpenter*

One of the more troubling consequences of the Balkan war was the marked deterioration of relations between the United States and two major powers in the international system, Russia and the People's Republic of China. Both countries vehemently opposed NATO's decision to use force against Serbia as unnecessary and counterproductive. They were especially upset at the alliance's bypassing the United Nations Security Council. From the standpoint of officials in Moscow and Beijing, that action set an extremely worrisome precedent. Possession of a veto power as permanent members of the Security Council would have little relevance if the United States and its allies could simply ignore the council's prerogative to approve or reject proposals to use coercive measures and act on their own. In other words, Russian and Chinese leaders saw NATO's unauthorized intervention in the Balkans as politically marginalizing their countries.

In addition to that shared concern, each government had its own reasons for opposing the substance of NATO's policy. Russia has significant economic, cultural, and religious links to the Serbs that go back more than a century. The Russian people did not welcome the sight of NATO bombs falling on fellow Slavs and Eastern Orthodox coreligionists. Moscow also worried about the broader implications of the Kosovo conflict. There are several ethnically based secessionist movements in the far-flung Russian federation, and although the West did not interfere when Russian forces attempted to squelch one of those movements (in Chechnya), if NATO's intervention in Kosovo went unchallenged there would be less certainty of a similar hands-off attitude should another crisis erupt elsewhere in the federation.

Given China's problems with restless ethnic minorities in Tibet and Xinjiang, Beijing likewise had reason to be apprehensive about the Kosovo precedent. Anything that so obviously diluted the sanctity of national sovereignty and made it clear that some members of the international community thought they had the right to intervene in the internal affairs of another country seemed to menace important Chinese domestic interests. In addition, Beijing saw the intervention in Kosovo as another piece of evidence that the United States was determined to be the global hegemon and run roughshod over any country that dared defy its wishes. According to that reasoning, NATO and America's bilateral alliances, such as those with South Korea and Japan, were institutional mechanisms for implementing Washington's global imperial policy.[1]

Moscow and Beijing were worried about the direction of U.S. and NATO policy even before the alliance began to move against Serbia. But the demands made on Belgrade, and especially the onset of the bombing campaign, greatly intensified the suspicions and the resulting anger. Although it is still too soon to say so definitively, there are ample indications that at least some of the damage to relations with Russia and China may be irreparable.

### Baiting the Bear

Moscow's reaction to NATO's military coercion of Serbia was even more strident than its response to the alliance's previous political inroads on Russia's western and southern flanks through, respectively, the expansion of NATO's membership and Washington's joint military exercises with Ukraine, Kazakstan, and other former Soviet republics.[2] Russia's more intense reaction to the intervention in the Balkans is not surprising. The bombing campaign discredited the West's soothing assurances that Russia had nothing to fear from NATO's enlargement because NATO was a purely defensive alliance. Whatever else one might conclude about the intervention in the Balkans, it showed unequivocally that NATO is now a proactive, offensive military association.

The importance of the change in NATO has not been lost on the Russians. Prime Minister Yevgeny Primakov turned his plane around in midflight across the Atlantic when it became clear that the alliance would proceed with air strikes even as he was scheduled to be in Washington for high-level talks. Alliance leaders could scarcely have chosen a more graphic way of displaying disdain for long-standing Russian interests in the Balkans or for Russia's status as a great power.

The Kremlin responded to the attack on Serbia by recalling Russian military officers from their liaison roles at NATO headquarters in Brussels and expelling their NATO counterparts from Moscow. Kremlin leaders denounced the assault on Serbia with the kind of shrill rhetoric not heard since the worst days of the Cold War. The harsh response was not confined to the political elite. Large and sometimes violent anti-NATO demonstrations erupted in Moscow and other cities.[3]

Pro-democratic Russian political leaders, such as Yegor Gaidar, Grigory Yavlinsky, Anatoly Chubais, and Alexi Arbatov, have warned their friends in the West that the Balkan war caused an unprecedented degree of genuine anti-Western (especially anti-American) sentiment among the Russian people. Those leaders fear that NATO's actions may produce another surge of domestic support for communist and ultranationalist factions, leading to their greater domination of the Duma and perhaps even victory in Russia's presidential elections in 2000. The comments of Chubais were typical of the dismay and despair expressed by pro-democratic Russian figures. "I have not in all my life seen such a scale of anti-Western sentiments as exist in Russia today." The communists and nationalists, he concluded, "could not have imagined a present of this scale."[4]

Although NATO allowed the Yeltsin government—specifically, former prime minister Viktor Chernomyrdin—to be the alliance's diplomatic intermediary in negotiations with Yugoslav president Slobodan Milosevic, there was no inclination to correct the blunder committed during the initial stage of the crisis and accord Russia greater respect. (That attitude seems especially inappropriate in light of postwar evidence that NATO's bombing did not destroy the Serbian military or compel Belgrade's capitulation and that Russia's diplomatic efforts may have played a very important role in bringing the fighting to an end.)[5] The continuing contemptuous dismissal of Russia as a European great power with significant Balkan interests became apparent at the end of the fighting when NATO leaders refused to give Russia a separate peacekeeping zone in Kosovo, despite the considerable service Moscow had performed in orchestrating a diplomatic solution to the conflict. The egregious nature of the snub was underscored by the fact that even Italy—barely a second-tier European power—was assigned a zone. Predictably, Russian political and military leaders reacted furiously to such treatment. One Russian liberal intellectual probably summarized the attitude of many of his countrymen when he accused the West of treating Russia like Pampers: "You use us for your dirty work and then throw us away."[6]

Privately, Western officials contended that it would have been dangerous to give the Russian army a separate zone to patrol, given Russia's pronounced pro-Serb sympathies. According to NATO alarmists, a Russian zone might lead to the de facto partition of Kosovo, just as Germany became divided after World War II.

Aside from the obvious rejoinder that today's democratic Russia is hardly the same country as the aggressively expansionist Soviet Union under Joseph Stalin, professed fears of a Russian-engineered partition of Kosovo seemed to be a pretext rather than a genuine reason for NATO's decision. The risk of an unauthorized partition could have been overcome by assigning the Russians a zone in the center of the province, surrounded by NATO-member zones. In other words, according Russia a peacekeeping zone would have been an easy concession to make—one, moreover, that would have enabled the Yeltsin government, and pro-democratic elements generally, to trumpet a prestige victory and overcome some of the domestic political damage caused by the war. The fact that the United States and its NATO allies stubbornly refused to make such a concession suggests that Western policy is either incredibly obtuse or dominated by Russophobes such as Secretary of State Madeleine Albright.

NATO's very public disdain for Russian sensibilities led to the stunning entry of Russian troops into Kosovo and their seizure of the Pristina airport before NATO troops could arrive. (It is still not clear whether that coup was authorized by the Yeltsin government or was a freelance operation by a Russian military command that had become disgusted with the tendency of civilian leaders to appease NATO at every turn. Neither interpretation bodes well for future Russian relations with the West.) The world was then treated to television images of British and Russian troops facing off at the airport and Russian armored personnel carriers racing up and down the runway to drown out the speech of British general Sir Michael Jackson, commander of the NATO peacekeeping force in Kosovo.

It was not exactly a symbol of NATO-Russian harmony and coopera-tion. The extent of the tensions can be gauged by the extraordinary testimony of NATO's supreme commander, Gen. Wesley Clark, before the Senate Armed Services Committee that "officials at levels above mine" decided against forcibly blocking the Russian entry into Kosovo—a step that Clark later indicated to some senators he would have favored.[7]

There is evidence that the Russians intended to reinforce their garrison at Pristina with several thousand additional troops, create a de facto Russian peacekeeping zone, and present NATO with a fait accompli.[8] That strategy was apparently thwarted when the United States exerted pressure on Hungary, Romania, Bulgaria, and other countries to deny overflight rights to Russian transport planes.[9] Prevented from adding to its small garrison, Moscow had little choice but to accept the crumbs offered by NATO—the right to have some Russian troops conduct patrols in zones controlled by NATO mem-bers.[10] Subsequently, Moscow also agreed to restore its liaison ties with NATO.[11] The humiliation remains, however, and the episode underscores the extent of the deterioration in relations between Rus-sia and the Western powers.

NATO leaders (and much of the Western foreign policy commu-nity) appear to be succumbing to the temptation to dismiss Russian anger at their policies, in the Balkans and elsewhere, as of no great consequence. After all, given Russia's pervasive economic woes, its continuing dependence on financial aid provided by the Western-controlled International Monetary Fund, and the disarray in its mili-tary, there is no way that Moscow can challenge NATO directly.[12] That is all true, but it would be a serious mistake to base U.S. or NATO policy on the assumption that Russia will remain weak for-ever. One should never equate a hibernating bear with a dead bear.

Moreover, even in its weakened state, Russia can take relatively low-cost, high-leverage actions calculated to make life difficult for the United States and its NATO allies. Even before the Balkan war, Moscow responded to NATO's encroachment by forging closer ties with both Iran and Iraq and undermining U.S. policy throughout the Middle East. Russia also concluded a deal to sell sophisticated S-300 anti-aircraft missiles to Cyprus, almost certainly realizing that the sale would provoke severe tensions between NATO members Greece and Turkey. Russia even engaged in talks with China and

India to create a counterhegemonic coalition implicitly directed against the United States and a U.S.-led NATO. While on a state visit to New Delhi, Primakov spoke of the possibility of a "triangular alliance" of those three powers to prevent global domination by any country.[13]

Even more worrisome than such diplomatic maneuvers is the Kremlin's decision to increase Russia's reliance on nuclear weapons—including tactical (battlefield) nuclear weapons.[14] That step hardly advances the goal of people who had hoped that the post–Cold War world would be a more peaceful place than its predecessor. Again, there is little doubt that Russia's actions are a response to NATO's eastward expansion and, even more, to the alliance's use of military force in the Balkans. Foreign Minister Igor Ivanov, one of the more pro-Western officials remaining in the Yeltsin government, warned that the United States and NATO risk provoking a new nuclear arms race with Moscow if they "seek to impose their will on the rest of the world." He considered it unacceptable that "countries which have set up an elite club" have the right to "order all the rest about."[15] Given Russia's current economic malaise, Ivanov's threat to respond with a new nuclear arms race has little substance in the short term. Indeed, Russia may have trouble maintaining its existing nuclear arsenal (along with the core of its conventional forces). But the danger over the long term is much greater, especially if someone who regards the restoration of Russia's military prowess as the highest priority is elected president. Both Primakov and Gen. Alexander Lebed fit that description—and there may be others lurking in the political wings.

If the United States and its NATO allies drift into a confrontational relationship, much less a new cold war, with Russia because the alliance insists on meddling in the convoluted disputes of the Balkans, that will go down as one of the colossal policy blunders of all time.

## Bombing the Panda

The Balkan intervention also intensified China's suspicions about America's global intentions and caused U.S.-PRC relations to decline to their lowest point since the Tiananmen Square massacre in 1989.[16] The principal catalyst for that deterioration was the U.S. bombing of the Chinese embassy in Belgrade on May 7. Although President

Clinton and other officials immediately sought to apologize for what Washington described as a horrible accident, the PRC was unforgiving. Chinese leaders openly charged that the attack was deliberate, perpetrated by elements within the U.S. military and foreign policy bureaucracy that view China as an enemy and want to destroy relations between the United States and the PRC.[17] Some of the anger and suspicion was undoubtedly genuine, and there is an outside chance that the attack was not accidental.[18]

An upsurge in anti-U.S. sentiment was inevitable, as was a tangible sign of Beijing's displeasure; China promptly suspended high-level military contacts and human rights dialogues and banned U.S. military aircraft from landing and U.S. warships from docking in Hong Kong.[19] But what occurred in the days following the bombing went far beyond a normal negative reaction. Mobs of Chinese young people attacked American businesses and other targets in Shanghai, Beijing, and other cities. Not only did the PRC government tolerate such excesses, there are indications that it abetted them.[20] Some participants in the mob violence directed at the U.S. embassy and ambassador's residence in Beijing—a barrage of rocks, bottles, and firebombs so severe that Ambassador James Sasser dared not leave the residence for three days—were bused in from other parts of the country. Such a logistic undertaking would have been impossible without the approval of the Chinese government. For that matter, a regime that butchered hundreds of demonstrators in Tiananmen Square a decade earlier, and has squelched any anti-regime demonstrations since then, can hardly plead that it was unable to break up mobs or ensure that demonstrations remained peaceful on this occasion. The conclusion seems inescapable that the PRC leadership whipped up nationalist emotions and allowed the mobs to attack U.S. targets because it wanted to send Washington a message of extreme displeasure with U.S. policy.

True, there were signs of the PRC's growing unhappiness with the United States in the months immediately preceding the bombing campaign in the Balkans. Disagreements between Washington and Beijing had flared on numerous issues, ranging from the PRC's intensified crackdown on political dissidents to the U.S. proposal for a regional shield against ballistic missile attacks in East Asia.[21] More and more official and "semiofficial" articles, studies, reports, and speeches emanating from the PRC warned that the United States

83

was using its power to achieve global domination, and that such hegemony posed a threat to important Chinese interests. Another subtle but unmistakable signal came in February 1999 when the PRC representative on the UN Security Council vetoed the extension of the UN's peacekeeping mandate in Macedonia. The conventional wisdom in the United States was that Beijing's veto was petty retaliation for Macedonia's decision a few weeks earlier to extend diplomatic recognition to Taiwan. Although that was undoubtedly a factor, the official explanation for the veto was broader—that an internal conflict in a province of Yugoslavia did not pose "a true threat" to Macedonia or other neighboring countries.[22] Again, Beijing seized an opportunity to emphasize the distinction between external aggression (which might justify international action) and internal quarrels and problems (which do not). The subsequent Balkan war increased the PRC's concern that that distinction was being erased.

As it did in the case of relations with Russia, the Clinton administration has gone to great lengths to foster the impression that relations with China are back on track.[23] The resumption of high-level meetings between officials of the two countries is touted as proof of a rapprochement, and it is true that both Washington and Beijing have made an effort to prevent a complete breach in the relationship.[24] The value of bilateral trade ties alone—now in excess of $80 billion annually—provides a significant incentive for both sides not to let the animosity get out of hand.

Nevertheless, it would be naive to assume that the Balkan episode did not leave scars. The overall tone of comments coming out of Beijing about relations with the United States has become noticeably more negative and hostile in recent months. One need look no further than the pages of Foreign Affairs Journal, published by the Chinese People's Institute of Foreign Affairs, an affiliate of the Foreign Ministry. In marked contrast to most earlier issues, recent issues of the journal have featured numerous strongly anti-U.S. articles. That was especially true of the June 1999 issue. It contained not only an entire section on the PRC government's reaction to the embassy bombing but several other critical articles as well. Although one denounced the recently released Cox report on alleged Chinese espionage at U.S. nuclear weapons laboratories and another was critical of the U.S.-Japanese alliance, an unusual number dealt with NATO and the war in the Balkans. Those articles included "New NATO in the 21st Century," "NATO Lifts Its Mask of Humanitarianism," "'Fighting for Values' an Excuse for War," and "NATO's New Strategic Concept Threatens World Peace."[25]

Such an intense focus by an East Asian power on an ostensibly Euro-Atlantic alliance seems more than a little peculiar—except that Beijing fears that an increasingly assertive U.S.-led network of alliances might use the Bosnia and Kosovo precedents to intervene in similar problems of direct interest to China. In particular, Chinese officials fret that NATO's Balkan policy is the harbinger of a global humanitarian interventionist doctrine that someday might be applied to such problems as Taiwan and Tibet. Indeed, President Jiang Zemin specifically underlined his government's determination never to let Taiwan become "an Asian Kosovo."[26]

The chill in Beijing's relations with the United States is apparent in subtle but important policy changes as well. For example, the PRC had previously been helpful in attempting to discourage North Korea from pursuing a nuclear weapons program or improving its ballistic missile capabilities.[27] In the aftermath of the Balkan war, Beijing has been somewhat less helpful. China's ambassador to Seoul defended North Korea's "sovereign right" to conduct launch tests of its new Taepodong 2 missile—a three-stage missile with a range that would enable it to strike U.S. territory. The ambassador further accused the United States of exaggerating the threat posed by such a missile.[28] Even more troubling, there is evidence that Chinese companies have recently transferred sophisticated missile components to North Korea.[29] Indeed, one of China's "contributions" to solving the problem of Pyongyang's destabilizing behavior has been to warn *Japan* not to exacerbate tensions on the peninsula.[30] Such an attitude is reminiscent of the knee-jerk hostility to Japan that characterized PRC policy under Mao Zedong.

The conventional wisdom holds that Washington's strong support of Beijing's position on the "one-China" issue following Taiwanese president Lee Teng-hui's assertion that relations between Taiwan and the mainland henceforth would be conducted on a state-to-state basis has repaired much of the damage to the U.S.-PRC relationship.[31] There may be some truth to that, but comments and actions by Beijing in the summer of 1999 conveyed, at best, a mixed message. Although Chinese leaders expressed appreciation for Washington's strong adherence to the one-China policy, they also gave unusually blunt warnings not to deviate from that policy. PRC foreign minister Tang Jiaxuan told Secretary of State Albright that the United States "should say little and act with great caution."[32] Moreover, any softening of Beijing's attitude certainly did not carry over to other political and security issues. In an address to a meeting of the Association of Southeast Asian Nations, Tang condemned countries that bypass the United Nations and "bully" others in the name of human rights. In an unmistakable swipe at the United States and its NATO allies, he stated that "claims such as 'the supremacy of human rights over sovereignty' and 'there is no national boundary in safeguarding human rights' are in essence excuses for strong countries to bully weak ones."[33] A few weeks later, Jiang explicitly denounced U.S. "gunboat diplomacy."[34]

Although it is impossible to precisely measure the extent or probable duration of the damage that the Balkan war—and especially the bombing of the Chinese embassy—inflicted on U.S.-PRC relations, there is little doubt that the damage is considerable. Gone are the expressions of exuberant good feelings that led Clinton and Albright in 1997 and 1998 to speak repeatedly of a "constructive partnership" and even a "strategic partnership" (in an apparent effort not to be upstaged by the warming Russian-PRC relationship) with China. Gone likewise is the spirit of collaboration that produced the astonishing sight of U.S. and PRC officials issuing joint statements chastising Washington's long-time Asian ally, Japan, for its economic policies.[35] The relationship is now characterized by wariness, if not overt suspicion and hostility.

## A Moscow-Beijing Axis?

A policy that alienated either Russia or China would have been bad enough, but NATO's Balkan war succeeded in alienating both countries simultaneously. That intervention helped to intensify what had already been a worrisome development: the growing, tangible political and military links between Russia and the PRC. Even before the frictions with the West caused by the Balkan war, Moscow and Beijing had begun to speak openly of a "strategic partnership," and China had become Russia's largest arms customer—something that would have been unthinkable a few years ago, given the long-standing tensions between the two Asian giants.[36] Reports leaked to two Hong Kong newspapers in September 1999 indicated that Russia was even considering selling two Typhoon-class nuclear-powered submarines to the PRC. Those submarines carry SSN-20 ballistic missiles capable of reaching the United States.[37] Such a sale would be a far more relevant indicator of Moscow's true strategic intentions than the resumption of Russia's liaison with NATO.

Thanks to the West's Balkan crusade, the coordination of Russian-PRC policies on a range of issues—perhaps even leading to a Moscow-Beijing axis—has acquired additional momentum.[38] A new agreement to pool resources in the development of military-related high technology was concluded in late June 1999, and even more troubling, diplomatic sources in Beijing reported that Russian officials had approached their PRC counterparts about creating a full-scale military alliance.[39] Foreign Minister Ivanov boasted in July 1999 that the strategic partnership with China had "noticeably strengthened" and that a "further widening" of Russian-Chinese cooperation could be expected. Ivanov contended that such a development would be "an important stabilizing factor for the world." What he meant by a stabilizing factor was all too apparent. "Our two states were the first in the world to declare with full voice in a joint declaration the necessity of building a multipolar world."[40] At a summit meeting in August 1999, Yeltsin and Jiang emphasized their commitment to multipolarity. They chastised certain powers (unnamed) for acting as though the world was not multipolar and for the "new display of hegemony relying on force."[41] The goal of a multipolar international system was a direct challenge to Washington's swaggering status as the sole remaining superpower and a global system that scholars have described as unipolar.

From the standpoint of American interests, a Moscow-Beijing entente—much less a full-blown alliance—would be a deeply disturbing development. It would signal a major shift in the configuration of global political, military, and economic power that would make the United States less secure. China is a rapidly rising great power, and Russia, although at the moment a great power in distress, retains serious military capabilities and a vast economic potential. If those two powers arrayed themselves against the United States, the world could become a decidedly less secure and friendly place for American interests in the coming decades.

Moreover, a Russian-PRC partnership could become the organizational core of an even larger counterhegemonic coalition directed against the United States. One possible version would be Primakov's proposed triangular alliance of Russia, China, and India.[42] Other nations alarmed at the aggressive posture adopted by a U.S.-led NATO might be tempted to cooperate with such a coalition. Americans are strangely oblivious to the reality that, in most parts of the world, the air strikes on Serbia were viewed, not as the prosecution of a just war to prevent genocide, but as a brutal attack on a small nation that was incapable of striking back.[43] That pervasive attitude provides the raw material for constructing a counterhegemonic coalition.[44]

In any case, it was extraordinarily myopic to pay the price of jeopardizing NATO's (and more specifically, America's) relations with not one but two great powers to pursue a humanitarian intervention in the Balkans. That approach should not have survived even a cursory cost/benefit calculation. Indeed, to sacrifice relationships with Russia and China merely for the emotional satisfaction of dictating the political status of an obscure province in a small Balkan country is akin to a chess player's sacrificing a knight and a queen to capture a worthless pawn. One does not have to be a chess grand master to recognize that such a move is appallingly bad strategy. Yet that is the kind strategy that the United States and NATO adopted to achieve "victory" in the Balkans.

## Notes

1. John Pomfret, "China Rethinks Security after NATO Attack," *Washington Post*, June 11, 1999, p. A16; and Peter Montagon and James Kynge, "Beijing Re-evaluates Relationship with U.S.," *Washington Times*, June 11, 1999, p. A17.

2. Useful discussions of Russia's reaction to the expansion of NATO include Susan Eisenhower, "The Perils of Victory," in *NATO Enlargement: Illusions and Reality*, ed. Ted Galen Carpenter and Barbara Conry (Washington: Cato Institute, 1998), pp. 103–19; Anatol Lieven, "The NATO-Russia Accord: An Illusory Solution," in ibid., pp. 143–56; and Craig R. Whitney, "NATO Ties with Russia Soured before Bombing," *New York Times*, June 19, 1999, p. A6. Sergo A. Mikoyan, a senior researcher at a prominent Moscow think tank, notes that the United States has concluded bilateral military agreements with Ukraine, Azerbaijan, Kazakstan, and Georgia. Since all of those countries were already in NATO's Partnership for Peace program, Russians were doubly suspicious about the motives for separate bilateral agreements—especially when they were combined with arms sales, training missions, and other measures. According to Mikoyan, U.S. moves "can only be interpreted in Moscow as actions designed to undermine the newly independent states' relationships with Russia." Indeed, at times Washington's goal in the Caucasus and Central Asia appears to be to "force Russia out altogether." Sergo A. Mikoyan, "Russia, the U.S. and Regional Conflict in Eurasia," *Survival* 40, no. 3 (Autumn 1998): 119.

3. Alan Rousso, "Kosovo and U.S.-Russian Relations: A View from Moscow," Carnegie Endowment for International Peace, May 6, 1999; David Hoffman, "Attack Stirs Cold War Feelings in Russia," *Washington Post*, April 4, 1999, p. A1; and Roy A. Medvedev, "Why They Say Nyet," *Washington Post*, May 2, 1999, p. B4.

4. Quoted in David Hoffman, "War Costs U.S., West Support in Russia," *Washington Post*, May 17, 1999, p. A11. See also Michael Wines, "Hostility to U.S. Is Now Popular with Russians," *New York Times*, April 12, 1999, p. A1; and Erik Eckholm, "It's Not the Cold War, But There's a Chill in the Air," *New York Times*, May 16, 1999, p. WK1.

5. Tim Butcher and Patrick Bishop, "NATO Admits Air Campaign Failed," *Telegraph* (London), July 22, 1999.

6. Comment of Alexander Pikayev, at the time a guest scholar at the Carnegie Endowment for International Peace, during a forum at the Atlantic Council of the United States, Washington, June 8, 1999.

7. Quoted in John Donnelly, "Air War Leader Greeted Coolly by Senators," *Boston Globe*, July 2, 1999. Former national security adviser Zbigniew Brzezinski also favored a highly confrontational response. Zbigniew Brzezinski, "NATO Must Stop Russia's Power Play," *Wall Street Journal*, June 14, 1999, p. A20.

8. Robert G. Kaiser and David Hoffman, "Russia Had Bigger Plan in Kosovo," *Washington Post*, June 25, 1999, p. A1.

9. Nigel Vincent, a military analyst with the Royal United Services Institute in London, aptly summarized the episode: "Basically, Hungary, Romania and Bulgaria were phoned up and told, 'If you get a request from Russia for overflights, simply refuse them.' And that's exactly what happened." He added, "What was new was that NATO effectively banned Russian use of airspace throughout southeastern Europe." Quoted in Luke Hill, "Agreement Gives Russian Troops Leeway with NATO Orders," *Defense News*, July 26, 1999, p. 50.

10. Steven Lee Myers and Michael Wines, "Accord with NATO Lets Moscow Add Troops in Kosovo," *New York Times*, July 6, 1999, p. A1.

11. "Recalled Russian General Holds Talks with NATO," Reuters, September 1, 1999.

12. James Meek, "U.S. Views Russian Bear as Largely Declawed," *Washington Times*, January 27, 1999, p. A1.

13. Sanjiv Miglani, "Primakov Eyes 3-Way Alliance," *Washington Times*, December 22, 1998, p. A13; and Martin Sieff, "Primakov Puts Russia in a Strategic Spot: Ties to India, China Check U.S. Hegemony," *Washington Times*, December 27, 1998, p. C1.

The fact that Yeltsin later dismissed Primakov for domestic reasons should offer little comfort to Western governments. Indeed, Primakov's political star may be rising, not falling. Moscow mayor Yuri Luzhkov, a major power broker and once considered a leading candidate for president in 2000, has thrown his support to Primakov. Luzhkov's backing now makes Primakov, who already was popular among Russian voters, the most likely successor to Yeltsin.

14. "Russia Upgrades Nuclear Defense," United Press International, April 30, 1999.

15. Quoted in "Russia's Ivanov Warns U.S. of New Arms Race," Reuters, July 27, 1999.

16. Eckholm.

17. That official skepticism did not abate with the passage of time. Matt Forney, "U.S. Envoy Fails to Persuade China That Embassy Bombing Was an Error," *Wall Street Journal*, June 17, 1999, p. A4; and Michael Laris, "U.S. Details Embassy Bombing

for Chinese: Beijing Officials Remain Skeptical at Washington's Explanation of Accidental Attack," *Washington Post,* June 17, 1999, p. A30.

18. There is evidence that the embassy was the PRC's espionage center for the entire southeast European region and may have been passing along information on NATO military maneuvers to Yugoslavia—something that would have enraged U.S. military and Central Intelligence Agency leaders and created an incentive to "take out" such a listening post. Knut Royce, "NATO May Have Hit Spy Center," *Denver Post,* June 25, 1999; see also Eric Schmitt, "Two Victims in U.S. Raid Reportedly Were Spies," *New York Times,* June 25, 1999, p. A13.

19. Jane Perlez, "China Suspends Some Ties As Bombing Adds Strains to Already Tense Relations," *New York Times,* May 10, 1999, p. A8.

20. Matt Forney, Ian Johnson, and Marcus W. Brauchli, "For Beijing, Protests against NATO Attack Are a Political Tool," *Wall Street Journal,* May 10, 1999, p. A1; and John Pomfret, "A Protest Beijing Can Endorse," *Washington Post,* May 10, 1999, p. A18.

21. Jane Perlez, "Hopes for Improved Ties with China Fade," *New York Times,* February 12, 1999, p. A6.

22. Quoted in Nicole Winfield, "China Vetoes Macedonia Resolution," Associated Press, February 25, 1999. See also Matt Pottinger, "China Avoids Taiwan Issue in Macedonia Veto," Reuters, February 25, 1999.

23. Carol Giacomo, "Albright Says Talks Ease U.S.-China Tensions," Reuters, July 25, 1999; Leslie Lopez, "Albright Welcomes Eased Tension with China and Chastises Taiwan," *Wall Street Journal,* July 26, 1999, p. A19; John Pomfret, "Albright, Chinese Foreign Minister Hold 'Very Friendly Lunch,'" *Washington Post,* July 26, 1999, p. A1; and Jane Perlez, "U.S. and China Say They Are Mending Post-Bombing Rift," *New York Times,* July 26, 1999, p. A1.

24. Ibid.

25. Zhu Muzhi, "NATO Lifts Its Mask of Humanitarianism," *Foreign Affairs Journal* 52 (June 1999): 48–49; Xin Hua, "'Fighting for Values' an Excuse for War," ibid., pp. 50–51; and Liu Jiang, "NATO's New Strategic Concept Threatens World Peace," ibid., pp. 52–53. Wang Naicheng, "New NATO in the 21st Century," ibid., pp. 1–10, provides a more comprehensive but equally hostile overview of NATO's role.

26. Quoted in "Jiang Calls for Action on 'Taipei Conspiracy,'" *South China Morning Post,* July 14, 1999.

27. Georgetown University professor Victor Cha noted a "remarkable détente between China and South Korea" and argued that engaging China further was a promising factor in reducing tensions on the Korean peninsula, although Beijing was unlikely to completely abandon its support of North Korea. Victor D. Cha, "Engaging China: Seoul-Beijing Détente and Korean Security," *Survival* 41, no. 1 (Spring 1999): 73–98.

28. John Burton, "China Defends N Korea Rocket Launches," *Financial Times,* July 23, 1999, p. 4.

29. Bill Gertz, "Missile Parts Sent to North Korea by Chinese Companies," *Washington Times,* July 20, 1999, p. A1.

30. "China Warns Japan Not to Inflame Korea Tensions," Reuters, July 25, 1999.

31. For an example of that conventional wisdom, see Helene Cooper and Ian Johnson, "Taiwan Flap Brings China Closer to U.S.," *Wall Street Journal,* July 28, 1999, p. A18.

32. Quoted in James Kynge, Sheila McNulty, and Moore Dickey, "China Warns U.S. Not to Interfere over Taiwan," *Financial Times,* July 26, 1999, p. A1.

33. Quoted in Laurinda Keys, "China Minister Criticizes Nations," Associated Press, July 27, 1999.

34. Quoted in Thaksina Khaikaew, "Chinese Leader Criticizes U.S.," Associated Press, September 4, 1999.

35. The ties between Beijing and Washington became so close during that period that they began to cause other Asian countries to worry about a possible U.S.-PRC condominium—an implicit division of much of the world into respective spheres of influence. Ted Galen Carpenter, "Roiling Asia: U.S. Coziness with China Upsets the Neighbors," *Foreign Affairs* 77, no. 6 (November–December 1998): 1–6.

36. For the extent of Russian military sales to China—and coproduction agreements with the PRC—even before the Balkan war, see Ted Galen Carpenter, "Managing a Great Power Relationship: The United States, China and East Asian Security," *Journal of Strategic Studies* 21, no. 1 (March 1998): 4–5. For discussions of the broader nature of the political and military cooperation between the two powers and its possible implications, see Stanley Kober, "Russia's Search for Identity," in *NATO Enlargement: Illusions and Reality,* pp. 135–39; National Institute for Defense Studies, *East Asian Strategic Review, 1998–1999* (Tokyo: National Institute for Defense Studies, 1999), pp. 171–72; and Richard Bernstein and Ross H. Munro, *The Coming Conflict with China* (New York: Knopf, 1997), pp. 68–77, 181–82.

37. "Russia May Sell Nuke Subs to China," Associated Press, September 1, 1999.

38. "Moscow, Beijing Hold Constant Consultations on Yugoslavia," Itar-Tass, April 1, 1999.

39. Willy Wo-Lap Lam, "Beijing and Moscow in High-Tech Arms Pact," *South China Morning Post,* June 26, 1999.

40. Quoted in "Russia Hails Strengthening Relations with China," Reuters, July 26, 1999.

41. Quoted in Vladimir Isachenkov, "Russia, China Seek Closer Alliance," Associated Press, August 25, 1999.

42. One development that makes such a scheme something more than a fantasy has been the concerted effort by long-time bitter adversaries India and China to improve their relations. Amy Louise Kazmin, "India and China Mend Fences," *Financial Times,* June 20, 1999, p. 4. That rapprochement is all the more surprising in light of India's unveiling in 1998 of its nuclear weapons program, which New Delhi justified in large part by the alleged threat posed by China, and which Beijing regarded with considerable hostility. See Carpenter, "Roiling Asia," pp. 2–3.

43. Anthony Faiola, "Bombing of Yugoslavia Awakens Anti-U.S. Feelings around the World," *Washington Post,* May 18, 1999, p. A1.

44. Even the prime minister of Pakistan, a nation that was once a staunch U.S. ally, issued a joint statement with his Russian counterpart agreeing to coordinate efforts to prevent the emergence of a unipolar world. "Nawaz, Primakov Vow to Oppose Unipolar World," *The Nation* (Pakistan), April 21, 1999.

# 7. Another Blow to America's Constitution

*Stanley Kober*

The war in the Balkans has been justified as "reaffirming NATO's core purpose as a defender of democracy, stability and human decency on European soil."[1] That justification is not without merit. There can be no question that Slobodan Milosevic's regime is incompatible with any American definition of democracy. Americans believe in *e pluribus unum* (out of many, one). Our conception of democracy is based on the inherent and equal worth of all people, whatever their religious or ethnic background. As President George Washington put it in his extraordinary letter to the Hebrew Congregation in Newport, Rhode Island: "It is now no more that toleration is spoken of, as if it was by the indulgence of one class of people, that another enjoyed the exercise of their inherent natural rights."[2] In place of the divine right of kings, the United States established the divine rights of the people—all of them.[3] One important motivation for the NATO intervention was to uphold that principle.

But another principle of democracy—not to mention a specific provision of the U.S. Constitution—was all but shattered by the war. The president initiated an attack on a foreign country on his own authority—indeed, even delegated the power to issue the actual order to the secretary general of NATO, who is not even a U.S. citizen—without obtaining the approval of Congress. Even as a vote in Congress failed to provide endorsement of the action (the House of Representatives tied on a resolution approving the air strikes, which meant they were not approved), the White House insisted the president could order a ground offensive as well. "The whole idea of approval and authority raises a series of constitutional questions," presidential press spokesman Joe Lockhart explained.[4]

Indeed, it does. When President Clinton took the war power upon himself, ignoring the explicit constitutional delegation of that power to Congress, he violated one of the most important legacies of the

93

Framers of our founding document. "In no part of the constitution is more wisdom to be found than in the clause which confides the question of war or peace to the legislature, and not to the executive department," James Madison stressed. "The executive is the department of power most distinguished by its propensity to war: hence it is the practice of all states, in proportion as they are free, to disarm this propensity of its influence."[5] Significantly, that was the view of Bill Clinton himself during the Vietnam War, when he characterized the U.S. government as a "limited, parliamentary democracy" in describing his opposition to the draft.[6]

## Where Were the Critics of the Imperial Presidency?

The support of people who opposed the Vietnam War, on both sides of the Atlantic, for the war in Kosovo has not received the attention it deserves, for if anything the legal case for the intervention in Vietnam was stronger. The United States as a member of NATO was under no legal obligation to intervene in Kosovo, and its intervention in the absence of UN Security Council authorization "raises very serious issues of international law," noted International Court of Justice presiding judge Christopher Weeramantry.[7] By way of contrast, "the United States undertook an international obligation to defend South Viet-Nam in the SEATO Treaty," according to the State Department's legal memorandum of March 4, 1966.[8] Not everyone agreed with that interpretation of U.S. obligations, and it may further be argued that the collective security defense provision applies only until the Security Council can consider the dispute. Nevertheless, defense of a treaty ally is allowed in the absence of Security Council authorization, whereas intervention in the absence of such a commitment is on much shakier legal ground.

The domestic legal case for the Vietnam War was also stronger because President Lyndon Johnson in 1964 asked for and received permission to use military force in the Gulf of Tonkin resolution. That resolution was not without its flaws: the events that occurred in the Gulf of Tonkin were not accurately represented to Congress, and the resolution itself may have been of dubious constitutional merit because of its broad grant of authority to the president.[9] It was, however, better than nothing—and it was certainly more legal than conducting military actions in the teeth of congressional votes refusing to approve them, as Clinton did in Kosovo. The need for congressional authorization undoubtedly imposes a barrier to the use of military power, but that has always been the case—indeed, it was the idea. "Suppose Congress was asked to declare war and said no?" *New York Times* columnist Anthony Lewis asked during the buildup to the Gulf War. "The answer is that that risk is the price of living under our constitutional system—and the benefits as Madison understood them."[10]

If that was the correct position then, why is it not the correct position now? Yet Lewis and many other critics of the "imperial presidency" backed Clinton's presidential war in the Balkans. Indeed, most liberals in Congress voted against measures to enforce the War Powers Resolution and reassert congressional control over the war power.[11] Some liberal commentators even implied that the legislative effort was unpatriotic.[12]

## Why the Founders Gave the War Power to Congress

The provision of the Constitution delegating the war power to the legislature and not to the president has become perhaps the most violated part of the Constitution, in part because it is so misunderstood. For example, it is commonly argued that wars are no longer declared because of the legal complications that emanate from such an action. But that argument reflects a fundamental misunderstanding of the reasoning behind the Constitution, which also delegates the authority to "grant letters of Marque and Reprisal" to Congress. Letters of marque and reprisal are no longer issued (and even declarations of war had become unusual by the time the Constitution was written), but the Constitution's delegation of the authority to begin actions short of full-scale war was meant to signify Congress's total control over the initiation of *any* military action short of self-defense. Indeed, when the original language of the Constitution was changed to give Congress the authority to "declare" rather than "make" war, it was simply to clarify the president's authority to use the armed forces "to repel sudden attacks."[13] Anything beyond that required congressional authorization. *"The whole powers of war being,* by the Constitution of the United States, *vested in Congress,* the acts of that body alone can be resorted to as our guides," the Supreme Court ruled in *Talbot v. Seeman* (1801). *"Congress may authorize general hostilities,* in which case the general laws of war apply to our situation; *or partial hostilities,* in which case the laws of war, so far as they actually apply to our situation, must be noticed."[14]

The reasoning behind this provision is simple: the question of war or peace is one of the most fundamental that can confront a government and a nation, and it is simply too important to be left to a single individual, even if elected. When a participant in the Constitutional Convention suggested giving the president the power to make war, arguing that the executive "will not make war but when the Nation will support it," his proposal evoked shock, and another participant replied that he "never expected to hear in a republic a motion to empower the Executive alone to declare war."[15] Abraham Lincoln elaborated on that reasoning in a letter to his law partner, who thought, in the context of the war with Mexico, that the president should have the authority to use the armed forces in defense of the national interest without first getting the approval of Congress.

> Allow the President to invade a neighboring nation, whenever *he* shall deem it necessary to repel an invasion, and you allow him to do so *whenever he may choose to say* he deems it necessary for such purpose—and you allow him to make war at pleasure. Study to see if you can fix *any limit* to his power in this respect, after you have given him as much as you propose. . . .
>
> The provision of the Constitution giving the war-making power to Congress, was dictated, as I understand it, by the following reasons. Kings had always been involving and impoverishing their people in wars, pretending generally, if not always, that the good of the people was the object. This, our Convention understood to be the most oppressive of all Kingly oppressions, and they resolved to so frame the Constitution that *no one man* should hold the power of bringing this oppression upon us. But your view destroys the whole matter, and places our President where kings have always stood.[16]

Lincoln's distinction between kings and presidents also addresses another claim that is often made on behalf of presidential war power: that the president is the commander in chief of the armed forces and therefore does not need the authorization of Congress to send them into battle. The proper distinction was drawn very clearly by Alexander Hamilton. The president has "a right to command the military and naval forces of the nation," he wrote in *Federalist* no. 69, whereas the king of Great Britain "in addition to this right, possesses that of *declaring* war." James Madison was even more emphatic. "Those who are to *conduct a war* cannot in the nature of things, be proper or safe judges, whether a *war ought* to be *commenced, continued,* or *concluded,*" he stressed in his Helvidius letters. "They are barred from the latter functions by a great principle in free government, analogous to that which separates the sword from the purse, or the power of executing from the power of enacting laws."[17]

Unless one believes Hamilton and Madison were misguided or dishonest, it is impossible to conclude that the Founders wanted the president's power as commander in chief to include the war power. Rather, it appears that the president's designation as supreme commander of the armed forces was designed to prevent any military usurpation of the government. "One of the grievances in the Declaration of Independence was that George III had 'affected to render the military independent of, and superior to, the civil power,'" notes historian Ernest R. May. "The example of a command[er]-in-chief not subject to political control may have remained vivid in the minds of some of the Constitution's framers."[18] And it was not only the British experience, or their experience as colonists, that influenced them. Although it has been all but forgotten, there almost was a military coup in the United States in 1783, which was prevented at the last moment by the personal intervention of George Washington—and even then, just barely. As Thomas Jefferson commented, "The moderation and virtue of a single character probably prevented this Revolution from being closed, as most others have been, by a subversion of that liberty it was intended to establish."[19] That close brush with disaster must have been on the minds of the Framers who gathered in Philadelphia just a few years later and led them to specifically designate the president commander in chief to create an enduring constitutional chain of command, thereby reducing to the extent they could the possibility that America's civilian government could be overturned by the military.

Another popular argument invoked by defenders of presidential war making—that if Congress votes funds for a war, it is thereby effectively approving that war—is also erroneous. Our legislative control over the war power may be said to have originated with an effort by taxpayers to control the burdens that were imposed on them. "[King] John's increasing readiness to reveal the reality of force which lay behind the legal facade of government was matched by an open admission that this financial oppression was geared directly to his war plans on the continent," writes J. C. Holt in his history of Magna Carta. "Hitherto this connexion had often been implied rather than openly stated. Now John emphasized the close interrelation of war and finance ... he was financing war ... by financial pressures which subjected a man to burdens near or beyond his powers of repayment and threatened his estate and patrimony." The barons decided they could bear no more, which led to the famous confrontation at Runneymede, where John was obliged to make the concessions they demanded. Magna Carta specifies that "no scutage or aid [i.e., tax] is to be levied in our realm except by the common counsel of our realm."[20]

Thus, Magna Carta was, among other things, an effort to mandate that people could not be taxed without the consent of their representatives (the common counsel of the realm), and it was prompted in large part by the abuse inherent in unrestricted executive control over the war power. That issue reemerged with a vengeance in the 17th century, when the tension between king and parliament led to civil war, the execution of one king (Charles I), and the overthrow of another (James II) in the Glorious Revolution of 1688, which established parliament's ultimate supremacy. Nevertheless, the linkage between taxation and war continued to plague Britain and ultimately led to the American Revolution. When the colonists were taxed to offset the costs of the Seven Years War (known in the United States as the French and Indian War), they protested that they could not be taxed without their consent. When the mother country did not agree, the issue once again led to war.

The outcome of that dispute is well-known, and the history that led to it had a profound impact on the U.S. Constitution. In the United States, treaties—some of which could oblige the United States to go to war in defense of allies—require the support of two-thirds of the Senate. As Hamilton explained in *Federalist* no. 75, "The history of human conduct does not warrant that exalted opinion of human virtue which would make it wise in a nation to commit interests of so delicate and momentous a kind, as those which concern its intercourse with the rest of the world, to the sole disposal of a magistrate created and circumstanced as would be a President of the United States." Indeed, in his Pacificus debate with Madison, Hamilton explicitly acknowledged that even the fulfillment of treaty obligations constitutionally requires a decision by Congress. Because he is commonly regarded as the most prominent advocate of presidential power among the Founders, and because he was taking that position in this debate, his views deserve to be quoted at length.

> If the Legislature have a right to make war on the one hand—it is on the other the duty of the Executive to preserve Peace till war is declared.... The Executive ... is consequently bound, by faithfully executing the laws of neutrality, when that is the state of the Nation, to avoid giving a cause of war to foreign Powers....
>
> ... [I]f the[re] had been a Treaty of alliance *offensive* [and] defensive between the UStates and [France], the unqualified acknowlegement of the new Government [of France after the Revolution] would have put the UStates in a condition to become an associate in the War in which France was engaged—and would have laid the Legislature under an obligation, if required, and there was otherwise no valid excuse, of exercising its power of declaring war....
>
> ... the Legislature can alone declare war, can alone actually transfer the nation from a state of Peace to a state of War....
>
> In this distribution of powers the wisdom of our constitution is manifested. It is the province and duty of the Executive to preserve to the Nation the blessings of peace. The Legislature alone can interrupt these blessings, by placing the Nation in a state of War.[21]

In short, while acknowledging the executive's ability to make decisions that would influence Congress's decision to authorize war, Hamilton was firm in maintaining that the final decision nevertheless belonged to Congress. In contrast to those who argue today that Congress has an effective right of veto by virtue of its control over the purse, Hamilton maintained that a power of veto is all the president has if Congress wants to initiate war. "The Executive indeed cannot control the exercise of that power [of war]—further than by the exer[c]ise of its general right of objecting to all acts of the Legislature; liable to being overruled by two thirds of both houses of Congress."[22]

To swing the balance the other way would mean that Congress's power to declare war would be reduced to stopping war only by cutting off supplies to troops already fighting in the field, thereby placing them in jeopardy. Such a position is completely unrealistic and was rejected by Lincoln during the Mexican War. "I have always intended, and still intend, to vote supplies," he wrote to his law partner. "The locos are untiring in their effort to make the impression that all who vote supplies, or take part in the war, do, of necessity, approve the President[']s conduct in the beginning of it; but the whigs have, from the beginning, made and kept the distinction between the two."[23]

## Modern Views of the War Power

A similar distinction was acknowledged by the D.C. Circuit Court with regard to the Vietnam War. "A Congressman wholly opposed to the war's commencement and continuation might vote for the military appropriations and for the draft measures because he was unwilling to abandon without support men already fighting," wrote federal appellate judges Charles Wyzanski and David Bazelon. "An honorable, decent, compassionate act of aiding those already in peril is not proof of consent to the actions that placed and continued them in that dangerous posture. We should not construe votes cast in pity and piety as though they were votes freely given to express consent."[24]

Finally, it is incorrect to assert that legislative control over the war power might have been useful 200 years ago but is outdated now. In the first place, such an attitude demonstrates contempt for the rule of law, which is the only guarantee against arbitrary rule by those who hold power, elected or not. In addition, however, legislative control over the war power proved its contemporary worth by helping to end the Cold War. "Most acts of aggression have been committed by expansionist countries under the pretext of acquiring 'lebensraum,'" an article in *Izvestia* declared in 1988. "It is difficult now to imagine a government in any highly developed country with an effectively operating parliamentary system of control over executive power being politically capable of such actions."[25] That article, which was not unusual, presaged the changes Mikhail Gorbachev attempted to implement in the Soviet Union. "The use of armed forces outside the country without sanction from the Supreme Soviet or the congress is ruled out categorically, once and for all," he emphasized when he was sworn in as the Soviet president in

March 1990. "The only exception will be in the case of a surprise armed attack from outside."[26]

World War II demonstrates the danger inherent in unchecked executive control over the war power. Adolf Hitler, it must be remembered, came to power by competing in elections. When he was accused of being undemocratic, his reply was scathing: "I became Chancellor in Germany under the rules of Parliamentary democracy. . . . Mr. Churchill and these gentlemen are delegates of the English people and I am delegate of the German people—the only difference lies in the fact that only a fraction of the English votes were cast for Mr. Churchill, while I can say that I represent the whole German people."[27]

The difference, of course, was that Hitler used his initial democratic legitimacy to concentrate all power in his hands under the *Führerprinzip,* or leader principle. The role of parliament was reduced to a rubber stamp following the Reichstag fire, when it approved the Law for Removing the Distress of People and the Reich, which effectively transferred its power to Hitler. "Thus was parliamentary democracy finally interred in Germany," noted journalist William Shirer in his famous history of the Third Reich. "Parliament had turned over its constitutional authority to Hitler."[28] Hitler then faced no constitutional barrier to the war he intended to unleash, and his unrestricted power legitimized even greater atrocity. When Adolf Eichmann's Israeli interrogators asked him whether he ever thought of disobeying orders, he replied that they were lawful because they came from Hitler. "According to the then prevailing interpretation, which no one questioned, the Führer's orders had the force of law," he explained. "That is common knowledge. The Führer's orders have the force of law."[29]

### Conclusion

The history of our century demonstrates the wisdom of our Founders. "Executive powers," Madison argued at the Constitutional Convention, "do not include the Rights of war & peace &c. but the powers shd. be confined and defined—if large we shall have the Evils of elective Monarchies."[30] Control of the war power by an executive, even if elected, is simply incompatible with the American conception of democracy. The Kosovo war ultimately resulted in a NATO victory, but it set a worrisome precedent for countries that

101

look to the United States as a model of democracy. When Russia sent its troops into Pristina unexpectedly, not only did President Yeltsin fail to inform NATO beforehand, he did not bother to get the approval of his legislature. "The hasty deployment of Russian troops in Kososvo contravenes Russia's own constitution," complained Igor M. Stepanov, a leading Russian constitutional authority. "Maybe they no longer bother to check their actions against the text of the constitution."[31] If the Russians and others conclude that executive rather than legislative control over the war power is the proper model, we shall have lost one of the greatest benefits of the end of the Cold War, and it is doubtful the world will be safer as a result.

President Clinton fought the war in Kosovo for a noble purpose, but that was what President Lyndon Johnson thought during the Vietnam War—and Bill Clinton saw no reason then why he should automatically obey the president. On the contrary, he was a war protester, and it should be remembered that many of those who opposed the war did so, at least in part, because they thought the president had assumed powers properly belonging to Congress. "One of the great tragedies of the Vietnam war has been that there has never been a clear-cut, up-or-down vote by Congress on war," Sen. George McGovern (D-S.D.) lamented. "Without such a 'yes' vote by Congress, made in an explicit and unambiguous manner, any large-scale military action taken by the president alone is unconstitutional."[32]

We should not allow the military victory in the Kosovo war to dull our memory. Proposals for repeating the Kosovo model of intervention elsewhere are already being heard, but the consequences of Vietnam are still with us—and they should not be forgotten, especially by those who protested that war. It is not as if we have not been warned. "The tyranny of the legislature is the most formidable dread at present, and will be for long years," Thomas Jefferson wrote to James Madison in 1789. "That of the executive will come in its turn."[33] Although it would be an exaggeration to say that the United States now suffers from tyranny of the executive, unchallenged executive control of the war power has dreadful potential, as we have seen in other countries, and the example we set may come back to haunt us.

# Notes

1. Secretary of State Madeleine Albright, quoted in Walter Isaacson, "Madeleine's War," *Time,* May 17, 1999, p. 28.

2. George Washington, *Writings* (New York: Library of America, 1997), p. 767.

3. The promise of Washington's letter was not fulfilled at the time he wrote, since slavery still existed in the United States. That contradiction between America's ideals and its reality was addressed by Abraham Lincoln in his speech on the *Dred Scott* decision: The Declaration of Independence "meant to set up a standard maxim for free society, which should be familiar to all, and revered by all; constantly looked to, constantly labored for, and even though never perfectly attained, constantly approximated, and thereby constantly spreading and deepening its influence, and augmenting the happiness and value of life to all people of all colors everywhere." Abraham Lincoln, *Speeches and Writings 1832–1858* (New York: Library of America, 1989), p. 398.

4. Quoted in Sean Scully, "House Refuses to Back Air War on Serbs," *Washington Times,* April 29, 1999.

5. Marvin Meyers, ed., *The Mind of the Founder: Sources of the Political Thought of James Madison,* rev. ed. (Hanover, N.H.: University Press of New England, 1981), pp. 212–13.

6. William Clinton, "A Letter by Clinton on His Draft Deferment: 'A War I Opposed and Despised,'" *New York Times,* February 13, 1992. Ironically, although Clinton did not impose a draft for the Kosovo war, his stop-loss order prohibiting people already in the armed forces from retiring on schedule amounted to the same thing, although it applied to a more limited pool of people. "'Stop loss' is essentially a draft—a draft of military members who no longer want to serve. The irony that Bill Clinton is the president to institute this de facto draft—and for something the administration refused to call a war—is not lost on our service members." Chris Stewart and David Forsmark, "If Clinton Won Kosovo War, Why Did He Invoke a New Draft?" *Detroit News,* June 17, 1999. Or in the words of a posting on an America Online message board: "I am currently 2 months from leaving the military after 4 years of volunteer service . . . my husband is 3 months away after 5 years as a military intelligence officer. Now, because of the severe shortage in troops, we may be forced to remain in the military until the end of this crisis. Meanwhile, people who have never volunteered, or sacrificed themselves will use the freedom that I have fought for . . . how ironic is that?" Pickens77, "Re: No Draft/Ground Troops," April 29, 1999, at 19990429189431.20736.00000162@ng-cd1.aol.com.

7. Quoted in "World Court Declines Request to Halt Bombing," *South China Morning Post,* June 2, 1999.

8. See John Norton Moore, *Law and the Indo-China War* (Princeton, N.J.: Princeton University Press, 1972), p. 615. Although that interpretation might be simply dismissed as a legal rationalization, it apparently was sincerely believed by President Lyndon Johnson. "We are party to a treaty," he told Sen. Richard Russell (D-Ga.) in a private conversation, "and if we don't pay attention to this treaty, why, I don't guess they think we pay attention to any of them." Quoted in Michael R. Beschloss, ed., *Taking Charge: The White House Tapes, 1963–1964* (New York: Simon & Schuster, 1997), p. 364. In his memoirs, Secretary of State Dean Rusk made the connection between SEATO and NATO explicit. "On another occasion at a NATO foreign ministers' meeting, my German, British, and French colleagues expressed misgivings about the

U.S. effort in Vietnam and concern that we might someday neglect Europe. I told my colleagues, 'You cannot expect the United States to be a virgin in the Atlantic and a whore in the Pacific.' I reminded them that Britain and France shared our treaty commitments in Southeast Asia and that the United States, as a two-ocean country, had to treat its commitments in the Pacific with the same seriousness as those in the Atlantic." Dean Rusk, *As I Saw It*, ed. Daniel S. Papp (New York: Penguin, 1990), p. 455.

9. On the latter point, see Alexander M. Bickel, "The Constitution and the War," *Commentary*, July 1972, pp. 49–55.

10. Anthony Lewis, "War in the Gulf?" *New York Times*, October 22, 1990.

11. By a vote of 249 to 180, House members approved a Republican-sponsored bill that would have prohibited the president from using Pentagon funds to send U.S. ground troops into Yugoslavia without authorization from Congress, but only 45 Democrats voted in support of the bill. On a measure to support the undeclared war, 187 Republicans voted no, but only 26 Democrats joined them. "2 House Votes Point to Lack of Support for Balkan Action," *Los Angeles Times*, April 29, 1999, p. A1.

12. *Crossfire* cohost Bill Press, for example, asserted that in voting for such bills, "Republicans undermined the authority of both the President and the Pentagon. Telling them, in effect, you can't ever use ground troops, without getting our permission first.... The Republicans' message is clear—to Yugoslav President Slobodan Milosevic ... the message is: Don't worry about winning this war, we'll win it for you by cutting the legs out from under our president and our troops." Bill Press, "Which Side Are You On, Boys?" *Los Angeles Times*, April 30, 1999, p. B7. Marianne Means, a commentator with the Hearst News Service, claimed that Republicans looked "cranky, small-minded, and unpatriotic" for not supporting the war. Marianne Means, "Petulant Republicans Are Sore Losers," *Des Moines Register*, June 17, 1999, p. 9.

13. The quotation is from James Madison's notes on the Constitutional Convention and is his description of the proposal he and Elbridge Gerry put forward for the change in language. Max Farrand, ed., *The Records of the Federal Convention of 1787*, rev. ed. (New Haven, Conn.: Yale University Press, 1966), vol. 2, p. 318.

14. 5 U.S. (1 Cranch) 1, 28 (1801). Emphasis added.

15. Farrand, vol. 2, p. 318.

16. Lincoln, pp. 175–76. Emphasis in original.

17. *The Mind of the Founder*, pp. 206–7. Emphasis in original.

18. Ernest R. May, "The President Shall Be Commander in Chief," in *The Ultimate Decision*, ed. Ernest R. May (New York: George Braziller, 1960), p. 9.

19. Quoted in James Thomas Flexner, *Washington: The Indispensable Man* (New York: New American Library 1984), p. 178.

20. J. C. Holt, *Magna Carta*, 2d ed. (New York: Cambridge University Press, 1992), pp. 192, 196, 455.

21. Alexander Hamilton, Pacificus no. 1 (1793), in *Selected Writings and Speeches of Alexander Hamilton*, ed. Morton J. Frisch (Washington: American Enterprise Institute for Public Policy Research, 1985), pp. 401–3. Emphasis in original.

22. Ibid., p. 402.

23. Letter to William H. Herndon, February 1, 1848, in Lincoln, pp. 172–73.

24. *Mitchell v. Laird*, 488 F.2d 611, 615 (DC Cir. 1973), cited in Louis Fisher, "The Spending Power," in *The Constitution and the Conduct of American Foreign Policy*, ed.

David Gray Adler and Larry N. George (Lawrence: University Press of Kansas, 1996), p. 230.

25. S. Blagovolin, "The Strength and Impotence of Military Might: Is an Armed Conflict between East and West a Real Possibility in Our Time?" *Izvestia,* November 18, 1988, in *Current Digest of the Soviet Press,* December 14, 1988, p. 3.

26. "Excerpts from Gorbachev Speech on Presidency," *New York Times,* March 16, 1990.

27. Adolf Hitler, *My New Order,* ed. Raoul de Roussy de Sales (New York: Reynal & Hitchcock, 1941), pp. 554–56.

28. William L. Shirer, *The Rise and Fall of the Third Reich* (New York: Simon & Schuster, 1960), p. 199.

29. Jochen von Lang, ed., *Eichmann Interrogated,* trans. Ralph Manheim (Toronto: Lester & Orpen Dennys, 1983), p. 124. It is worth noting that the "Nuremberg defense" of obeying orders was addressed early in American history in the case of *Little v. Barreme,* decided by the Supreme Court in 1804. In 1799 an American naval officer, following the order of President John Adams during the quasi-war with France, seized a vessel sailing from a French port. Congress, however, had authorized seizure only of vessels sailing to French ports. The Court decided the president's order had exceeded the authority granted by Congress and therefore should not have been obeyed. "That implicit obedience which military men usually pay to the orders of their superiors, which indeed is indispensably necessary to every military system, appeared to me strongly to imply the principle that those orders, if not to perform a prohibited act, ought to justify the person whose general duty it is to obey them, and who is placed by the laws of his country in a situation which in general requires that he should obey them," wrote Chief Justice John Marshall. But the president's "instructions cannot change the nature of the transaction, or legalize an act which without those instructions would have been a plain trespass." 6 U.S. (2 Cranch) 170, 179 (1804).

30. Rufus King, Notes of June 1, 1787, in Farrand, vol. 1, p. 70.

31. Quoted in Richard C, Paddock, "Russia Confronts Results of Hasty Deployment in Kosovo," *Los Angeles Times,* June 16, 1999.

32. George S. McGovern, introduction to *Unquestioning Obedience to the President: The ACLU Case against the Illegal War in Vietnam* by Leon Friedman and Burt Neuborne (New York: W. W. Norton & Company, 1972), p. 18.

33. Thomas Jefferson, Letter to James Madison, March 15, 1789, in *The Origins of the American Constitution: A Documentary History,* ed. Michael J. Kammen (New York: Penguin, 1986), p. 378.

# 8. Setting Dangerous International Precedents

*Stanley Kober*

The Kosovo war has been described as a unique war, a war fought for humanitarian purposes. Those who supported it argue that because it was fought for a noble purpose, the normal rules that prohibit attacks against a foreign country did not apply. When a government violates the rights of its citizens the way the Milosevic regime violated the rights of the Albanians, the international community has a right, and even an obligation, to intervene with military force. Sovereignty, it is alleged, is no longer sacrosanct; when fundamental human rights are being violated, sovereignty must yield.

That argument is not new. The Peace of Westphalia that is commonly recognized as the inauguration of our system of sovereign national states also prescribed principles of fundamental rights that rulers were obliged to observe. Because the Thirty Years War that led to the peace was rooted in religious differences, the treaty specified principles of religious tolerance that had to be observed. "All others of the said Confession of Ausburg [*sic*], who shall demand it, shall have the free Exercise of their Religion," states Article 28 of the treaty signed at Munster on October 24, 1648. It also placed the signatories under an obligation to restore the free trade that had been impeded by the war. "Above all, the Navigation of the Rhine shall be free," commands Article 89. "It shall not be permitted to impose upon the Rhine new and unwonted Tolls, Customs, Taxes, Imposts, and other like Exactions." Violations of these and other articles specifying limits to sovereignty were to be dealt with by the international community of the time. According to Article 123, "all Partys in this Transaction shall be oblig'd to defend and protect all and every Article of this Peace against any one, without distinction of Religion."[1]

In short, it is incorrect to argue that our modern state system is based on inviolable state sovereignty, for sovereignty was subject to certain restrictions, based on fundamental human rights, at its very inception. The reason that system fell into disuse, and even disrepute, is that it was subject to misuse. Aggressors typically do not announce their intent to commit evil; they try to cloak their designs with the appearance of reasonableness. A good example is Munich, the 20th-century experience that is frequently invoked as the precedent for Kosovo. But the full analogy is broader than the part that is usually invoked: that it is both dangerous and morally wrong to appease an "aggressor." It is important to remember that Hitler's claims against Czechoslovakia were based on alleged violations of the fundamental rights of the Sudeten Germans. His accusations of the mistreatment of the ethnic Germans were purposely exaggerated and distorted to inflame public opinion; he even invoked the specter of ethnic cleansing to justify his ultimatum. "We see the appalling figures: on one day 10,000 fugitives, on the next 20,000, a day later, already 37,000," he declared on September 26, 1938. "Whole stretches of country were depopulated, villages are burned down, attempts are made to smoke out the Germans with hand-grenades and gas."[2]

NATO's justification for its military intervention in Kosovo is remarkably similar to Hitler's justification for military intervention in Czechoslovakia. Hitler's concern for the Sudeten Germans, of course, was manufactured; the Sudeten German territory was just a steppingstone to seizing the rest of Czechoslovakia and ultimately even greater "living space" in Europe. NATO's leaders, on the other hand, were genuinely concerned by Milosevic's treatment of the Albanians in Kosovo, especially after the massacre in Racak early in 1999. Nevertheless, by acting on their own, and by justifying their unilateral action as both legitimate and necessary in the name of protecting a beleaguered ethnic minority, NATO's leaders risked legitimizing a process that in the past had led to tragedy.

That point must be stressed because it is so important. Governments are not, and should not be, allowed to violate the fundamental rights of their citizens with impunity. Outside parties may be justified in intervening, not only to protect the helpless innocent, but also to protect themselves, since a country that does not respect the rights of its citizens is unlikely to respect the sovereignty of its neighbors if it becomes militarily strong.[3] Nevertheless, the process by which such a decision is reached must have a recognized legitimacy or it is likely to be counterproductive. That is why the Peace of Westphalia prescribed a procedure for such intervention. "If it happens any point shall be violated, the Offended shall before all things exhort the Offender not to come to any Hostility, submitting the Cause to a friendly Composition, or the ordinary Proceedings of Justice," it concludes. "Nevertheless, if for the space of three years the Difference cannot be terminated by any of those means, all and every one of those concern'd in this Transaction shall be oblig'd to join the injur'd Party, and assist him with Counsel and Force to repel the Injury."[4]

Such a procedure is extremely difficult to implement. In particular, the identities of the offended and the offender are often a matter of dispute. That is why countries are loath to base their security on such arrangements and frequently seek additional protection by membership in alliances. It was the explicit provision for such alliances in the Peace of Westphalia that was the basis of the claim to sovereignty, for only sovereigns can form alliances with other sovereigns to provide for their security. Even here, however, the treaty insisted that "such Alliances be not against the [Holy Roman] Emperor, and the Empire, nor against the Publick Peace, and this Treaty, and without prejudice to the Oath by which every one is bound to the Emperor and the Empire."[5] That provision is similar to Article 52 of the UN Charter, which permits regional security arrangements so long as "their activities are consistent with the Purposes and Principles of the United Nations."

### Problems with Collective Security

In short, it is erroneous to argue that the legal system allowing humanitarian intervention is a recent innovation, for its historical roots may be found in the Peace of Westphalia, the foundation of our system of sovereign states. The problem is that it did not work as intended, and the reason is the same now as it was then: the overarching authority—then the Holy Roman Empire, now the United Nations—lacks real power and respect, and alliances fill the vacuum. Reliance on alliances led to the elaboration of the concept of the balance of power as a mechanism by which weaker states could avoid being overpowered by a stronger one. Initially, the balance of power was viewed as an advance. "Enormous monarchies are, probably, destructive to human nature," wrote the Scottish Enlightenment philosopher David Hume, whereas "the maxim of preserving the balance of power is founded so much on common sense and obvious reasoning."[6]

Yet the balance of power has its own problem, as alliances provoke the formation of counteralliances. George Washington was more cautious than Hume in his assessment of alliances, which he feared could spawn unnecessary wars by locking countries into confrontation. "'Tis our true policy to steer clear of permanent Alliances with any portion of the foreign world," he advised the American people in his Farewell Address, although "we may safely trust to temporary alliances for extraordinary emergencies."[7] For Washington, alliances were an evil that might on occasion be necessary, but they could not be the foundation of an enduring peace. His viewpoint seemed vindicated by World War I, when the division of Europe into two "permanent" alliances—the Triple Alliance and the Triple Entente—established the conditions that allowed a minor conflict to expand into the greatest war the world had ever seen.

That catastrophe set the pendulum moving again. "Is the present war a struggle for a just and secure peace, or only for a new balance of power?" President Woodrow Wilson asked on January 22, 1917, shortly before Germany's campaign of unrestricted submarine warfare brought the United States into the war. "There must be, not a balance of power, but a community of power; not organized rivalries, but an organized common peace." And that common peace had to rest on the recognition that denial of fundamental human rights leads to war. "Henceforth inviolable security of life, of worship, and of industrial and social development should be guaranteed to all peoples," Wilson continued. "Any peace which does not recognize and accept this principle will inevitably be upset."[8] Once again, the principle of human rights was seen as more important than the sovereignty of states; the only question was how to create a system that would effectively safeguard those rights. As we have seen, Hitler manipulated the principle of national self-determination, which Wilson had thought one of those fundamental rights, so that the democracies confronted him later than they otherwise might have done.

The establishment of the United Nations after World War II was an attempt to reconcile all these competing imperatives, to create a system that would guarantee both peace and human rights. But the victorious allies fell out, and the world divided the way Europe had divided earlier in the century. Perhaps even more important, a vast part of the world fell under the tyranny of communism. Recognizing the limits of their power, the Western allies did not interfere in the areas where communism held sway, but by their policy of containment they did attempt to prevent the spread of its tyranny. That policy ultimately led to the war in Vietnam.

## Vietnam Doves Become Kosovo Hawks

The war in Kosovo has been praised by its supporters as an attempt to learn from history, to ensure that the appeasement of Munich that preceded World War II would not be repeated. "The great lesson of this century is that when aggression and brutality go unopposed, like a cancer, they spread," Secretary of State Madeleine Albright told the American Jewish Committee during the war against Yugoslavia. "And what begins as the sickness in one part of the body can become a grave danger to the whole."[9] When one of her aides suggested she compromise during a negotiation session, she snapped, "Where do you think we are, Munich?"[10]

The war in Vietnam was justified on the same basis. In the words of one of Secretary Albright's predecessors, Dean Rusk, in 1964:

> So what is our stake [in Vietnam]? ... Can those of us in this room forget the lesson that we had in this issue of war and peace when it was only 10 years from the seizure of Manchuria to Pearl Harbor; about 2 years from the seizure of Czechoslovakia to the outbreak of World War II in Western Europe? Don't you remember the hopes expressed those days: that perhaps the aggressor will be satisfied by this next bite. ... But we found that ambition and appetite fed upon success and the next bite generated the appetite for the following bite. And we learned that by postponing the issue, we made the result more terrible, the holocaust more dreadful. We cannot forget that experience.[11]

Similarly, the Kosovo war has been praised by its supporters because it was not a war for territory but a war to defend the fundamental rights of people who faced persecution. But how is that different from the war in Vietnam? After the United States lost that war, communist movements swept to power in all three states of Indochina. One of the greatest massacres of the 20th century then occurred in Cambodia. It is impossible to imagine that slaughter would have taken place if the United States had won the war. And the violence was not confined to Cambodia. Just as hundreds of thousands of people fled Kosovo, hundreds of thousands fled Vietnam after the South Vietnamese government fell. Their journey, like that of the Kosovars, was fraught with terror. Because their story has received so little attention, the story of one young refugee from Vietnam deserves to be quoted at length as an example of what they endured. This account begins with his boat coming under fire as it approached an island.

> I never felt any physical pain, but when I looked down I saw that I was lying in blood. Whatever entered the side of my upper thigh is still there today.
>
> While lying there, I saw five people swimming from the island to the boat. . . .
>
> All of us were in a state of shock. Only the presence of the five newcomers kept us from being paralyzed with inactivity. We listened as they told us of the terrifying events that had occurred during the hours before we had reached the island. . . .
>
> They had left the coastal city of Nha Trang, in Central Vietnam, in a wooden fishing boat that carried 120 refugees. Their journey was uneventful until they reached the fateful fog-shrouded island around 3:00 A.M. . . .
>
> Suddenly, brilliant beams of light flashed and focused on the beach. At the same time, a great number of Vietnamese Communist soldiers with automatic rifles stepped out into the light and surrounded the people on the beach. . . .
>
> Not long after, two huge explosions shattered the boat, direct hits from shells fired fore and aft. Bodies, blood, wood, and metal flew into the air. When they heard the explosions, the prisoners on the beach panicked. As they dashed for the water or for cover away from the beach, the soldiers opened fire on them. Very few survived. . . .
>
> About three hours after the shooting began, our boat approached the island. At first we heard no shots; indeed, the first ones we heard were those that ripped into our boat and killed the captain's daughter. For about 30 minutes after that, the Communists continued shooting. We saw people running along the beach, and we saw them shot down in their tracks.[12]

What is striking is that so many people who opposed the Vietnam War—President Clinton, NATO secretary general Javier Solana, German chancellor Gerhard Schroeder, and German foreign minister

Joschka Fischer, to name a few—fervently believed in the war in Kosovo. But what is the difference? If the Munich analogy applies to Kosovo, why didn't it apply to Vietnam? If it is unacceptable to allow people to be killed as part of a campaign of ethnic cleansing, why is it acceptable to allow them to be killed as part of a campaign of ideological cleansing?

Those questions illuminate the difficulty with the new doctrine of humanitarian intervention. To justify the war in Kosovo, one has to ignore the war in Vietnam, because there is no difference in the humanitarian issue involved. "[T]hose of us who opposed the American war in Indochina should be extremely humble in the face of the appalling aftermath: a form of genocide in Cambodia and horrific tyranny in both Vietnam and Laos," William Shawcross, the journalist who detailed the secret bombing of Cambodia, has acknowledged. "After the Communist victory came the refugees to Thailand and the floods of boat people desperately seeking to escape the Cambodian killing fields and the Vietnamese gulags. Their eloquent testimony should have put paid to all illusions."[13]

That is not to say that the U.S. intervention in Southeast Asia was warranted—much less that it was wise and prudent. There were good strategic rationales for opposing such an investment of American blood and treasure, however justified the intervention might have been on the basis of abstract morality. The point is that proponents of the war in Kosovo who railed against the war in Vietnam cannot have it both ways, at least not without an explanation.

## Global Fears of a New Imperialism

The very fact that so many of those in power who oversaw the Kosovo war opposed the Vietnam War exposes the difficulty with the doctrine of humanitarian intervention: what appears as humanitarian intervention to some seems like imperialist aggression to others. Although supporters of the Kosovo war claim they represented the international community, opposition to the war outside the NATO members and those countries aspiring to NATO membership was widespread.[14] That was true even in the Islamic nations, which might have been expected to enthusiastically back a military intervention in support of the largely Muslim Albanian Kosovars. Yet despite President Clinton's contention that "through our efforts in the Balkans we have also helped to bridge the gulf between Europe

113

and the Islamic world, the source of so much trouble over the last millennium, and the source of troubling tensions still today," the Kosovo war appears to have strengthened suspicions about NATO's intentions in the Islamic world.[15] "The most offensive part of the accord was the overstepping of the UN Security Council thus rising [sic] NATO [to] something parallel to or above the world body," wrote a commentator in *Pakistan Today*. "Obviously Russia, China, India, Ukraine and other Central Asian countries, and a silent majority of the world community opposed this anarchy by [a] few powerful countries that were bent on undermining the authority of the United Nations."[16] An article in Egypt's semiofficial *Al-Ahram* expressed similar views. "Far from reassuring the world, this display of absolute American might is deeply disquieting," it argued. "The real future opened up by the events of the past few weeks is one in which the UN has effectively granted the US a mandate to interfere any time, anywhere. . . . Perhaps it is time for the peoples of the world to learn to read the writing on the wall. As they say in Hollywood: Coming soon to a strategically-sensitive war zone near you."[17]

Even in Jordan, which was more supportive of NATO's action, some observers questioned the alliance's motivation. According to Jamil Abu Baker, a member of the Executive Committee of the Muslim Brotherhood, Milosevic's "ethnic cleansing policy is a serious violation against mankind," but "we know that what NATO is doing is not defending Muslims but the strategic interests of the USA and Europe." An academic at the University of Israa' similarly questioned the purpose of NATO's intervention. "If we, for one moment, think that the forces of the great powers care about the Muslim refugees then we are wrong," insisted political science professor Husni Al Shayab. "The Western powers, which have the latest military technology on earth, want to be in control and replace the United Nations."[18] That theme—the inadmissibility of NATO's overriding the United Nations, even in the defense of Muslims—was repeated again and again. "Kosovo has witnessed unimaginable atrocities," acknowledged Mohamed Sid-Ahmed in *Al-Ahram*, but NATO "is not empowered to carry out punitive raids against a sovereign state without the authorization of the United Nations, the only universally recognized and genuinely global organization backed by international law."[19]

The reaction of the Islamic world is not the only surprise. In Ukraine, a country that has been intensively wooed by NATO as part of its expansion campaign, the reaction was similarly negative. When NATO began bombing Yugoslavia, the Ukrainian parliament voted 231–46 to encourage the government to reconsider the country's nonnuclear status, claiming that NATO's attack amounted to "aggression against a sovereign state."[20] To be sure, the Ukrainian reaction was also motivated by sympathy for fellow Slavs who were enduring NATO bombing. According to Ivanna Klympush, a NATO expert at the East-West Institute in Kiev, "with the Kosovo crisis, it is a lot harder for pro-westerners to raise arguments for European integration now the people are emotionally engaged with their Slavic brethren."[21]

Ukraine may well have been affected by Slavic ties, but other countries reacted similarly even without bonds of kinship. "NATO is indulging in naked aggression against Yugoslavia," accused India's prime minister Atal Behari Vajpayee. "In doing this, NATO has disregarded the United Nations completely." Significantly, Vajpayee's reaction was the same as that of the Ukrainian parliament: if NATO is the threat, the solution must rest with a nuclear deterrent. "Who is safe in this world? It is a worrisome situation. In this situation, we cannot let our defenses slip. Nuclear weapons are the only way to maintain peace."[22]

The mounting enthusiasm for nuclear weapons is one of the most disturbing consequences of NATO's military actions. "NATO's war over Kosovo has also complicated efforts to persuade nations to forgo nuclear weapons," notes the *Washington Post*. "According to participants [in a U.S.–North Korean meeting], the North Korean leaders replied, in essence: Why should North Korea give up those weapons? If it did, the United States might start complaining about human rights in North Korea and bomb it into oblivion like Serbia."[23] Perhaps that is just posturing, but the fundamental point nevertheless holds: if countries feel NATO (or other American alliances) reserves the right to initiate military action unilaterally, they will seek to protect themselves, which could lead to a reliance on nuclear weapons that otherwise might not occur.

But if all those consequences of the Kosovo war are noteworthy, possibly the most important reaction is in the members of the Security Council whose vetoes were ignored. If Russia and China conclude that NATO will not respect their rights in the Security Council, they will do what David Hume considered "obvious" in his essay on the balance of power: they will join together to try to balance NATO. Indeed, that process is well under way. "After the air strikes against Serbia began, Boris Yeltsin told Beijing that unless China and Russia joined forces, the American military machine could not be stopped," an official of the Chinese armed forces told Hong Kong's *South China Morning Post*. "The Jiang leadership decided to make a move after the Chinese Embassy in Belgrade was bombed," and an agreement for a massive Russian arms sale to China was quickly reached.[24] Although the Chinese government is still resisting Russia's proposals for a formal military alliance, the Chinese people might be more receptive. "In an online poll by Sohu, one of China's biggest Internet portals, 94 percent of those responding said the[y] believe that the American explanation of the embassy bombing was not plausible," the *Washington Post* reported in late June 1999. "About 63 percent said that a restoration of a China-Russia alliance would restrain NATO and be beneficial to world peace."[25] Of course, such a poll is not comprehensive, but one would expect Chinese with Internet access to be biased toward the United States rather than Russia, which makes this result even more startling.

Indeed, one of the most significant trends of the 1990s is the growing alienation of the Russian and Chinese people from the United States. At the beginning of the decade, Russians embraced everything American and looked to a better future, but years of economic decline have ground them down and made them suspicious. "Are you American?" a Russian woman asked a correspondent for the *Washington Post*. "Your America, it seems, is very glad about these so-called reforms. Is that so? Are you glad we are falling apart? There was an opinion that there is gloating in America that we are becoming beggars."[26] The attack on Yugoslavia has heightened Russian suspicions, with two-thirds of Russians now telling pollsters they view NATO as a threat to Russia.[27] "At last Russia seemed to have found its new national idea: anti-Americanism," wrote Alan Rousso, director of the Moscow Center of the Carnegie Endowment for International Peace, during the Kosovo war. "Reading the Russian press and talking to Russians of every stripe reveals strikingly how widely shared and deeply felt anti-NATO sentiments are here."[28]

Similar shifts in opinion can be seen in China. "We are a very old and traditional nation," a Chinese government employee told the

*New York Times.* "If you do not show us respect, we will hate you." Astonishingly, students praised Chairman Mao as a symbol of national greatness. "Mao was the only Chinese leader who really dared to stand up to anyone," explained one protesting student following the embassy bombing. "He was very anti-American."[29] That sentiment is a long way from Tiananmen Square and the Goddess of Democracy, modeled on the Statue of Liberty. "The US is a democracy, but its conduct was not as perfect as students thought 10 years ago," another student told a British newspaper. "If this was the model, now we should not follow that model."[30]

The leaders of NATO have presented the outcome of the war as a basis for a more peaceful world, but if it alienates the Russian and Chinese peoples, thereby driving their countries (and possibly others) into closer military collaboration to oppose the United States and its allies, we will have seen the end of the post–Cold War world.[31] Instead, we will be back to the posture that characterized the Cold War, but with two major differences: the collaboration between Russia and China will be closer because they will not be competing for leadership of the communist world, and their peoples will share a hostility toward the United States rooted in their common conviction that we betrayed their hopes.

The stakes, in short, are very high, which means that we should get the questions as well as the answers right. To repeat, the issue is not the legitimacy of humanitarian intervention as such but rather the procedure by which such intervention is undertaken. The appropriate procedure is prescribed in Article 39 of the UN Charter: "The Security Council shall determine the existence of any threat to the peace, breach of the peace, or act of aggression and shall make recommendations, or decide what measures shall be taken in accordance with Articles 41 and 42, to maintain or restore international peace and security." If the United States and its allies now feel that, in the post–Cold War world, they no longer have to honor that provision of international law, they should have no illusions about the result. Other countries are not going to roll over and play dead. The world will divide once again, and the century will end the way it began, primed for major conflict.

The parallels are eerie. The century began when a great power delivered an ultimatum to Serbia and then attacked, thereby alienating the Russian people. That alienation led to decades of confrontation, which dominated the history of the 20th century. When the confrontation ended 10 years ago, there was a global sense of relief that the danger of nuclear war seemed to have passed. But now, once again, a great power has delivered an ultimatum to Serbia and then attacked, thereby alienating the Russian people. We can only hope that we are not seeing history repeat itself and that the parallels end there.

## Notes

1. "The Articles of the Treaty of Peace, Sign'd and Seal'd at Munster, in Westphalia, October the 24th, 1648," in *The Consolidated Treaty Series*, ed. Clive Parry (Dobbs Ferry, N.Y.: Oceana, 1969), vol. 1, pp. 327, 344–45, 354.

2. Adolf Hitler, *My New Order*, ed. Raoul de Roussy de Sales (New York: Reynal & Hitchcock, 1941), p. 529.

3. For more on the connection between domestic tyranny and foreign aggression, see Stanley Kober, "Idealpolitik," *Foreign Policy*, no. 79 (Summer 1990): 11–13.

4. "The Articles of the Treaty of Peace," p. 354.

5. Ibid., p. 338.

6. David Hume, *Essays Moral, Political, and Literary*, ed. Eugene F. Miller, rev. ed. (Indianapolis: Liberty Classics, 1987), pp. 340–41, 337.

7. George Washington, *Writings*, ed. John Rhodenhamel (New York: Library of America, 1997), p. 975.

8. Woodrow Wilson, *The New Democracy*, ed. Ray Stannard Baker and William E. Dodd (New York: Harper & Brothers, 1926), vol. 2, pp. 410–11.

9. "Text: Albright Remarks for American Jewish Committee Dinner," May 6, 1999, USIS Washington File, May 7, 1999.

10. Quoted in Walter Isaacson, "Madeleine's War," *Time*, May 17, 1999, p. 29.

11. *U.S. Department of State Bulletin*, March 22, 1964, p. 401, cited in Yuen Foong Khong, *Analogies at War: Korea, Munich, Dien Bien Phu, and the Vietnam Decisions of 1965* (Princeton, N.J.: Princeton University Press, 1992), p. 180.

12. "Perilous Journey: 1979," in *Hearts of Sorrow: Vietnamese-American Lives*, ed. James M. Freeman (Stanford: Stanford University Press, 1989), pp. 327–29. The narrator was 14 years old at the time and went on to join the U.S. armed forces.

13. Quoted in Stephen S. Rosenfeld, "The Shawcross Apology," *Washington Post*, May 21, 1999.

14. Even within NATO, public opinion was divided; in Greece, public opinion was overwhelmingly against the war.

15. "Remarks by the President at United States Air Force Academy Commencement Ceremony," June 2, 1999, www.pub.whitehouse.gov.

16. Nisar Ahmad, "Russia-US Synergy Key to a Secure Europe," *Pakistan Today*, Internet edition, June 25, 1999.

17. Gamal Nkrumah, "The Pristina Precedent," *Al-Ahram Weekly*, Internet edition, June 17–23, 1999.

18. Quoted in Ibtisam Awadat, "Refugee Crisis in the Balkans: beyond Arab Apathy," *Star* (Jordan), Internet edition, May 13, 1999.

19. Mohamed Sid-Ahmed, "Primacy of NATO over the UN?" *Al-Ahram Weekly*, Internet edition, April 1, 1999.

20. "Ukraine's Parliament Denounces NATO, Raises Nuclear Threat," *Dow Jones International News*, March 24, 1999.

21. Quoted in Charles Clover, "Ukraine Caught between West and Slav Brethren," *Financial Times*, May 8, 1999.

22. Quoted in "Nuclear Arms Prevent Aggression, India Says," *Washington Times*, May 10, 1999.

23. Steven Mufson, "Losing the Battle on Arms Control," *Washington Post*, July 17, 1999.

24. Quoted in Willy Wo-Lap Lam, "Beijing and Moscow in Hi-tech Arms Pact," *South China Morning Post*, Internet edition, June 26, 1999.

25. John Pomfret, "China's Surfers Make Waves," *Washington Post*, June 23, 1999.

26. Quoted in Sharon LaFraniere, "Capitalist Reality Comes Home to Roost in Russia," *Washington Post*, October 26, 1998.

27. "Russians Still Buy American Products," *Washington Times*, April 15, 1999.

28. Alan Rousso, "Kosovo and US-Russian Relations: A View from Moscow," Carnegie Endowment for International Peace, fax, May 6, 1999.

29. Quoted in Seth Faison, "Rage at U.S. Is Sign of Deeper Issues," *New York Times*, May 13, 1999.

30. Quoted in Teresa Poole, "Me-Generation on the rise in China," *Independent* (London), Internet edition, June 2, 1999.

31. In this regard, discussion of a strategic triangle comprising Russia, China, and India is especially noteworthy. When the idea was first broached by Russia's then–prime minister, Yevgeny Primakov, during a visit to India in December 1998, the India-China side of the triangle seemed questionable. The Kosovo war, however, seems to have sparked some reconsideration in both New Delhi and Beijing. On June 14, 1999, during a visit by Indian foreign minister Jaswant Singh to Beijing, the two countries announced they had decided to establish a "security dialogue" to resolve the issues, notably concerning the border, dividing them. Although such a dialogue is certainly unobjectionable to resolve differences that have led to war in the past, it should be noted that Indian media have indicated it is also motivated by the concerns that the two countries share regarding NATO's military action in the Balkans. "India and China took a common stand on NATO action in Kosovo—both worried about the bypassing of the UN system by the U.S.-led Western alliance. This fear of growing unilateral action by the U.S. perhaps prompted China to suggest a security dialogue. Faced with increasingly testy ties with the U.S., China may find it convenient to improve ties with India." Seema Guha, "China, India to Set Up Security Dialogue," *Times of India*, Internet edition, June 15, 1999. Shortly afterward, in an interview with the *Australian Financial Review*, the Chinese ambassador to Australia hinted at the development of a strategic triangle. "The U.S. has a powerful military, but it is a big world and the U.S. should not try to extend its power in Asia in this way. Asia is not Europe," emphasized Ambassor Zhou Wenzhong, adding pointedly, "China, Russia, India and other countries are very concerned about such a policy of putting human rights above national sovereignty." See "U.S. Warned against Trying 'Kosovo Formula' in Asia," *Hong Kong Standard*, Tigernet, August 6, 1999.

PART III

WHERE DO WE GO FROM HERE?

# 9. Stabilizing Borders in the Balkans: The Inevitability and Costs of a Greater Albania

*Michael Radu*

Most outsiders, and not a few people inside the Clinton administration, have criticized the political decisions that led to the war in Kosovo. The reason for that quasi-consensus is the explicit or implicit acknowledgment that the Rambouillet texts—they cannot be called "accords" because there was no negotiation, let alone accord, between the relevant parties, Serb nationalists and Albanian irredentists—were, to quote a familiar Washington phrase, "dead on arrival."

The Rambouillet and Paris texts of February–March 1999 resembled what used to be called a diktat—a unilateral decision by the great powers to solve the squabbles of the small ones for them. The 1878 Congress of Berlin, which cut short the dreams of a Greater Bulgaria, is a perfect example. The problem with Rambouillet was that there was no decision, except to postpone a decision on the key issue: the permanent status of Kosovo. Instead of a new Congress of Berlin, Rambouillet was a repetition of the Dayton Accords, which postponed determination of the permanent status of Bosnia-Herzegovina in general and that of the disputed city of Brcko in particular.

## Rambouillet's Lack of Realism

Why the timidity and lack of decisiveness at Dayton and Rambouillet? There were many reasons, some related to the mentality of the principal actors, some to tactical mistakes, and some to particular circumstances (such as coming elections in the United States), all of which contributed to those failures. The most important reasons, however, were ignorance of Balkan history and nationalism and the inability to choose between the territorial integrity of sovereign states and the often poorly defined rights of ethnic minorities. Hence,

Serbian nationalism was dismissed as "Milosevic's propaganda," while Albanian irredentism was winked at and allowed to hide behind both real and alleged victimhood. The "solution" to the sovereignty vs. minority rights dilemma at both Dayton and Rambouillet was to simply sidestep it. But how long can such matters be evaded? NATO forces are deployed in Bosnia to prevent a majority of that "country's" population (Serbs and Croats) from seceding and joining Serbia and Croatia, respectively. Yet NATO bombed Serbia on behalf of Albanian separatism.

Rambouillet provided for a return to the autonomous provincial status that Kosovo enjoyed from 1974 to 1989—a status that gave Kosovo Albanians a veto over Serbian affairs but did not give Belgrade a comparable veto over the decisions of the Kosovo Albanian regime that often denied non-Albanians legal and police protection.[1] Not surprisingly, the Serbs refused to accept a return to that situation. Their refusal was fueled by the fact that the implied, and logically inevitable, outcome set in motion at Rambouillet was some form of a vote on Kosovo's permanent status in three years. That vote, however, was to be by the population of Kosovo alone, not that of Serbia as a whole, and thus the results were preordained, considering the Albanians' overwhelming numerical majority and equally overwhelming irredentist sentiments. Thus, at best, Rambouillet offered the Serbs a face-saving step toward losing Kosovo permanently.

NATO's demands reflected an incredible misunderstanding of Serbian nationalism. No matter how unpopular Slobodan Milosevic and his Marxist true believer wife may be (particularly with urban voters), he cannot dismount the nationalist tiger he decided to ride in 1989 without losing power and, most likely, much more. Not surprisingly, given the Serbian political universe, which is cavalierly dismissed by NATO politicians and generals alike, Milosevic's most popular political rival is the anti-communist nationalist Vojislav Seselj of the Radical Party, and his most serious immediate threat is the Yugoslav army's ultranationalist officer corps.

Moreover, the socially and politically influential Serbian intelligentsia—from opposition journalists persecuted by Milosevic to opposition leader Vuk Draskovic (who, like Seselj, was once arrested and beaten by the police) to the respected Academy of Sciences—is almost to the last person more nationalist (albeit also Orthodox

Christian and anti-communist) than is Milosevic.[2] Finally, the Serbian Orthodox Church—the only one in Eastern Europe with credible anti-communist credentials—simply cannot conceive the loss of its most important and oldest shrines, from Pec to Visoki Decani, all of which are in "Old Serbia" (i.e., Kosovo). Patriarch Pavle, a former bishop of Prizren in Kosovo, has been beaten by Albanians, and the most influential bishops have long been on record protesting what they saw as Albanian anti-Serb abuses in Kosovo prior to 1989.[3]

Given those realities, the very first step toward any exit from the present morass in Kosovo should be a clear understanding and acceptance by President Clinton, NATO, and the Western news media that, rhetorical claims ("we did not fight against the Serb people, only against the Milosevec regime") or outbursts ("Milosevic equals Hitler") notwithstanding, NATO's policies and actions are arrayed against the Serbs, period. That certainly is the Serbs' perception and the one that matters. Since the real enemy is the Serbian nation, not just a single political leader, any negotiation to produce a lasting settlement has to deal with Serbian nationalism, regardless of the role Milosevic will, should, or could play. That is self-evident unless, of course, one accepts the *New Republic*'s theory that the Serbian people as a whole are guilty of crimes and thus should collectively be taught a lesson.[4]

Just as NATO's Serbian enemy is not just Milosevic, unsavory and criminally responsible for atrocities though he may be, but the Serbian nation, NATO's real protégé and the de facto ultimate beneficiary of the war's damage to Serbian military capabilities is not the refugees, the "Kosovars" (as if the only people in Kosovo are ethnic Albanian), or some generic victims of "Milosevic's ethnic cleansing." Instead, very specifically, concretely, and disturbingly, the real beneficiary is the Ushtria e Clirimtare e Kosoves, also known as the Kosovo Liberation Army.

### The Sources of KLA Power

The main reason the KLA is both the primary beneficiary of the NATO bombing of Serbia and the only plausible Kosovo Albanian government is simply that since the beginning of 1998 it has successfully eliminated all Albanian competition, political or military. Knowing the methods of the KLA's success, its origins, and goals is essential if postwar negotiations are to lead to a stable solution.

The origins and nature of the KLA were best and most recently examined by Christophe Chiclet, but they had been known both publicly and by the Western intelligence communities for some time.[5] Fundamentally, the KLA seeks a quite non-Marxist goal, a Greater Albania to include extensive areas of Macedonia, Greece, Montenegro, Serbia proper, and, of course, Kosovo. At the same time, it seeks to take advantage of the organization's roots in Marxism-Leninism; old ties with the late Enver Hoxha's ultra-Maoist Albanian regime and infamous Sigurimi secret police; and the backward clannish society of Ghegh Albanians in Kosovo, Macedonia, and northern Albania. Adem Demaci, the KLA's original ideological mentor and much trumpeted Albanian equivalent of Nelson Mandela, spent many years in Tito's prisons because he advocated the unification of Kosovo with Hoxha's Albania—at the time, the state closest to the perfect totalitarian model.

The KLA's funds, leadership, and weapons come from the half-million-strong Albanian diaspora in Switzerland, Germany, and North America. That diaspora is mostly emigrés from Kosovo and Macedonia, since Tito's relative liberalism allowed emigration, while Hoxha's communist fundamentalism did not. The two primary sources of the KLA's funds are well-known: The first is heroin trafficking in Europe; Kosovo Albanians share control of that traffic with Turkish Kurds, many of whom support the Marxist Kurdish Workers Party. The second is mass racketeering, including a (minimum) 3 percent "tax" on the income of all Albanians in the diaspora (most of them workers, waiters, and, in New York, building managers).[6]

By now we know enough about the KLA's modus operandi to have a good insight into what an "independent Kosovo," or a Greater Albania, under KLA control would look like. During the KLA's brief control over the Drenica region in central Kosovo at the end of 1997, the KLA banned all political parties and expelled non-Albanians—not only Serbs, but also Gypsies and Gorans (Slavic Moslems). In fact, the KLA's very first operation in 1996 was bombing refugee camps of the Krajina Serbs who had been expelled from Croatia and resettled in Kosovo. So much for the likelihood of President Clinton's stated goal of creating, via NATO's bombings, a "multiethnic, tolerant" Kosovo. Equally disturbing is the KLA's strategy after the beginning of 1998. The KLA provoked Serb atrocities—not that the Serbs needed much provocation—by fortifying villages and using civilians as shields. That strategy ultimately internationalized the conflict and led to the NATO intervention.

### Lines of Partition

NATO's bombing campaign and the parallel Serbian campaign of expelling as many Albanians as possible were not the beginning of the de facto division of Kosovo along ethnic lines. The process started long ago—encouraged or tolerated by Tito and obtaining a momentum of its own that continued after the dictator's death in 1980. Indeed, between 1961 and 1981, 1,154 of Kosovo's 1,445 communities became dominated by a single ethnic group; the number of Albanian communities grew by 250, that of Serbian ones declined by 61, and 78 previously mixed communities became totally dominated by one group or the other.[7] There were virtually no mixed marriages, in contrast to Bosnia or even Croatia, and the separation of Albanians from non-Albanians was exacerbated after 1991 by the decision of Ibrahim Rugova's Kosovo Democratic League to establish a de facto voluntary apartheid system in Kosovo.

Those are the circumstances in Kosovo with which a postwar NATO has to deal and the type of realities on the ground negotiators will have to start with if a stable solution is to be found. Thus, there seems to be little doubt that an eventual partition of Kosovo is the only solution. The only matters to be decided will be the lines of partition, the economics and logistics of the population resettlement partition inevitably involves, and the regional implications of partition.

For the Serbs, the bombings may well have made one big difference as far as retaining Kosovo is concerned, inasmuch as many may have decided that keeping all of the province at the cost of getting back the Albanian population is neither possible nor desirable. The Yugoslav army's apparent concentration of efforts in northern, northwestern, and eastern Kosovo during the war suggested an implicit decision to give up the central and southwestern areas, perhaps including such major towns as Prizren, Djakovica, Orahovac, and Urosevac. It is equally clear that in any postwar settlement the Serbs are not prepared to give up the cities of Pec and the Decani religious complex, Kosovska Mitrovica and areas north of it, and areas around Pristina, including Gracanica and the famous Kosovo Polje monument.

The KLA is on record, repeatedly, as opposing any partition of Kosovo; however, neither the KLA's dubious nature and ideology nor its poor military performance in the field should give it a credible veto over the idea or lines of partition. Moreover, if partition is to be part of a stable solution, there will be little or no Albanian presence in the areas of Kosovo remaining under Serb control (the residual Albanian population in Serbia proper has neither demonstrated enthusiasm for the KLA nor experienced Serbian repression). Without a recruiting and support base inside the new postpartition borders, the KLA would have no realistic chance of continuing hostilities, or, if it attempted to do so from rear bases across the Albanian border, it would only succeed in provoking devastating Serbian cross-border raids and thus threaten a rekindling of the conflict— to NATO's displeasure. For that matter, the KLA does not seem interested in control over Serbian religious sites, or even the viability of an independent Kosovo, since its goal is a Greater Albania, with an independent Kosovo as merely a first and temporary stage.

Obviously, for partition to become a stable solution, population exchanges have to be accepted, and they are already a fait accompli. Non-Albanians have already left, or will leave, any area expected to come under KLA control; and a return of ethnic Albanians to what would become Serbian Kosovo does not make sense if the present crisis is not to be repeated a few decades hence.

### Implications of Partition

The above scenario is to be seen, not as either easy or necessarily feasible, but just as the least unpalatable solution to a crisis largely produced by a chain of bad decisions by NATO, Belgrade, and the Albanians. Nor should it necessarily be seen as even a partial solution to the general problem of ethnic conflict in the central Balkans. There are ample reasons for at least some pessimism over the long term.

First, a diminished Serbia, following the loss of most of Kosovo, will remain a permanent irredentist factor in the region, unless the acknowledgment of the Albanians' right to secede from Belgrade is matched by that of the Bosnian Serbs' right to join Serbia—and, inevitably, recognition of the fact that Bosnian Croats have already joined a Greater Croatia in all but official international acceptance.

Indeed, largely Croat Herzegovina already uses the Croat currency, flag, and school manuals and is controlled by Croat national parties. Similarly, the Republika Srpska, notwithstanding opposition and dictates from Carlos Westendorp, the NATO/UN/EU proconsul, is closer to becoming an integral part of Serbia than Kosovo has been since the 1960s. Recognizing those realities is painful for NATO, and for the supporters of punishing the Serbs and pretending that Bosnia-Herzegovina is a real state, but realities they are, nevertheless.

The far more politically, strategically, and legally complicated issue is that of dealing with Albanian irredentism in general—that is, beyond the partial satisfaction of Albanian claims to Kosovo. The map shown here is used in refugee camp schools in Albania and by the KLA and its U.S. lobby, the Albanian American Civic League, led by former representative Joseph Dio Guardi (R-N.Y.).

There are several manifestations of Albanian irredentism. Perhaps the least threatening is the Albanian claim to Greece's northern Epirus region, including Ioánnina. Not only is Greece a NATO member, and thus presumably protected against Albanian claims, but it is strong enough to defend itself. Albanian claims against Montenegro, including the capital Podgorica, are also unlikely to result in more than a permanent reconciliation between Montenegro and Serbia and an Albanian defeat.

The most dangerous possible impact of a partition of Kosovo will be felt in Macedonia, where KLA-incited Albanian irredentism infects more than a third of the territory, including the capital Skopje and the historic city of Ohrid. The Macedonian Albanians have the same subethnic identity (they are mostly Ghegh) and obvious pro-KLA sympathies as their clan and family members in Kosovo. Under these circumstances, unification of Kosovo with Albania would almost certainly result in a repeat of the pattern of KLA irredentism, massive Slavic counteraction (with Serbian, Bulgarian, and Greek support), and internationalization of the conflict—sooner rather than later.

How NATO would deal with Macedonia is an open question, given the alliance's present implicit support of Kosovar irredentism, but the choices are clear—and so is the fact that they will have to be made at the time of negotiations over Kosovo, not later. One choice is to formally guarantee Macedonia's present borders at the cost of future irritation and hostility from Albanians. The other is

GREATER ALBANIA

SOUTHERN SERBIA

SOUTHERN MONTENEGRO

Podgorica

Pristina

KOSOVO

Skopje

WESTERN MACEDONIA

Tirana

ALBANIA

NORTHERN GREECE

to allow things to simmer, à la Dayton and Rambouillet, and witness a larger Balkan conflict pitting the Albanians against Macedonian Slavs, Bulgarians, and probably Serbs and Greeks as well. Contrary to some common versions of the domino theory, it is highly unlikely that Turkey would become involved; irredentism, even an Albanian version, is not something Ankara encourages, particularly when the KLA, which has no friends in Turkey, is involved.

Finally, and probably inevitably, a partition of Kosovo would have a major impact on Albania itself. The traditionally dominant Tosk ethnic group of the south would be seriously challenged by the numerous Gheghs (now a distinct minority centered around Shkodra) of Kosovo. The latter are richer; better educated; and control the diaspora and, with it, the lucrative heroin, cigarette, and emigrant smuggling rackets in Western Europe. They also have a tested leadership in control of an armed force. The present dysfunctional Albanian state would likely become even more so, as the Ghegh clans of the north, now led by pro-KLA former president Sali Berisha from his Tropoja clan stronghold, challenged the southern Tosk mafias of Vlore and their neocommunist or "socialist" representatives who now make up the Tirana "government." Such a "state" would almost certainly be unable to absorb, or use rationally and honestly, the amounts of aid NATO is now promising to the postwar Balkans. To the contrary, an Albania deconstructed along the lines of "independent" Chechnya or Somalia, divided among mafia gangs and ethnic groups, already visible, will become a permanent European feature—to the already acute discomfort of Italy, Germany, and Albania's Balkan neighbors. But that will be just a small part of the long-term price to be paid for the shortsighted NATO policies that led to the recent war.

### Notes

1. See, for instance, Marvin Howe, "Exodus of Serbs Stirs Province of Yugoslavia," *New York Times*, July 12, 1982, pointing out that 57,000 Serbs had left the region during the previous decade.

2. A good example is Dragoljub Zarkovic, the much persecuted editor of Belgrade's weekly *Vreme*, who wrote: "In this whole business as a matter of principle, we shouldn't give a toss for the latest political pirouettes of Yugoslav President Slobodan Milosevic. It is because of him that we are where we are. . . . There is something more important at stake here: the preservation of the international order and the preservation of Serbs as a political nation." Dragoljub Zarkovic, "Kosovo Transcends Milosevic," *Transitions*, November 1998, http://www.omri.cz/transitions/nov98/opinzarark.html.

3. For a recent analysis of the Serbian Church's position on Kosovo, see Xavier Ternisien, "Les voies célestes de la Grande Serbie," *Le Monde*, May 16, 1999.

4. See Stacy Sullivan, "Milosevic's Willing Executioners," *New Republic*, May 10, 1999, pp. 26–35; and Daniel Jonah Goldhagen, "A New Serbia," *New Republic*, May 17, 1999, pp. 16–18.

5. Christophe Chiclet, "Aux origines de l'Armée de Libération du Kosovo," *Le Monde Diplomatique*, May 1999.

6. Ibid.

7. Cf. Denisa Kostovic, "The Trap of the Parallel Society," *Transitions*, November 1998, http://www.omri.cz/transitions/thetrapl.html.

# 10. The Case for Partitioning Kosovo

*John J. Mearsheimer*

NATO appears to be in a political no-win situation in Kosovo despite the much-touted military victory.[1] To escape that dead end, the alliance must rethink its political goals. NATO continues to insist on a settlement based on autonomy for the Albanian Kosovars inside Serb-dominated Yugoslavia. But that goal is not only unattainable, it is also undesirable. Does anyone seriously believe that the Albanian Kosovars and the Serbs can live together again after all the bloodletting that has taken place? The interethnic violence that has already occurred in the immediate postwar period confirms how unrealistic that scenario is.[2]

Instead, NATO should pursue a settlement that partitions the province, creating an independent Albanian Kosovar state. This new state would control most of current Kosovo, while the Serbs would retain a slice of north and northwestern Kosovo. The Albanian-controlled portion could remain independent or unite with Albania if it chose.

Autonomy is a dead letter because there is no way to reconcile Albanians and Serbs to living together in one country. There is nearly unanimous agreement among Kosovo's Albanians that full independence is the only acceptable outcome. Even the moderate Ibrahim Rugova, an influential Albanian leader who advocates non-violence, says adamantly that autonomy within Serbia is not enough.[3] Serbian brutalities during the spring 1999 military offensive have only strengthened the Albanian insistence on full independence. Albanian Kosovars might be amenable to delaying a final decision on Kosovo's status for three years if, in the meantime, they receive significant autonomy and are protected from the Serbs by a large NATO force. But when the time is up, they will insist on independence.

The Serbs have demonstrated their attitude toward cohabitation by their savage ethnic cleansing of Albanians in Kosovo. The 800,000

Albanian refugees who fled Kosovo will hardly be satisfied to live indefinitely inside Serbia, whether Kosovo is autonomous or not, unless the United States stations sizable forces in Kosovo to police any autonomy agreement. But we cannot afford to tie our military down doing such police work. The world is full of civil wars, and the whole American military could soon be committed to peacekeeping if we made a general policy of such deployments.

One might argue that the United States could work to reconcile the Kosovar Albanians and the Serbs to living together in a multiethnic democracy and thus create the right conditions for the eventual exit of American troops. But that is a pipe dream. History records no instance of ethnic groups' agreeing to share power in a democracy after a large-scale ethnic civil war. Such wars end only with a dictatorship that restores order by the knout, or with partition.

### Democratic Power Sharing after a Major Ethnic Conflict Has No Precedent

The history of Yugoslavia since 1991 shows that ethnic separation breeds peace, while failure to separate breeds war. Slovenia seceded with little violence from Yugoslavia in 1991 and has since been at peace with itself and its neighbors. The key to its peace is its homogeneity: 91 percent of the people are Slovenes; fewer than 3 percent are Serbs. Croatia fought a bloody war of secession from 1991 to 1995, which was finally resolved when Zagreb expelled most of Croatia's sizable Serb minority at gunpoint. That expulsion set a poor example of how groups should separate, but it did bring an end to the Serb-Croat conflict. Separation did not end the deep hatred between Croats and Serbs, but it did stop the violence between them.

Bosnia saw fierce fighting among Croats, Muslims, and Serbs from 1992 to 1995, then an uneasy peace under the Dayton Accords. Dayton created a confederal Bosnia in which the three hate-filled groups were supposed to live together. Refugees were to be returned to their homes, and central Bosnian political institutions were to be built. However, Dayton has failed, quietly but quite completely. Few Bosnian refugees have returned to homes in areas where they are in the minority. Indeed, members of all three ethnic factions have left their homes since Dayton, because the boundaries it established made them minorities where they lived.[4]

Moreover, Bosnia still has no functioning central government. The Croat-Muslim Federation, which is supposed to be running half of the country, is a sham. The Bosnian Croats, who have effectively joined Croatia proper, largely refuse to cooperate with their Muslim partners. The Serbs likewise remain firmly committed to partition. Most observers agree that a savage new war would erupt if the large NATO peacekeeping force were withdrawn from Bosnia.[5] New ethnic cleansing would be likely. Croatia and Serbia might divide Bosnia between them, suppressing the Muslims by force and leaving them stateless.

Now Kosovo has been consumed by a war that stems from hatreds born of the great cruelties that Albanians and Serbs inflicted on each other in the past. The war could have been avoided if they had been separated by political partition at some earlier point, when Slobodan Milosevic might have been more amenable to the idea.

Under what circumstances would the Serbs accept such a partition today? The NATO bombing has seemingly exacerbated rather than reduced Serbian nationalism. Although the bombing campaign eventually compelled Belgrade to accept a dictated peace settlement, there is no evidence that the Serbs have abandoned their goal of keeping Kosovo part of Serbia.[6] NATO can prevent a renewed attempt by Belgrade to regain control of the province only if alliance peacekeeping troops garrison Kosovo indefinitely.

While Serbia will probably not be enthusiastic about a proposal for partition, it may accept partition if NATO offers Belgrade carrots as well as the stick. To entice the Serbs, NATO should offer a "grand bargain" that partitions Bosnia as well as Kosovo—moving Serbia toward its dream of a homogeneous Greater Serbia.

### Toward a Grand Bargain

Under this grand bargain Serbia would concede most of Kosovo to the Albanians. In return, the Serbs would be compensated with a portion of northern Kosovo that includes many Serbian historic sites. Serbia would also get the eastern portion of Bosnia, which is now populated mainly by Serbs. The rest of Bosnia would be transformed into an independent Bosnian Muslim state, save for the Herzegovina region, which should be allowed to become part of Croatia. NATO should also be willing to lift all economic sanctions against Yugoslavia if the Serbs take the deal. Finally, the United

States and its allies might consider helping to rebuild Serbia's war-damaged economy.

This is not a perfect solution by any means, but it addresses several important problems. First, it provides the Albanian Kosovars with their own homeland, where they can live free of Serbian terror. Second, it solves the refugee problem—and not just temporarily. Third, it does not require American troops to remain in Kosovo, since the Albanians and Serbs would be living separate lives, and the Albanians would have guns with which to protect themselves. Fourth, partitioning Bosnia would allow the United States to pull its troops out of that Potemkin state, thus removing the albatross of permanent occupation from America's neck.

Some observers warn that an independent Kosovo would spark secessionist violence among Albanians living next door in Macedonia. But an independent Kosovo would more likely dampen than spark violence in Macedonia. The main trigger for war in Macedonia would be the presence of a large radicalized Albanian refugee population. The solution to the continuing social and economic strains in Macedonia caused by the flood of refugees during the war is to achieve a settlement that returns the Albanian Kosovar refugees to their homes permanently, not just as long as NATO is willing to garrison the province. Only a partition offers such a settlement, and hence partition is more likely to pacify Macedonia than to enflame it.

Still, it may be that peace cannot be maintained in Macedonia. Macedonia's Slavic majority discriminates severely against the large Albanian minority, which is roughly 30 percent of the population. If the Slavs refuse to share more equally with the Albanians, violence is inevitable. To forestall this, NATO should consider calling for a plebiscite to determine whether the Albanians want to remain in Macedonia. If they do not, Macedonia should also be partitioned. That is feasible because the Albanians of Macedonia are concentrated in western Macedonia, next to Kosovo and Albania.

Others observers argue that an independent Kosovo would be too small to survive economically and politically as a sovereign state. That is not likely to be a problem, because an independent Kosovo would probably become part of a Greater Albania. But even if that marriage did not take place, Kosovo would probably be able to survive on its own. The two richest states in Europe today on a per capita basis are Lichtenstein and Luxembourg, both of which have less territory and smaller populations than would an independent Kosovo. The main threat to Kosovo's survival would be a direct military attack by Serbia. There are, however, three ways to minimize the likelihood of that unwelcome outcome. First, the Kosovar Albanians should be well armed so that they can defend themselves against a Serbian attack. Second, NATO should make it clear to the Serbs that they will pay a severe price if they start another war in Kosovo. Third, the United States should go to considerable lengths to ensure that Serbia is satisfied with the territorial concessions it receives in the grand bargain described above.

Still other observers caution that the United States cannot support partition in Kosovo because it will legitimize altering borders, which is a prescription for endless trouble. The unpleasant truth is that some borders are untenable and preserving them causes conflict, not peace. Moreover, the United States has never behaved as if borders were sacrosanct. Within the past decade, for example, the United States facilitated the breakup of the Soviet Union and Czechoslovakia, and it quickly recognized Bosnia, Croatia, Macedonia, and Slovenia when they broke away from Yugoslavia in 1991 and 1992. Why should the United States treat Kosovo any differently than those remnant states? Indeed, Kosovo almost seems a more appropriate candidate for partition than Croatia was in the early 1990s. Kosovo's population before the present conflict was nearly 90 percent Albanian and only 8 percent Serbian. Croatia's population in 1991 was approximately 72 percent Croatian and 12 percent Serbian.

Another possible criticism is that partition rewards ethnic cleansing. That charge is correct, but the sad truth is that there is no viable alternative to partition, if one is concerned about saving Albanian or Serbian lives. Also, the United States encouraged and rewarded ethnic cleansing of the Serbs by the Croats in 1995, so the United States does not have clean hands on this controversial issue.

Partition is an ugly formula for ending wars. It destroys communities and violates individual rights. It forces minorities that are trapped behind new borders to leave their homes. But there are only three other options in Kosovo: endless ethnic conflict and retribution, allowing the Serbs to win the struggle and cleanse Kosovo of Albanians permanently, or allowing the Albanian Kosovars to do the same to the Serbian minority. Partition is clearly better than any of those unacceptable choices. If we shrink from it, then we merely make the catastrophe that has already occurred in the Balkans even more devastating.

## Notes

1. This chapter is drawn from John J. Mearsheimer and Stephen Van Evera, "Redraw the Map, Stop the Killing," *New York Times*, April 19, 1999, p. 23; and John J. Mearsheimer, "A Peace Agreement That's Bound to Fail," *New York Times*, October 19, 1998, p. 17. See also John J. Mearsheimer, "Shrink Bosnia to Save It," *New York Times*, March 31, 1993, p. 23; John J. Mearsheimer and Stephen Van Evera, "Hateful Neighbors," *New York Times*, September 24, 1996, p. 25; John J. Mearsheimer, "The Only Exit from Bosnia," *New York Times*, October 7, 1997, p. 27; John J. Mearsheimer and Robert A. Pape, "The Answer: A Partition Plan for Bosnia," *New Republic*, June 14, 1993, pp. 22–28; and John J. Mearsheimer and Stephen Van Evera, "When Peace Means War," *New Republic*, December 18, 1995, pp. 16–21.

2. See Scott Glover, "Revenge Attacks Fill Police Blotter in Postwar Kosovo," *Los Angeles Times*, July 28, 1999, p. A1; "Federal Republic of Yugoslavia: Abuses against Serbs and Roma in the New Kosovo," Human Rights Watch Report 11, no. 10 (August 1999), http://www.hrw.org/hrw/reports/1999/kosov2; and "Destruction of Serbian Orthodox Churches and Monasteries in Kosovo and Metohija (June 13–July 27 1999)," http://www.decani.yunet.com/destruction.html.

3. See "Rugova Says Kosovo Will Never Again Be a Part of Serbia, Even if Milosevic Ousted," Associated Press, August 7, 1999. According to the article, Rugova says Kosovo's present status as a virtual international protectorate is a mere step to full independence. "We will have a referendum, at the very latest within three years time. After that the Serbs will have no alternative but to accept our independence," explains Rugova.

4. For an overview of the Dayton Agreement's failure, see Gary Dempsey, "Rethinking the Dayton Agreement: Bosnia Three Years Later," Cato Institute Policy Analysis no. 327, December 14, 1998.

5. For instance, according to James Lyon, a policy analyst with the International Crisis Group, "Within a year after the international community leaves Bosnia it will explode unless the international community is able to create structural reform here that is long lasting—and that will not happen under the current policy." See "Most of Dayton Peace Accord Is Failing, Balkan Expert Says; Three Ethnic Groups in Bosnia 'Essentially Refuse to Cooperate,'" *Baltimore Sun*, July 23, 1999, p. 17A.

6. Indeed, the commander of Yugoslavia's third army, Gen. Nebojsa Pavkovic, has said that Yugoslav forces could be sent back to Kosovo "at any moment" if the UN and NATO are judged to be failing to protect the province's non-Albanian populations and secure Yugoslavia's borders. "Preparations for the return of a certain number of members of the Yugoslav army and the police to Kosovo-Metohija are in full swing," explained Pavkovic, adding that such a move was legitimate under the military-technical agreement with NATO commanders. See "Yugoslav General Says Army Preparing for Return to Kosovo," BBC Worldwide Monitoring, July 23, 1999. See also Jason Goodwin, "Learning from the Ottomans," *New York Times*, June 16, 1999, p. 29; "Serbian Laws Apply in Kosovo, Justice Minister Says," BBC Worldwide Monitoring, July 26, 1999; and "Serbian Radicals Call for 'Liberation' from NATO Occupation," BBC Worldwide Monitoring, August 9, 1999.

# 11. Alternatives to a NATO-Dominated Balkans

*Gary Dempsey and Spiros Rizopoulos*

The Balkan peninsula is home to 12 countries, 5 of which have been independent for less than a decade. Conflicting ethnoreligious claims, border disputes, political turmoil, and economic hardship have all afflicted the region. NATO's air war has set Yugoslavia's economy back at least a decade; Macedonia has suffered under the weight of massive refugee flows from Kosovo; Bosnia's peace remains fragile; Albania is still struggling to recover from its near collapse in 1997; and Greece and Turkey still face unresolved issues, the most prominent of which involve Cyprus, islands in the Aegean, and territorial waters.

Given the pervasive instability of the region, there was considerable discussion at NATO's 50th anniversary summit meeting in Washington, D.C., in April 1999 about promulgating a "Marshall Plan for the Balkans." As NATO secretary-general Javier Solana indicated on the eve of the event:

> [W]e also need a comprehensive vision on the future of Southeastern Europe. . . . [L]ooking beyond Kosovo, the summit will launch work on a set of initiatives to enhance security in the wider Southeastern Europe. These initiatives could complement other efforts under way in the European Union and the Organization for Security and Cooperation in Europe. . . . We want to help the people in the Balkans to enjoy peace and prosperity, as part of the Euro-Atlantic community.[1]

No leader at the NATO summit, however, was prepared to put a total price tag on the plan. The leaders said that it was too early to do so. But rebuilding Kosovo alone could cost upwards of $5 billion.[2] And any comprehensive plan to stabilize the entire Balkan region could cost as much as $50 billion.[3]

139

The first formal meeting to sketch a working framework for a Marshall Plan for the Balkans was held on May 27 in Bonn. Representatives from NATO, the EU, the International Monetary Fund, the European Bank for Reconstruction and Development, and other international institutions attended. A follow-up meeting was held in July. European donors promised $2.1 billion for Kosovo's reconstruction and $403 million in economic aid to Yugoslavia's neighbors Romania, Bulgaria, and Macedonia.[4] A few days later, President Bill Clinton pledged $700 million to help rebuild the Balkans.[5]

According to experts who are familiar with the concept of a Marshall Plan for the Balkans, the plan would have three specific components:

- An economic component focusing on economic development and regional integration, both within the Balkans and between the Balkan countries and the more affluent parts of Europe to the north and west. The EU would take on the bulk of the responsibility for this component.
- A democracy-building component that would build institutions central to functioning democracies and encourage people-to-people programs between countries in the region. This responsibility would be taken on primarily by the Organization for Cooperation and Security in Europe.
- A security component designed to increase cooperation between NATO and non-NATO countries in the alliance's Partnership for Peace program. This component would build new institutions for conflict resolution and generate closer ties between the militaries of nations in the region. NATO would assume the central leadership role.

The idea of a Marshall Plan for the Balkans must be approached critically. Similar foreign aid plans have routinely failed. Indeed, since World War II the United States alone has provided $1 trillion in foreign aid to countries around the world. The result? According to the United Nations, 70 of the countries that received aid are poorer today than they were in 1980, and an incredible 43 are worse off than in 1970.[6] Good intentions must be matched by effective, corruption-free administration on the part of aid recipients.

In another example, Germany launched its own version of the Marshall Plan to rebuild communist East Germany after the fall of the Berlin Wall. Since 1990 the German government has spent more than $600 billion, and private firms, in response to special government incentives, have invested another $500 billion.[7] The outcome after the first 10 years? Mass unemployment, low productivity, uncompetitive industry, and minimal growth. "Never before in history," laments the chief economist at Frankfurt's Deutsche Bank, "has one country spent so much money building pyramids."[8]

The repeated failures are not so surprising if one studies the actual Marshall Plan experience more carefully. If massive government spending could work anywhere, it was in Europe in 1948: skilled labor was readily available, the rule of law and property rights had a long history, and the customs of a commercial society were readily recoverable. The only thing lacking was physical capital, since so much of it had been destroyed during the war. But even under those amenable circumstances, there is no conclusive evidence that the Marshall Plan by itself was responsible for Europe's regrowth. Indeed, U.S. assistance never exceeded 5 percent of the gross domestic product of any recipient nation, an assistance total that was minuscule compared to the growth that occurred in the 1950s, according to economist Tyler Cowen.[9] Moreover, there seemed to be an inverse relationship between economic aid and economic recovery. In fact, France, Germany, and Italy all began to grow before the onset of the Marshall Plan, and Great Britain, the recipient of the most aid, performed the most poorly.[10] The real lesson of the Marshall Plan is that the rule of law, property rights, free markets, and an entrepreneurial culture are necessary for economic success.[11]

## Recent Initiatives

Although they are not ideal, there are three recent initiatives in southeastern Europe that come closer to recognizing this reality than would any aid program: the Black Sea Economic Cooperation, the Southeast European Cooperative Initiative, and the Southeast European Brigade. Those three initiatives deserve the attention of U.S. policymakers because they advance the twin goals of promoting economic growth in the Balkans and discouraging European security dependence on the United States.[12] They will also promote the internal cohesion of the NATO alliance by increasing the interdependence of Greece and Turkey, both of which are taking leading roles in organizing and advancing the efforts.

*Background*

Increasing attention has being paid inside and outside the Balkans to the idea of promoting regional cooperation in southeastern Europe. But unlike regional initiatives of the past, such as the Little Entente and the Balkan Pact, the current initiatives are motivated, not by a common fear of the territorial aspirations of other countries, but by a common goal, namely regional cooperation and, eventually, membership in the EU.[13] Indeed, for many countries in the Balkans, regional cooperation is a necessary precursor to joining the economic and political structures of the Continent. That's because the present economic and political conditions inside most Balkan countries preclude them from entering the EU any time soon. It is widely believed, however, that the current regional initiatives will accelerate the economic and political development that will enable those countries to obtain membership in the EU.

For that reason the West must continue to clearly connect regional cooperation with eventual European integration. As Sophia Clément, research fellow at the Western European Union's Institute for Security Studies, points out, as far as these initiatives are concerned,

> their linkage to the broader European integration process remains for the countries of the region the main reason for their participation. It is essentially because these frameworks are perceived as a means and a first step towards further integration that they are considered available tools. Therefore, their future effectiveness heavily depends on a clearer (re)definition of regionalism, and its linkage to the broader European security context.[14]

As the only Balkan country that is a member of the EU, Greece can play an important role in this regard. Greece has the strongest economy in the region and conducts more commercial and trade activity in the Balkans than any other country. At present, there are 1,700 Greek businesses and joint ventures operating in Romania, 1,000 in Bulgaria, 200 in Albania, 150 in Yugoslavia, and 100 in Macedonia.[15] Greek exports to the other Balkan countries increased from $240 million in 1989 to $1.8 billion in 1997, and imports from the other Balkan countries to Greece reached $1.23 billion in 1997.[16]

What's more, Greece has given clear indications that it wants to transform itself from a Balkan country in Europe to a European country in the Balkans by assuming a leading role in promoting economic integration and security cooperation in southeastern Europe. According to Greek deputy minister of foreign affairs Yannos Kranidiotis, "The successful integration of the Balkan area into the European structures is of strategic importance to Greece.... Greece is ready to contribute to this common effort and will continue, to the best of its abilities, to promote stability and cooperation among the Balkan nations."[17]

In November 1997, Greece took a first step in the direction of promoting stability and cooperation when it convened a summit meeting of heads of state on the island of Crete. For the first time ever, national leaders from all over southeastern Europe were brought to the same table to discuss their mutual relations and common future. The Greek-organized summit produced a joint statement that declared, among other things:

> We aspire to transform our region in an area of cooperation and economic prosperity.... We shall intensify our efforts for the increase of our economic cooperation, the improvement of infrastructure for transport, telecommunications and energy as well as for the establishment of favorable conditions for investments.... We shall promote the cross border cooperation and to that effect we invite officials to meet regularly and Ministers of Economy or Finance, or other Ministers responsible for it.[18]

In October 1998, a second summit meeting of heads of state was held in Antalya, Turkey. This time the summit participants formally raised the idea of creating a Balkan free-trade zone and released a joint statement that declared:

> We reiterate our common opinion that enhanced economic and trade relations between our nations would best contribute to better understanding and cooperation in our region.... We shall, therefore, intensify our efforts for the increase of economic cooperation, reforms ... and transport infrastructure, including the realization of the Pan-European corridors.... Having reviewed the recent negative trends in the world economic situation, particularly in the financial markets and stock exchanges, we acknowledge their undesirable effects on the countries of Southeastern Europe.... We believe that there is still more to be gained from globalization, and protectionist measures should be avoided.... In this vein, we welcome the bilateral trade agreements which have

already been signed and/or being negotiated among the countries of the region. We agreed to continue this process with a view to gradually creating the conditions for the establishment of a [region-wide] free trade zone.[19]

Greece is not alone in promoting the idea that economic development is critical to encouraging regional stability and eventual membership in the EU. That is also the idea behind Turkey's Black Sea Economic Cooperation (BSEC).

## Black Sea Economic Cooperation

The Black Sea Economic Cooperation, which was inspired by Turkey's former prime minister Turgut Ozal, became a fully economic-oriented organization in April 1997. Current BSEC members include Albania, Armenia, Azerbaijan, Bulgaria, Georgia, Greece, Moldova, Romania, Russia, Turkey, and Ukraine—a total market of more than 350 million people.[20] Bosnia, Croatia, Cyprus, France, Jordan, Kazakhstan, and Slovenia have filed petitions for admission.

Like that of the EU, the goal of BSEC is to liberalize and harmonize the foreign trade regulations of member states, respect the rules and practices of the World Trade Organization, and implement agreements between members and the EU. BSEC also hopes to foster free trade among its members by eliminating many import tariffs and customs procedures. Turkey has already established its first free-trade zone in the Black Sea port of Rize in northeastern Turkey, and a second free-trade zone is under evaluation for Samsun, a Black Sea port in northern Turkey. Expanding this commitment to free trade across the region would not only be a great step toward promoting economic development in the Balkans; it would also bring rivals Greece and Turkey into tighter economic interdependence.

## Southeast European Cooperative Initiative

The Southeast European Cooperative Initiative was launched by the United States in December 1996. The initiative aims at encouraging cooperation among the countries of southeastern Europe and facilitating their economic growth, stability, and eventual integration into mainstream Europe.

SECI is not a bureaucratic wealth-redistribution scheme; it does not rely on any public financial commitments to defray the costs of its construction projects. Instead, it provides economic and financial assistance to promote better coordination of the private sector on projects that have private or European funding sources. SECI's Business Advisory Council has primary responsibility for this task. The council's members include key business leaders from inside and outside the region who strive to identify and mobilize private investment to support the initiative's programs. Moreover, "SECI does not organize ministerial conferences, meetings of heads of state, or events aimed at publicizing or promoting . . . itself." Rather, it "strives to produce concrete, viable results which will have a lasting impact on the entire region and Europe as a whole."[21]

The initiative has 11 participating states: Albania, Bosnia, Bulgaria, Croatia, Greece, Hungary, Moldova, Romania, Slovenia, Macedonia, and Turkey. SECI's activities are organized into eight projects that focus on issues like border-crossing facilitation, building regional securities markets, and developing transportation infrastructure.

Facilitating border crossings is one of SECI's most important projects. Long delays in transiting international borders are a serious obstacle to economic development and the timely movement of goods. Such delays are costly to people already engaged in international commerce as well as discouraging to those who would like to enter it. In light of this, the SECI working group on border-crossing facilitation has a four-pronged approach to the problem: (1) physical expansion of 30 border-crossing stations in the region to eliminate bottlenecks, (2) simplification and standardization of border-crossing procedures, (3) restructuring and reform of customs services and border police, and (4) combating cross-border crime and corruption.

SECI's security markets project was launched at the Istanbul Stock Exchange in Turkey in June 1998. This project aims to build an operational stock exchange in each SECI country. This step is essential if the Balkan economies are to join the international marketplace and attract needed foreign capital. The project will recommend ways of harmonizing the region's capital markets, improving the liquidity and reliability of market operations, linking exchanges to a single regional index, and raising capital for regional companies.

Many SECI countries, including those along the main international corridors, suffer from inadequate road and rail transport infrastructures. That results in reduced efficiency and increased costs of national and international transport, as well as in ultimately depressed economic development and competitiveness and a lower level of integration of the SECI countries. This project is identifying the strategic transport needs of the region and providing contact with outside financial institutions, like the European Bank for Reconstruction and Development, for development of specific projects. SECI could also prove useful in expediting the flow of machinery and construction supplies through the Balkans.

*Southeast European Brigade*

On September 26, 1998, the defense ministers of seven southeastern European countries met in Skopje, Macedonia, to sign a pact creating the Southeast European Brigade, a multinational military force that can be used for peacekeeping or aid operations in the Balkans and elsewhere. Three NATO members—Greece, Turkey, and Italy—joined Albania, Bulgaria, Macedonia, and Romania in creating the force, which will be a brigade with 3,000 to 4,000 troops divided into 14 companies. The seven countries, along with the United States and Slovenia as observer members, are part of what is called the Southeastern European Defense Ministerial, a cooperative forum launched by then–U.S. secretary of defense William Perry in 1996 as a way to promote military cooperation in southeastern Europe and stability in the Balkans. Turkey was instrumental in moving SEEBRIG from a concept to a reality, and Greece's strong support for the brigade helped overcome some potentially troublesome problems with its establishment.

The effective functioning of the brigade, of course, will require a significant upgrading of political and military consultation mechanisms among the participating countries. In this regard, a Politico-Military Steering Committee is being established to provide oversight and policy guidance for deployment of the force. This will help promote a common conception of Balkan security issues among member nations. What's more, the brigade will not only promote better relations among the Balkans nations by encouraging military staffs to address interoperability problems and train together; it will also be an opportunity for teamwork between Greece and Turkey. As Adm. T. Joseph Lopez, former commander in chief of U.S. Naval Forces in Europe and NATO commander of allied forces, southern region, has remarked, "SEEBRIG will not be a remedy for existing bilateral disputes, but it can help dispel the negative perceptions some countries have of others by broadening the dialogue among the member countries ... it is ... heartening to see Greece and Turkey working together harmoniously."[22]

Moreover, the length of time the multinational peacekeeping force will spend in Kosovo has not been determined. SEEBRIG could act as a follow-on force, reducing the time American troops will have to spend managing what is essentially a European problem.

## Operation Alba as a Precedent

The idea of a regional response to security problems in the Balkans is not entirely unprecedented. In early 1997 Albania underwent a profound political and economic crisis, sparked by the frustration of hundreds of thousands of people who lost their life's savings in bogus investment schemes. Civil unrest broke out all over the country and gradually led to the collapse of the central government. Criminal elements took advantage of the anarchy, and many Albanian citizens found themselves in open confrontation with the armed forces. In many cases soldiers simply abandoned their posts, leaving most military installations open to looting. Nearly 1 million weapons and millions of rounds of ammunition were stolen.

Concerned by the dangers posed by an imploding Albania, and recognizing that U.S. involvement would not be forthcoming, Europeans decided to respond to the Albanian situation themselves. By April 1997 Italy was leading Operation Alba, an eight-nation protective force to secure the roads and ports for the distribution of humanitarian aid in Albania. In total, more than 7,000 troops were involved.[23] The operation was organized under the auspices of the Organization for Security and Cooperation in Europe but was essentially a regional response that included Balkan nations Greece, Turkey, and Romania.

Operation Alba was largely a success, as it cleared the way for elections and the return of a working central government. Albanians voted out the discredited government of President Sali Berisha and replaced it with one led by Fatos Nano, who had formerly been imprisoned by Berisha's security services.

What is remarkable about Operation Alba is that it was the first peacekeeping operation conducted in Europe by a multinational military force that was composed of Europeans only, and the first

147

operation of its kind conducted by individual countries acting outside the umbrella of the United Nations or NATO.[24] The operation was also quite an accomplishment, given that Albania is a nation of 3.2 million people and was in a state of near anarchy when peacekeepers arrived. Most important, Operation Alba demonstrates that America's European allies are not helpless. When the United States makes it clear that it will not intervene, Europeans can and will pool their efforts to get the job done.

### Relevance to Greece and Turkey

Among their many potential benefits, BSEC, SECI, and SEEBRIG will encourage economic and security cooperation between rival NATO members Greece and Turkey. BSEC and SECI will foster Greco-Turkish economic and political interdependence, and the SEEBRIG initiative will improve the interoperability of the Greek and Turkish militaries and open channels of communication between them.

But U.S. diplomatic involvement must play an important role in supporting these initiatives, especially in promoting the economic liberalization envisioned by BSEC. In this regard, the United States should consider establishing a U.S. office for BSEC affairs. That office could be a springboard for greater U.S. economic influence in southeastern Europe. Indeed, it must not be forgotten that the United States would have benefited if it had secured its interests in Europe by participating in what started out as the European Coal and Steel Community in 1949 with only six member states. Today, the ESSC, now called the European Union, is the world's largest integrated economic community.

Moreover, economic development and foreign investment in southeastern Europe cannot be seriously expected unless the customs procedures of the countries in the region are simplified. To that end, the United States should continue to support SECI but tie its support directly to an assertive free-trade agenda to be carried out by BSEC.

Ideally, these regional frameworks will bring Greece and Turkey into tighter economic and security interdependence, and that economic and security foundation will promote wider Balkan stability.

### Relevance to the United States

Generally speaking, all of the aforementioned initiatives are aimed at developing a "security community" in the Balkans.[25] According to political scientist Karl Deutsch, a "security community" is a group of states "which has become integrated, where integration is defined as a sense of community, accompanied by formal or informal institutions or practices, sufficiently strong and widespread to assure peaceful change among members . . . with reasonable certainty over a long period of time."[26] Deutsch notes that such "security communities" arise out of a process of regional integration characterized by the development of transnational interests and mutually predictable behavior, and of "transaction flows," which involve the regular, institutionalized interaction, not only of national governments, but of nongovernment and commercial institutions as well. That interaction, in turn, leads to "dependable expectations of peaceful change." Member states come to believe that disputes among them will be settled not by force but by law and dialogue.[27] Thus, peace is cemented by the bonds of economic and political interdependence.

Although greater Balkan stability does serve U.S. interests, the primary responsibility for achieving that goal should rest with the Balkan countries themselves and with America's strategic partners Greece and Turkey, both of which are in a better position than is Washington to foster economic development and regional cooperation. As RAND scholar F. Stephen Larrabee argues:

> [I]ncreasing attention needs to be paid to [Balkan] economic construction and development. Without sustained economic growth and development, many of the democratic reforms in the region are likely to falter, plunging the countries of the region into a new round of political instability and violence. . . . This will require a joint effort, with the United States and Europe working in tandem. However the primary role should be played by the Europeans, working through the EU. . . . [G]reater regional cooperation, especially in key areas such as transportation and telecommunications, should be encouraged in order to create a broader network of trade and economic interaction.[28]

Although they should be primarily European enterprises, these initiatives are relevant to the United States. The SEEBRIG initiative, for example, presents the United States with an opportunity to begin moving away from a "NATO or nothing" approach to European security. That would help keep the United States from becoming unnecessarily entangled in purely regional security matters.

BSEC and SECI, too, could lessen the likelihood that U.S. forces will be called on to deploy to southeastern Europe. Linkage of political economy and security strategy is the ultimate goal of the initiative. As SECI's 1998 report puts it, the goal "is to create and implement viable mechanisms which would preclude military . . . solutions to regional contrarieties."[29]

Shifting the maintenance of Balkan stability to the Balkan countries themselves and to America's strategic partners in the area, especially Greece and Turkey, would go a long way toward easing Washington's overseas military commitments. Right now the United States has more than 225,000 soldiers stationed in 144 countries around the globe, and since 1988 the U.S. military has conducted 29 significant overseas operations, compared with 10 over the preceding 40 years.[30] The U.S. percentage of worldwide defense spending is currently 32 percent and rising; Americans spend nearly two and a half times more on defense than do all their potential adversaries combined.[31] Moreover, during NATO's recent air war against Yugoslavia, U.S. pilots flew more than 80 percent of the combat sorties, and American taxpayers have already picked up more than half of the $20 billion bill for NATO's Bosnia peacekeeping operation, which entered its fifth year in December 1999.[32]

Fewer commitments would also lessen the tax burden on America's citizens and economy. This is of extreme importance because America's well-being in the 21st century is far more likely to depend on its economic competitiveness than on its defense spending. As Ronald Steel, professor of international relations at the University of Southern California, explains: "Tomorrow's America will not, like Cold War America, be dealing with a world it dominates. It will be part of a complex of market economies, some of which will be democratic and some not—but all will be unyielding competitors with their own [economic] agendas. The days of deference by allies to American military power are over."[33] By encouraging these regional initiatives wholeheartedly, the United States can begin to move its institutional relationships with Europe away from security issues to economic matters in which it is absolutely critical that the United States be engaged.

Moving away from a "NATO or nothing" approach would also benefit Russian-American relations and transatlantic security by reducing the direct confrontation inherent in expanding the alliance further eastward, and especially in replicating the Kosovo intervention elsewhere. The NATO-centric approach is reviving old dividing lines with Russia and playing into the hands of militaristic and reactionary forces there who argue that the Soviet empire must be restored to maintain Russian security and prevent further encroachments by NATO.

In the post–Cold War era, the United States must carefully choose its security commitments in Europe, defining itself as the power of last resort, not the power of only resort. Encouraging the development of regional economic and security initiatives, such as those now emerging in southeastern Europe, is an important first step in that needed transformation of U.S. foreign policy.

## Notes

1. Javier Solana, "NATO Is Upholding Our Values," *Globe and Mail* (Toronto), April 22, 1999, p. A15.

2. Tony Czuczka, "Balkans Plans Face Big Hurdles," Associated Press, July 25, 1999.

3. "Europe's Time to Pay," *Investor's Business Daily*, June 9, 1999.

4. Peter James Spielmann, "Donors Pledge $2B to Help Kosovo," Associated Press, July 28, 1999; and Ann Compton, "Rebuilding the Balkans," *ABC News*, July 30, 1999.

5. Arshad Mohammed, "Clinton Offers $700m Package to Help Balkans," Reuters, July 30, 1999.

6. Doug Bandow, "A Look behind the Marshall Plan Mythology," *Investor's Business Daily*, June 3, 1997, p. A28.

7. Ibid.

8. Quoted in "Gamble on East Germany: Will Bonn's Huge Investment in Ex-Communist State Pay Off?" *Pittsburgh Post-Gazette*, April 20, 1997, p. A6.

9. Tyler Cowen, "The Marshall Plan: Myths and Realities," in *U.S. Aid to the Developing World: A Free Market Agenda*, ed. Doug Bandow (Washington: Heritage Foundation, 1985), pp. 61–74.

10. Ibid., pp. 73–74.

11. See Ian Vásquez, "Marshall Plan, Two Views: More Harm Than Good," *Journal of Commerce*, June 4, 1999.

12. It is worth noting, too, that BSEC and SECI are consistent with Article 2 of the NATO treaty, which states that member countries, in this case Greece and Turkey, "will seek to eliminate conflict in their international economic policies and will encourage economic collaboration between . . . them." www.nato.int/docu/basictxt/treaty.htm. According to the *1998 NATO Handbook*, this article is based on the premise that "political cooperation and economic conflict are irreconcilable" within the alliance, and "there must therefore be a genuine commitment among [NATO] members to work together in the economic, as well as political field." www.nato.int/docu/handbook/1998/index.htm.

13. For a summary of past initiatives, see Levent Bilman, "The Regional Cooperation Initiatives in Southeast Europe and Turkish Foreign Policy," *Perceptions* 3, no. 3 (September–November 1998): 60–67.

14. Sophia Clément, "Sub-Regional Cooperation in the Balkans," in *The Southeast European Handbook 1997–98*, ed. Thanos Veremis and Dimitrios Triantaphyllou (Athens: Hellenic Foundation for European and Foreign Policy, 1998), p. 224.

15. Vasso Papandreou, former Greek minister of development, "Greece's Leading Role in Southeastern Europe," Remarks delivered at the Western Policy Center, Washington, January 22, 1999.

16. Statistics provided by Office of the Economic Counselor, Embassy of Greece, Washington, February 9, 1999.

17. Yannos Kranidiotis, "Greece and Co-Operation among the South-East European Countries," *Thesis* 1, no. 3 (Autumn 1997): 10, 13.

18. "Joint Statement by the Heads of State and Government of Countries of South-Eastern Europe, Heracleion, Crete, November 4, 1997," www.greekembassy.org/press/pressreleases/nov0497b.html.

19. "Summit Declaration of the Countries of Southeastern Europe (Antalya, 12–13 October 1998)," *Thesis* 2, no. 3 (Autumn 1998): 48.

20. Starting as an economic cooperation initiative, BSEC first convened in July 1992. The 11 members agreed to establish the organization's Trade and Development Bank. This bank is permanently headquartered in Thessaloniki, Greece's major northern port; BSEC's permanent secretariat is based in Istanbul, Turkey. All member countries have a financial obligation to the bank. Those financial subsidies are determined by each country's level of economic growth and stability and are ranked at three levels. At the first level, Russia, Greece, and Turkey each is obligated to contribute 16.5 percent of the organization's projected budget. At the second level, Bulgaria, Ukraine, and Romania each is obligated to contribute 13.5 percent. Finally, at the third level, Moldova, Albania, and Armenia each is obligated to contribute 2 percent. BSEC has established a currency, the Special Drawing Rights (SDR), adopted for internal transactions and communication. One SDR is equal to $1.35. The BSEC bank is expected to initially fund the organization's operational needs, and subsequently projects established by BSEC. BSEC anticipates that through those projects it will be able to improve trade, commerce, and energy relations among the member states and, through this improvement, to increase the economic stability and wealth of the member states, especially those that have not been able to stabilize their economies since the end of the Cold War. The bank began operation in the middle of 1999.

21. Southeast Europe Cooperative Initiative, "Activity Report," February 10, 1999, www.unece.org/seci/seci.htm.

22. T. Joseph Lopez, "A Politico-Military Success in the Balkans," Western Policy Center *Strategic Regional Report*, October–November 1999.

23. "Unrest Quelled: Albania Struggles for Tenuous Grip on Normality," *San Diego Union-Tribune*, August 17, 1997, p. 26.

24. Andrew Gumbel, "Italy Ready for Mission Impossible," *Independent* (London), April 7, 1997, p. 15.

25. See Palmen Pantev, "Strengthening of Balkan Civil Society: The Role of the NGOs in International Negotiations," April 24, 1997, www.isn.ethz.ch/isis/resstu04.htm.

26. Karl Deutsch, "Security Communities," in *International Politics and Foreign Policy*, ed. James Rosenau (New York: Free Press, 1961), p. 98.

27. Karl Deutsch, *Political Community in the North Atlantic Area* (Westport, Conn.: Greenwood, 1969), passim.

28. F. Stephen Larrabee, "Security Challenges on Europe's Eastern Periphery," in *America and Europe: A Partnership for a New Era*, ed. David Gompert and F. Stephen Larrabee (Cambridge: Cambridge University Press, 1997), pp. 184–85.

29. Southeast Europe Cooperative Initiative.

30. See "Worldwide Manpower Distribution by Geographical Area," U.S. Department of Defense, March 31, 1997; and Bradley Graham and Eric Pianin, "Military Readiness, Morale Show Strain," *Washington Post*, August 13, 1998, p. A1.

31. See "Last of the Big Time Spenders: U.S. Military Budget Still the World's Largest, and Growing," Center for Defense Information, February 1, 1999, www.cdi.org/issues/wme/spendersFY'00.html.

32. See Anthony Cordesmann, "The Lessons and Non-Lessons of the Air and Missile War in Kosovo," Center for Strategic and International Studies, Washington, July 29, 1999, p. 9, www.csis.org/Kosovo/LessonsExec.pdf; and "White House Already Spending Budget Surplus . . . And NOT for Social Security," Republican Policy Committee, March 10, 1998, p. 3.

33. Ronald Steel, *Temptations of a Superpower* (Cambridge, Mass.: Harvard University Press, 1995), p. 127.

# 12. Silver Lining: Renewed Interest in European-Run Security Institutions

*Jonathan G. Clarke*

Among the more enduring of the lessons spawned by the Kosovo war's instant analysis industry is the revelation of dramatic qualitative differences between the militaries of the United States and its European allies. American comment has been harsh. The conclusion of *Washington Post* correspondent William Drozdiak is typical: "The Kosovo war revealed a profound gap between the military capabilities of the U.S. and its European allies that could soon lead to serious friction over how to share defense burdens. The triumph of the air campaign against Yugoslavia was tempered at NATO headquarters by the stark realization that Europe has fallen so far behind the U.S. in the use of precision-guided weapons, satellite reconnaissance and other modern technologies that the allies are no longer equipped to fight the same way."[1] According to a study by the Center for Strategic and International Studies, the imbalance between the United States and its allies was striking in all aspects of the war. "It is clear that the U.S. flew over 60% of all the sorties in the air and missile campaign, flew over 80% of the strike-attack sorties, carried out over 90% of the advanced intelligence and reconnaissance missions, flew over 90% of the electronic warfare missions using dedicated aircraft, fired over 80% of the precision guided air munitions, and launched over 95% of the cruise missiles."[2]

Influential Europeans have already drawn the same lesson. Reflecting on the Kosovo experience, British defense minister George Robertson stated, "While Kosovo showed how far Europe has come since Bosnia in responding to conflicts on its own doorstep, it also embarrassingly highlighted the collective weakness of European defense capabilities."[3] Loud alarm bells have also sounded in France. "For the first time in 200 years, one country—a 'hyper-power,' to use an expression coined by the French foreign minister, Hubert Védrine—overwhelmingly dominates the world in the five key areas of political, economic, military, technological and cultural power. That country, the U.S., sees no reason to share or accept limits on its hegemony when it can exercise it without restriction, unchallenged by anyone, not even the UN."[4] Nonofficial comment has echoed those sentiments. According to a London *Times* correspondent, "The lesson for Europe is clear: America remains crucial for our peace and security but Europe has got to assume more responsibility for its own defense."[5]

Alongside the public breast-beating, there have been some signs that the Kosovo experience may prompt the Europeans to move in the positive direction of taking greater responsibility for security problems on the Continent. It appears that Europe not only acknowledges the need to remedy its military deficiencies but is going to go beyond agonized rhetoric to take the practical steps required to make a genuine European defense capability a reality.

At the June 3–4, 1999, European Council summit, it was decided that "the [European] Union must have the capacity for autonomous action, backed up by credible military forces, the means to decide to use them, and a readiness to do so, in order to respond to international crises without prejudice to actions by NATO. The EU will thereby increase its ability to contribute to international peace and security in accordance with the principles of the UN Charter." The same declaration committed the EU to a buildup of its military capabilities: "We therefore commit ourselves to further develop more effective European military capabilities from the basis of existing national, bi-national and multinational capabilities and to strengthen our own capabilities for that purpose." At the same meeting, it was announced that Javier Solana, then NATO's secretary general, would leave his post to become the first EU high representative for foreign affairs.[6] To ensure that this is not simply a paper appointment, Britain and Italy have proposed that a permanent committee be established to support the high representative.[7]

So far so good—at least at the level of rhetoric. European ambitions to build a defense community alongside their economic community date back to the earliest days of the European integration movement. Boilerplate remarks about the need for a more self-confident Europe based on a more self-sufficient European defense capability have been a routine feature of Euro-Atlantic gatherings for a number of years. The classic example is the 1991 statement of then–foreign minister of Luxembourg Jacques Poos in connection with Bosnia: "This is the hour of Europe."[8]

Actual outcomes have limped far behind the rhetoric, however. Trying to learn the lessons of the Bosnia debacle, which indicated that Europe was still woefully underprepared for such contingencies, member states of the Western European Union agreed in May 1996 to strengthen their military cooperation through the Combined Joint Task Force system, under which European forces would be available for deployments in which the United States did not wish to participate.[9] The concept of a European defense capability was given official blessing in the 1997 EU Amsterdam treaty and was further endorsed at NATO's 50th anniversary summit in April 1999. The new Strategic Concept adopted at that summit stated that "the Alliance fully supports the development of the European Security and Defense Identity within the Alliance by making available its assets and capabilities for WEU-led operations. . . . The increase of the responsibilities and capacities of the European Allies with respect to security and defense enhances the security environment of the Alliance."[10]

### Are the Europeans Serious?

Contrary to the numerous European promises, however, overall resources in the European defense budgets have continued to decline with no sign that European governments are ready to cut into civilian programs to make up for the defense shortfall. On July 2, 1999, for example, German defense minister Rudolf Scharping defended further reductions in German military spending by stating: "The armed forces must contribute to the unavoidable necessity of reducing public spending. Only in this way can we ensure that prosperity, growth, and social security are maintained in our country." The British government's July 1998 Comprehensive Spending Review, setting limits on public expenditures up to the year 2002, made the same point: "In Defence and the Foreign Office, we have achieved the changes necessary to provide us with the defence and diplomatic capability we need while making the savings necessary."[11]

Of particular concern is the share of European government research and development spending devoted to the military. This continues to lag seriously behind U.S. levels. For example, U.S. spending on military-related R&D is seven times that of France, the nearest competitor. That gap produces a troubling result. Although

Western Europe's combined military spending is two-thirds that of the United States, that level of spending enables the Europeans to deploy only a quarter of the U.S. deployable fighting strength.[12] It is right to question, therefore, whether on this occasion the Europeans have finally decided to be serious about correcting the problem.

An indication that they may be serious can be found in the meeting at Saint-Malo, France, in December 1998 between British prime minister Tony Blair and French president Jacques Chirac. Representing as they do the two European countries most willing and able to take military action, their agreement about the need to revamp European defense so that action independent of the United States would be possible is important. The two leaders agreed that "in order for the European Union to take decisions and approve military action where the Alliance as a whole is not engaged, the Union must be given appropriate structures and a capacity for analysis of situations, sources of intelligence, and a capability for relevant strategic planning. . . . In this regard, the European Union will also need to have recourse to suitable military means (European capabilities pre-designated within NATO's European pillar or national or multinational European means outside the NATO framework)." The agreement included practical measures: "Europe needs strengthened armed forces that can react rapidly to the new risks, and which are supported by a strong and competitive European defense industry and technology."[13] This agreement reflected long-standing French concerns that Europe should build defense infrastructure systems, such as military satellites, that would give it capabilities independent of the United States.

Germany is also part of this emerging consensus on the need for specific new operational capabilities. Speaking in Washington on March 14, 1999, Defense Minister Scharping stated, "I feel there is a need for us to start thinking about the European members creating a strategic reconnaissance capability, as well as a strategic air transport component available for independent European operations—supplementing the corresponding U.S. capabilities within the integrated NATO structure."[14] The Kosovo intervention broke new ground for Germany in as much as it was the first deployment outside Germany of German forces in an offensive capacity since World War II. The deployment enjoyed marked public support and was welcomed by Germany's international partners; thus the Kosovo campaign operated as a sort of rehabilitation of the German military and has established a precedent for other similar German military interventions. A formidable new weight has been added to European intervention capabilities. Commentators in and outside Germany certainly believe so. Chancellor Gerhard Schroeder has noted: "Germany's integration in the western community of nations is part and parcel of our raison d'être. We do not want a separate lane for Germany. And we must recognize that Germany's role has changed following the collapse of state socialism. We cannot shirk our responsibility. German soldiers are engaging in a combat mission for the first time since the end of World War Two." In Britain *The Economist* commented, "The Germans have crossed a big psychological and physical boundary."[15]

A further indication of Europe's seriousness of purpose may be found in the recent softening of U.S. attitudes. After years of suspicion about or barely concealed hostility toward an independent European defense "pillar," American policymakers now openly acknowledge the virtues of a more robust European capability. On April 6, 1999, Secretary of State Madeleine Albright confirmed the new trend when she stated: "We also support the strengthening of the European pillar of our Alliance. It is in America's interest to see a more integrated Europe, able to act effectively and cohesively, willing to assume a greater share of our common responsibilities. So we welcome and support efforts to improve European capabilities."[16]

Perhaps more important, those sentiments are also being heard in the hardheaded commercial world of the defense industry. Here, in the wake of the Kosovo campaign, the Defense Department has initiated a program of encouraging the emergence of a strong European defense industry. Jacques Gansler, under secretary of defense for acquisition and technology, has observed: "We have to be more willing to share our technology with our allies and they have to be more willing to control it. . . . The lesson of Kosovo is that we are going to be fighting coalition warfare."[17] Once again, though, a word of caution against any expectation of instant results is in order. The tangled history of national rivalries and politically motivated decisionmaking underlying such initiatives as the Eurofighter project shows that a genuine Europe-wide defense industry is still a long way off.

## The Opportunity for the United States

Despite the apparent discrepancy between European rhetoric and the willingness of the European allies to make hard resources available for military purposes, there is little doubt that the post-Kosovo environment presents a favorable moment for the United States to make real progress on an important national interest: furthering the emergence of Europe as an entity capable of handling such substrategic challenges as Bosnia and Kosovo as well as those emerging elsewhere in Eastern Europe and Central Asia. Today, there is a real sense of embarrassment in Europe about its second-class military status. Moreover, the institutional and political factors are coalescing around the need to do something substantial.

For that to happen, however, U.S. policymakers will have to play their part. Three things are of particular importance:

- The United States must signal to Europe that it not only welcomes European efforts to develop a security and defense identity but that it actively *expects* that to happen. A readily understandable way of demonstrating that attitude would be for the United States to start withdrawing military assets from Europe.
- At the same time as it encourages the Europeans to stand on their own feet, the United States must resist the temptation to second-guess European decisions. A good case can be made that in 1992 and 1993 Washington's failure to support the EU's Bosnian mediation effort, led initially by Lord Carrington and later by David Owen, caused those initiatives to fail and thereby unleashed an unnecessary war.[18] When left alone by the United States, Europe has shown itself fully capable of resolving regional crises, as was demonstrated by the Italian- and Greek-led intervention that calmed the civil war in Albania in 1996.
- The United States must maintain a fierce focus on European defense spending. As indicated above, European willingness to match rhetoric with resources is suspect. European public opinion is certainly not being conditioned to the need for increased military spending.[19] Luckily, the amount spent on defense is quantifiable and is public knowledge. The United States should insist that Europe undertake the necessary increases, especially for military R&D.

If, under U.S. prodding, a stronger European military capability does in fact emerge, that will in turn affect how security issues are handled in Europe. Given that in the past decade the United States has twice found itself engaged on the ground in a European shooting war, it is clearly central to American interests that any new security arrangements minimize the likelihood that that pattern will repeat itself. A further lesson of the Kosovo conflict is that the United States should also take a fresh look at security structures in Europe. Now that the first (and extremely transient) flush of victory that NATO enjoyed has passed, there is every incentive to examine means to ensure that the Europeans are ready and willing to handle future Kosovos without inevitably and helplessly turning to Washington.

This requires an examination of the role of NATO, in which the United States is dominant and will remain so for the conceivable future. Far from solving the Kosovo crisis, NATO's involvement in the Balkans made the very difficult situation all the more intractable. That was true for three reasons: (1) NATO's involvement militarized an essentially political problem; (2) placing the alliance's "credibility" on the line made military intervention almost inevitable, even against the better judgment of some of NATO's members; and (3) because of the U.S. domination of NATO, America was drawn into a conflict that might have been better handled by the European powers.

## The OSCE and Europe's Future Security

Given that Europe's present and future problems are much more likely to involve issues more analogous to Kosovo than to the major strategic threat that NATO was originally meant to counter, the search for fresh structures that may be better adapted to contemporary needs should start today. A possible starting model is the Organization for Security and Cooperation in Europe. Both before the NATO bombing campaign started and now that it is finished, OSCE was and is providing the backbone of the long-term civilian civil-society-building skills that will be needed if Kosovo and the wider region are to regain stability. In addition to its practical, detailed contribution to Kosovo, the OSCE is Europe-wide and has conflict mediation skills. If those desirable assets could be combined with some of the cooperative features of the Partnership for Peace and other European structures such as the WEU, and if OSCE procedures and capabilities were upgraded, OSCE could become the basis of a new European-led security system that would address future sub-strategic conflicts like the one in Kosovo.

There are some indications that Western policymakers are thinking along those lines. The April 1999 NATO summit declaration set out the foundation for the possibility that OSCE might emerge as a premier security institution. The declaration drew attention to some of OSCE's virtues, noting that "the OSCE, as a regional arrangement, is the most inclusive security organization in Europe . . . , and plays an essential role in promoting peace and stability, enhancing cooperative security, and advancing democracy and human rights in Europe. The OSCE is particularly active in the fields of preventive diplomacy, conflict prevention, crisis management, and post-conflict rehabilitation. NATO and the OSCE have developed close practical cooperation, especially with regard to the international effort to bring peace to the former Yugoslavia."[20] Days before the Kosovo bombing campaign started, Deputy Secretary of State Strobe Talbott praised OSCE's contribution to peace in Kosovo. "OSCE," he stated, "through its verification mission, remains on the ground in Kosovo to help keep the parties from each other's throats." Three months previously, he had praised OSCE as "unique, and it is indispensable. It is not only the most inclusive of our Euro-Atlantic institutions—it is also the premier mechanism for the prevention of conflicts before they occur, for the management and amelioration of conflicts when they occur, and for reconciliation after they occur."[21] Later events were to prove him tragically prescient. The withdrawal of the OSCE monitors, starting on March 19, 1999, opened the way to the bombing campaign and the worst refugee and humanitarian crisis in Europe since World War II. Had OSCE been allowed to remain and do its job, the Kosovo tragedy might have been averted.

As the Cold War wound down and in the decade after the end of that confrontation, the OSCE compiled a respectable track record. Its performance in managing the issues of the Cold War endgame and interbloc reconciliation was excellent. Its performance in post–Cold War security also shows a creditable score. Also on the positive side, it has enjoyed some success in mediating disagreements between the Baltic nations and Russia on the pace of Russian troop withdrawals and citizenship issues. Throughout 1998 and 1999 OSCE officials continued to provide mediation efforts on the citizenship issue; they even drafted proposals for adoption by the Latvian parliament. OSCE's role in assisting the October 1998 Latvian referendum on citizenship drew praise from the State Department.[22] The engagement of OSCE monitors in Kosovo while the war in Bosnia was at its height played a role in keeping ethnic tensions in Kosovo from erupting into full-scale war. The same pattern has been repeated in mediating Georgia's difficulties with the breakaway provinces of Abkhazia and South Ossetia and Moldova's similar problems with Transdniestria. The fact that those problems rarely make the headlines is a tribute to OSCE's patient behind-the-scenes negotiation.

Former secretary of state Warren Christopher praised those successes, conceding that "OSCE's innovative work on crisis management and conflict prevention is one of the most promising security experiments underway in Europe today."[23] Secretary Albright has echoed those words: "We want the OSCE to continue evolving into an organization that is more operational than conversational. We want it to be an organization that produces not just reports, but results."[24]

Successful OSCE initiatives over the past three years include the January 1997 OSCE mission to Serbia led by former Spanish prime minister Felipe Gonzalez. That mission played a key role in persuading President Milosevic to recognize the municipal election victories of opposition parties. Since the 1995 Dayton Accords, the OSCE has provided the crucial administrative infrastructure for the construction of a civil society in Bosnia-Herzegovina, including supervising the 1997 municipal elections. Had the West expanded and deepened that approach instead of resorting to NATO, the contemporary landscape in the Balkans might look very different.

In the Caucasus, the OSCE "Minsk group," which includes the United States, is performing useful work in actively mediating the dispute between Armenia and Azerbaijan on the breakaway Armenian-dominated enclave of Ngorno-Karabakh. As noted in a State Department statement on June 15, 1999, that mediation effort is keeping the conflict from spiraling out of control.[25] Given the involvement of religious animosities; Caspian energy-resources-related strategic concerns; and international competition among Russia, Iran, and Turkey, that is no mean achievement.

On the debit side, the OSCE performed no better in the early stages of the conflict in the former Yugoslavia than did anyone else.

Nor was it able to prevent the tragic war in Chechnya, although it did play a useful institutional role once the conflict was resolved.

In view of an overall creditable performance by the organization, it is perhaps surprising that the United States has not used the OSCE to its maximum potential. Instead, Washington has usually maneuvered to keep the OSCE in the background and to discourage it from challenging NATO's primacy in European defense structures. In the run-up to the Paris conference of December 1990 (at the time the OSCE was still called the Conference on Security and Cooperation in Europe, or CSCE), the Bush administration was concerned not to allow the organization to supplant NATO as Europe's principal security organization. (Similarly, the PFP was seen as merely an interim measure in the lead-up to NATO expansion, not as an alternative to expansion.)

A strong measure of NATO-centricity endures today. For example, Secretary Albright has stated that "the response to Milosevic would not have been possible without NATO."[26] President Clinton had earlier made the same point at the NATO summit, stating, "The crisis in Kosovo has underscored the importance of NATO."[27]

During the Cold War, an insistence on NATO primacy may have been the correct policy in the face of the threat of Soviet invasion. But events in the Balkans have shown that the threat has changed. The altered strategic context, in which intrastate rather than interbloc conflict is the most likely challenge to regional stability, means that the time has come for Washington to take a less negative attitude toward the OSCE.

The organization enjoys some significant conceptual and structural strengths that, if developed, would allow it to make a major contribution to overall European security and to become the key organization for tackling what Warren Christopher termed "the root causes of European security problems."[28] Its membership includes the full NATO membership, but it also includes all the countries in the former Warsaw Pact and the various former Soviet republics. It has developed specialized expertise in arms control, confidence building, and conflict mediation and resolution. Its infrastructure—a Secretariat in Prague, a Conflict Prevention Center in Vienna, and an Office for Democratic Institutions and Human Rights in Warsaw—continues to consolidate.

That is a promising foundation, but the OSCE is still vulnerable to the criticism that it remains stuck at the "talking-shop" stage.

There is an opportunity at the next OSCE summit for the emergence of an imaginative U.S. policy designed to remedy that deficiency. The organization now needs to develop structures that will enable it to exert significant influence over the behavior of its members. Three steps in ascending order of complexity might be considered.

*Modus Operandi*

The OSCE has traditionally operated by consensus. There are good reasons for that, but it has also proved a weakness. Both the Soviet Union and the federal government of Yugoslavia, for example, were able to block substantive discussion or mediation of the impending Bosnian conflict in the early 1990s. A procedure that enabled discussion to proceed on the basis of a qualified majority (that is, something less than unanimity but still substantially in excess of a simple majority and with safeguards for regional and large-country interests— a system that already exists in the European Council of Ministers) would address that weakness. At the very least, no party to a dispute should be allowed to block mediation procedures.

Such a reform still falls short of the proposals for legally binding arbitration, which have been discussed within the OSCE but never adopted. Enforcement would remain a problem, with contravening states able simply to ignore OSCE resolutions.

A way around that problem would be to enhance OSCE's membership benefits, particularly in the military sphere. That could be done by expanding OSCE's responsibilities to include such operational matters as joint planning, coordinated exercises, and common procurement policies. An international military staff along NATO lines would be needed to carry out those tasks. The lessons derived from both NATO's long experience in this regard and the PFP's more recent experience may be useful. OSCE membership could confer significant military benefits, which would make suspension or exclusion from the organization a more potent threat.

*OSCE Forces*

As the concept of OSCE as an increasingly powerful executive agency took root, the creation of forces answerable to the OSCE Council of Ministers for Foreign Affairs might become desirable. NATO has already indicated its willingness to undertake military missions at OSCE's behest. The logical next step would be to enhance and empower the OSCE secretariat to carry out such tasks directly rather than through an organization that does not include the full OSCE membership.

The creation of OSCE forces requires careful definition. The goal should not be to perpetuate NATO under another name by creating a new collective defense structure or exacting wider security commitments from current NATO members. There is no need to establish a standing OSCE army. Nor should the goal be to turn the OSCE into a war-making organization to the detriment of its central mission of conflict prevention and resolution. Instead, feasible reform proposals would place in the hands of the Council of Ministers an instrument with which in the last resort it could back up OSCE resolutions. The organization's inability to put trained personnel quickly into the field weakened its response in the early days of Yugoslavia's demise.[29] Likewise, in October 1998, the OSCE had difficulty finding sufficient unarmed monitors to fulfill the terms of the Holbrooke-Milosevic agreement. What is needed is for OSCE's European member nations to earmark components of their forces for OSCE emergency deployment.

Equipped with such extra abilities, the OSCE would be transformed into a "one-stop" mediation and peacekeeping institution. If, as the Bosnia and Kosovo examples indicate there may be, there is a growing need for long-term "peace protectorates" to address ethnic conflict in former communist bloc countries—in Europe and elsewhere—an OSCE force would provide the required troops. For example, as the pace of negotiations on Cyprus accelerates with the new G-8 initiative launched in June 1999, there is likely to be a need for a postsettlement troop presence on the island. In Cyprus and other problem areas, troops from a Europe-wide organization rather than a specifically Western group such as NATO would be both more acceptable to non-NATO countries and more effective.

A greater emphasis on the OSCE would enable the United States to transfer responsibilities to an organization that is much more finely calibrated than any existing organization to respond to today's problems in Europe. An additional benefit to American interests would be that missions undertaken by a pan-European security body might avoid some of the legal uncertainty arising from NATO's circumvention of the United Nations during the Kosovo intervention.

*Regional Subgroups*

Within the OSCE, it would make sense for the United States to promote the creation of regional subgroups. The challenges in southern

Europe and the eastern Mediterranean are, for example, very different from those in the Baltic republics. Such problems need local and subregional solutions, not a centralized, all-purpose approach directed by NATO. Luckily, there are many such initiatives under way, notably the Balkan Foreign Ministers Conferences led by Greece and similar initiatives in Central Europe and the Black Sea region. The Black Sea Economic Cooperation organization, for example, brings together all of the states in the Black Sea area.

In adopting a less NATO-centric policy, the United States would guard against repeating some of the mistakes made in the war over Kosovo. Of course, institutional reform is not by itself the Holy Grail of a new generation of peace. There are too many entrenched hatreds, claims, and counterclaims for that to be a realistic prospect. In addition, the OSCE, like NATO, will be only as effective as its membership wishes it to be. Nonetheless, by encouraging a more robust OSCE, or a new security mechanism based on its structure, the United States would be facilitating the development of a real organization to deal with the real problems of the Continent.

## Kosovo's Silver Lining

In the immediate aftermath of the Kosovo conflict, some people trumpeted it as a model for future Western interventions. Sensible second thoughts have now asserted themselves with Albright's stating that "some hope, and others fear, that Kosovo will be a precedent for similar interventions around the globe. I would caution against any such sweeping conclusions."[30] However, the need for rational security arrangements in Europe endures, as the lengthy list of current problems makes clear. Many of the lessons from Kosovo are gloomy, especially those that illuminate Washington's overcommitment and lack of a coherent strategic approach. But a new interest on the part of the Europeans in providing for themselves and taking greater responsibility for the security of their region would be a major compensation. The United States should seize this opportunity to encourage the Europeans as they move in this direction.

### Notes

1. William Drozdiak, "War Showed U.S.-Allied Inequality," *Washington Post,* June 28, 1999, p. A1.

2. Anthony Cordesmann "The Lessons and Non-Lessons of the Air and Missile War in Kosovo" p. 9, http://www.csis.org/kosovo/Lessons.html.

3. George Robertson, Speech to Royal United Services Institute, London, June 29, 1999, http://www.mod.uk/news/speeches/sofs/99-06-29.htm.

4. Ignacio Ramonet, "New World Order," *Le Monde Diplomatique*, June 1999.

5. Peter Ridell, "Europe Must Learn to Defend Itself," *Times* (London), June 28, 1999, p. 14.

6. Declaration of the EU Cologne Summit, Annex III, para. 1-2, http://ue.eu.int/newsroom/main.cfm?LANG=1.

7. Robin Cook, British Foreign Secretary, Speech at the General Affairs Council, Brussels, July 19, 1999, http://www.fco.gov.uk/news/speechtext.asp?2655.

8. Quoted in William Drozdiak, "Europe Follows American Lead, *Washington Post*, March 26, 1999, p. A1.

9. See the WEU Birmingham Declaration of May 7, 1996, http://www.weu.int/eng/index.html.

10. Article J7 of the Amsterdam Treaty reads in part: "The common foreign and security policy shall include all questions relating to the security of the Union, including the progressive framing of a common defense policy." http://ue.eu.int/Amsterdam/en/treaty/treaty.htm. See also "The Alliance's Strategic Concept Approved by the Heads of State and Government Participating in the Meeting of the North Atlantic Council in Washington D.C. on the 23rd and 24th April 1999," NATO press release NAC-S(99)65, April 24, 1999, para. 18, http://www.state.gov/www/regions/eur/nato/nato_990424_stratcncpt.html.

11. For the proposed reductions in German defense spending, see Zukunfts program 2000, http://www.bundesfinanzministerium.de/. On the British situation, see Statement by the Chancellor of the Exchequer on the Comprehensive Spending Review, July 14, 1998, www.official-documents.co.uk/document/cm40/4011/4011.htm.

12. Stockholm International Peace Research Institute, *1998 Yearbook* (Stockholm: SIPRI, 1998), chap. 6; and Peter Rodman "The Fallout from Kosovo," *Foreign Affairs* 78, no. 4 (July–August 1999): 50.

13. Joint Declaration issued at the British-French Summit, Saint-Malo, France, December 3-4, 1998, para. 2-3, http://www.fco.gov.uk/news/newstext.asp?1795.

14. Rudolf Scharping, "The Future of Transatlantic Security Cooperation," Speech at the Trilateral Commission's 1999 Annual Meeting, March 14, 1999, Washington, http://www.bundeswehr.de/presse/news/1999rede_99_s2htm. On the new German attitudes toward intervention, see "Germany Comes out of Its Post-War Shell," *The Economist*, July 10, 1999, p. 43.

15. Gerhard Schroeder, Policy Statement Delivered in the German Bundestag on the Current Situation in Kosovo, April 15, 1999, http://www.bundesregierung.de/english/01/newsf.html; and "Rudolf Scharping, Measured German Warrior," *The Economist*, April 3, 1999, p. 46.

16. Madeleine Albright, "A New NATO for a New Century," Speech to Brookings Institution National Issues Forum April 6, 1999, http://secretary.state.gov/www/statements/1999/990406.html.

17. Quoted in Elizabeth Becker, "Defense Department Urges Industry to Cooperate with Europe," *New York Times*, July 8, 1999, p. A10.

18. Owen makes this case in David Owen, *Balkan Odyssey* (London: Brace, Harcourt, 1995), p. 151 ff.

19. In a June 1999 public opinion survey by MORI, only 16 percent of British voters responded that foreign and defense affairs were an "important issue." http://www.mori.com.

20. "The Alliance's Strategic Concept," para. 16.

21. Strobe Talbott, "A New NATO for a New Era," Address at Royal United Service Institute, London, March 10, 1999, http://www.state.gov/www/policy remarks/ 1999/990310 talbott nato.html; and Strobe Talbott, Intervention at the OSCE Ministerial Meeting, Copenhagen, Denmark, December 18, 1997, http://www.state.gov/ www/policy_remarks/971218_talbott_osce.htm.

22. James P. Foley, deputy spokesman, Statement of October 5, 1998, http://secretary.state.gov/www/briefings/statements/1998/ps981005a.html.

23. Warren Christopher, "U.S. Leadership after the Cold War: NATO and Transatlantic Security," Intervention at the North Atlantic Council Ministerial Meeting, Athens, Greece, June 10, 1993, http://dosfan.lib.uic.edu/ERC/briefing/dossec/ 1993.9306/930610/dossec.hmtl.

24. Madeleine K. Albright, Statement to the OSCE Permanent Council, Vienna, Austria, September 3, 1998, http://secretary.state.gov/www/statements/1998/ 980903.

25. James P. Rubin, spokesman, Statement of June 15, 1999, http://secretary.state.gov/www/briefings/statements/1999/ps990615ahtml.

26. Madeleine Albright, "After Kosovo: Building a Lasting Peace," Remarks to the Council on Foreign Relations, June 28, 1999, http://secretary.state.gov/www/ statements/1999/990628.html.

27. William Jefferson Clinton, Remarks to the Opening Session of the North Atlantic Council Summit, April 24, 1999, http://www.whitehouse.gov/WH/New/NATO/ 19990424-27660.html.

28. Warren Christopher, Intervention at the North Atlantic Council Ministerial Meeting at Noordwijk, Netherlands, May 30, 1995, http://dosfan.lib.uic.edu/ERC/ briefing/dossec/1995/950530dossec.hmtl.

29. Susan Woodward, *Balkan Tragedy* (Washington: Brookings Institution, 1995), p. 162 ff.

30. Madeleine K. Albright, Remarks and Q&A Session with the Council on Foreign Relations, New York, June 28, 1999, http://secretary.state.gov/www/statements/ 1999/990628.html.

# 13. Kosovo as an Omen: The Perils of the "New NATO"

*Ted Galen Carpenter*

When NATO was first established in 1949, it was explicitly an alliance to defend the territorial integrity of its member states. Indeed, Article 6 of the North Atlantic Treaty described the region to be covered, lest there be any implication that the United States was undertaking more wide-ranging obligations (such as protecting the colonial holdings of its new West European allies). NATO forces never fired a shot in anger during the Cold War, and the alliance's first military operation did not involve the defense of a member from attack. Instead, that initial mission took place in Bosnia, with NATO aircraft bombing Bosnian Serbian positions and the alliance trying to prop up the Muslim-dominated government in Sarajevo. Later, NATO took responsibility for implementing the Dayton Accords by deploying a peacekeeping contingent in Bosnia, where it remains to this day.

Not content with the futile and seemingly endless nation-building mission in Bosnia, NATO is now deeply involved in the conflict between Serbia and its restive, predominantly Albanian province of Kosovo. The bombing campaign against Yugoslavia was an even more dramatic expansion of NATO's post–Cold War mission than was the intervention in Bosnia. At least in the latter case, the alliance was asked to take military action by the Bosnian government (admittedly a regime of dubious legitimacy that controlled less than half the country's territory). In the latest intervention, NATO launched air strikes on a sovereign state that had not attacked or threatened to attack an alliance member or, for that matter, even a neighboring state. NATO, in other words, asserted the right to bomb a country for refusing to accept an alliance-dictated peace settlement to an internal dispute.

Kosovo itself has become, as Bosnia before it, a de facto NATO colony. Alliance forces (KFOR) patrol the province, maintaining an

171

uneasy peace between a triumphant Albanian Kosovar majority and a steadily shrinking and dispirited Serbian minority. Those peace-keeping troops have already had to intervene on numerous occasions to prevent returning Albanian refugees from venting their anger and committing acts of revenge against their Serbian neighbors. KFOR has been decidedly less successful in preventing the Kosovo Liberation Army from waging a campaign to cleanse the province of its non-Albanian inhabitants—not just Serbs but Gypsies and other minorities as well. Although most of the Albanian population regards the NATO occupation favorably at the moment, it is not certain that that attitude will persist if the alliance sticks to its official position that Kosovo should enjoy enhanced autonomy but not inde-pendence. Indeed, KFOR's efforts (half-hearted though they have been) to protect Serbian residents have already led to several ugly attacks on peacekeeping units by disgruntled Albanian Kosovars.[1]

Even the most optimistic experts concede that the peacekeeping and nation-building mission in Kosovo will last for years. Absent is the naive optimism that led proponents of the Bosnian mission to predict that the military component of the Dayton peace accords would be fully implemented in a year, allowing NATO forces to go home. Now, international officials and other advocates of nation building in Bosnia admit that the NATO-led stabilization force may have to remain for as long as 15 to 20 years.[2] And few people would dare predict that the occupation force in Kosovo will be able to depart sooner.

The missions in Bosnia and Kosovo are not NATO's only obliga-tions in the Balkans. For all intents and purposes, both Macedonia and Albania are now NATO protectorates. Indeed, both countries were more active participants in the war effort against Yugoslavia than were Greece, the Czech Republic, and several other official NATO members. Both countries also host a sizable postwar NATO military presence and are the beneficiaries of financial assistance from the alliance. Indicative of NATO's increasingly prominent role in the Balkans, alliance leaders at the 50th anniversary summit meet-ing in April 1999 pledged to guard Yugoslavia's neighbors against any act of aggression that might emanate from Belgrade. The alliance is well on its way to playing the role of an imperial stabilizing power—the de facto successor to the defunct Ottoman and Austro-Hungarian empires—throughout the entire region.[3]

## NATO's New Strategic Concept

Long-time observers of NATO—to say nothing of ordinary Americans—would be justified in wondering how and why the alliance has become the baby sitter of the Balkans. But the adoption of that role is not surprising. The Bosnia and Kosovo missions are the models of what NATO's principal focus is likely to be in the coming decades.

Even before NATO launched its war against Yugoslavia, many supporters of the alliance were insisting that a new NATO—something more akin to a collective security organization than to a traditional military alliance—should evolve and was, in fact, evolving. That line of thinking was evident in President Clinton's May 1997 comment that "NATO, initially conceived to face a clear-cut and massive threat, is now a lighter, more flexible organization adapted to its new crisis management and peacekeeping missions."[4] The objective was apparent as well from another comment Clinton made in the spring of 1997: "We are building a new NATO. It will remain the strongest alliance in history, with smaller, more flexible forces, prepared to fight for our defense, but also trained for peacekeeping." He added, "It will be an alliance directed no longer against a hostile bloc of nations, but instead designed to advance the security of every democracy in Europe—NATO's old members, new members, and non-members alike."[5]

Likewise, the alliance's new Strategic Concept, approved at the April 1999 summit, reflected an unmistakable shift of emphasis from the traditional mission of collective defense to the far more amorphous new mission of crisis management and "out-of-area" interventions. The Strategic Concept's section on security challenges and risks begins with the admission that "large-scale conventional aggression against the Alliance is highly unlikely," although a future threat might conceivably emerge.[6] But the absence of such a threat does not mean that NATO faces no security difficulties. According to the authors of the Strategic Concept, "The security of the Alliance remains subject to wide variety of military and nonmilitary risks, which are multi-directional and often difficult to predict." As if that notion of security threats were not vague enough, the document goes on to describe the nature of such "threats" in a manner that makes the hoary and discredited domino theory seem an example of analytical restraint and precision:

These risks include uncertainty and instability in and around the Euro-Atlantic area and the possibility of regional crises at the periphery of the Alliance, which could evolve rapidly. Some countries in and around the Euro-Atlantic area face serious economic, social and political difficulties. Ethnic and religious rivalries, territorial disputes, inadequate or failed efforts at reform, the abuse of human rights, and the dissolution of states can lead to local and even regional instability. The resulting tensions could lead to crises affecting Euro-Atlantic stability, to human suffering, and to armed conflicts. Such conflicts could effect the security of the Alliance by spilling over into neighbouring countries, including NATO countries, or in other ways, and could also affect the security of other states.[7]

Several things are remarkable about that passage. First, the phrase "in and around the Euro-Atlantic area" is never defined and is in fact so vague that it could apply not only to developments anywhere in Europe but to events in North Africa, the Middle East, and even Central Asia as well. Second, the concept of a security threat is made so elastic that it now covers everything from a slowdown in economic reforms in (unnamed) countries to (undefined) human rights abuses. Finally, the daisy-chain reasoning is breathtaking: "tensions" could lead to "crises" that "might affect" neighboring countries or "in other ways" cause problems that might then adversely affect the security of NATO members or "other states." One would be hard-pressed to find any unpleasant development within several thousand kilometers of a NATO member that could not arguably be considered a potential security issue for the alliance under those criteria.

The underlying logic—and the implications for NATO's military forces—is expressed in another section of the Strategic Concept: "An important aim of the Alliance and its forces is to keep risks at a distance by dealing with potential crises at an early stage. In the event of crises which jeopardize Euro-Atlantic stability and could affect the security of Alliance members, the Alliance's military forces may be called upon to conduct crisis response operations."[8]

## An Obsolete Alliance Searches for Relevance

Throughout the Cold War, NATO had an unambiguous primary purpose: to keep a major strategic and economic prize (Western

Europe) out of the orbit of what seemed to be an aggressively expansionist totalitarian superpower. During the initial decade or so of its existence, NATO was an institutional arrangement that enabled the United States to shield a war-ravaged and demoralized Western Europe from either Soviet conquest or (more likely) Soviet intimidation. Later, NATO became a more genuinely collaborative effort to stabilize relations between the two political-military blocs and prevent a miscalculation that might produce a third world war.

To be sure, NATO's purpose was always a bit broader than merely containing Soviet expansionism. The pithy comment of Lord Hastings Ismay, NATO's first secretary general, that the alliance existed to "keep the Russians out, the Americans in, and the Germans down" succinctly captured the essence of that wider mission.[9] Scholars likewise noted that NATO implicitly had a "double containment" policy—directed against possible German revanchism as well as possible Soviet aggression.[10] Nevertheless, the main goal was always to deter Moscow.

The end of the Cold War may have been a boon to humanity in general, but it created an immediate institutional crisis for NATO. Abruptly, NATO's primary—and most visible—mission was no longer compelling or even terribly relevant. That point became increasingly apparent with the disintegration of the Soviet Union, the deepening economic malaise in Russia, and the rapid unraveling of Russia's conventional military capabilities. A military force that could not subdue a secessionist rebellion in Chechnya did not pose a credible threat to the security of Western Europe—or even Central and Eastern Europe.

Institutions rarely volunteer to disband, however, even when their original purpose is no longer relevant. The end of the Cold War spawned a multiyear—and at times desperate—search for an alternative mission that would make NATO appear relevant in the post–Cold War era. Gradually, two proposed new missions began to dominate the discussions. One was to enlarge the membership of the alliance to include some or all of the Soviet Union's former satellites. The other was to have the alliance undertake out-of-area missions—to become a proactive force beyond the territory of the member states. Linking those two prospective missions was the goal of thwarting the specter of "instability" in Central and Eastern Europe and perhaps beyond. Former secretary of state James Baker provided a concise case for transforming the alliance along those lines even before the Clinton administration fully embraced the goal. Baker urged the administration "to work with its Western European allies to broadly redefine the North Atlantic Treaty Organization's mission to encompass preserving peace and stability in Europe. That redefinition should permit NATO military action anywhere and under any circumstances when that peace and stability are threatened."[11]

Even some supporters of NATO's traditional role have expressed uneasiness about the venture into out-of-area missions in the Balkans or elsewhere. "Is NATO to be the home for a whole series of Balkan NATO protectorates?" former secretary of state Henry Kissinger asks. He also tacitly acknowledges a significant gap between America's interests and those of the European members of the alliance. "Kosovo is no more a threat to America than Haiti was to Europe—and we never asked for NATO support there."[12] Most NATO partisans, however, have swept such concerns aside.

For the advocates of out-of-area missions, the ability of NATO to deal effectively with the various crises in the former Yugoslavia is a crucial test case.[13] That was an important factor that led the alliance to launch air strikes on Serbia when the Belgrade regime refused to accept a NATO-imposed settlement of the Kosovo dispute. President Clinton warned that if the alliance failed to act—and to succeed—it "would discredit NATO" and make it impossible to secure a democratic and united Europe.[14] British prime minister Tony Blair was equally apocalyptic, asserting that there is "no alternative to continuing until we succeed. On its 50th birthday NATO must prevail."[15]

### Rapidly Expanding Ambitions

Even the out-of-area interventions in the Balkans do not fully satisfy the ambitions of some "new NATO" enthusiasts. Former secretary of state Warren Christopher and former secretary of defense William Perry suggest that the alliance become an instrument for the projection of force anywhere in the world the West's "collective interests" are threatened.[16] In a moment of exuberance, Madeleine Albright stated that NATO should become a force for peace "from the Middle East to Central Africa."[17] Such rhetoric understandably impelled *Jane's Defence Weekly* correspondent Marc Rogers to ask whether NATO was going global.[18]

U.S. and NATO leaders are already showing an interest in a stabilization role outside the Balkans. Through the Partnership for Peace program, NATO has already conducted joint military exercises with Kazakstan, Ukraine, and other former Soviet republics. The U.S. general who commanded the mission in Kazakstan boasted that it showed the ability of the United States to deploy effective military power in any region of the world. Georgia and Azerbaijan have asked to join NATO, and Azeri leaders have suggested that the United States establish a military base in their country. Although U.S. policymakers thus far decline that invitation, they hint that American forces might be willing to use bases that remained under Azeri control. According to a Pentagon official: "A real American base in Azerbaijan is impractical. . . . If they were to request military assistance or military advisers, that would be a different thing. There would even be the possibility of taking over an old Soviet base and using it as a joint American and Azerbaijan facility."[19] Finally, at the NATO summit meeting in April 1999, the foreign ministers of the alliance issued a statement expressing NATO's concern about the continuing violence in the Caucasus and urged Georgia, Armenia, and Azerbaijan to settle their problems.[20] That was a not terribly subtle declaration that the Caucasus, like the Balkans before it, is now a region in which NATO has a legitimate interest.

The ongoing geographic expansion of Washington's and NATO's areas of responsibility is not the only troubling development. At least as alarming is the nearly open-ended rationale for increased activism. The boldest expression of the new rationale was an April 22, 1999, speech by Prime Minister Blair. "The most pressing foreign policy problem we face is to identify the circumstances in which we should get actively involved in other people's conflicts," Blair asserted.[21] Although he conceded that noninterference in the internal affairs of countries had long been considered an important principle of international order that the West should not want to jettison "too readily," the prime minister argued that the principle "must be qualified in important respects." Predictably, he insisted that "genocide can never be a purely internal matter." Since Blair assumed that the 2,000 deaths in Kosovo in the 12 months before NATO launched its air strikes constituted "genocide," that exception would likely be very broad indeed. But another exception he cited was even broader. "When oppression produces massive flows of refugees which unsettle neighboring countries, then they can properly be described as 'threats to international peace and security.'" Moreover, he noted that whenever regimes "are based on minority rule they lose legitimacy," implying that the mere existence of such regimes might be cause for outside intervention.[22]

Blair's notion of when the principle of noninterference could be "qualified," if taken seriously, would be a mandate for an extremely proactive stance by NATO. Since any sizable armed conflict produces extensive refugee flows, that exception alone could provide a virtual blank check for NATO intervention. Equally worrisome, Blair's concept of humanitarian intervention would not give rise to short-term ventures. "In the past we talked too much of exit strategies," he complained. "But having made a commitment we cannot simply walk away once the fight is over; better to stay with moderate numbers of troops than return for repeat performances with large numbers."[23] Those who fear that NATO might be mired in the Balkans for many years—or perhaps even decades—find their worst fears confirmed by Blair's comments. It is also not comforting that NATO is contemplating establishing a new command—the first since the end of the Cold War—for the Balkans. That step would be a tacit admission at the crucial operational (bureaucratic) level that the alliance intends to maintain a long-term presence in the region.

### America's Limited European Interests

Proponents of a U.S. leadership role in the "new NATO" typically argue that whatever costs and risks are entailed in humanitarian interventions pale in comparison with those that would occur if the United States were drawn into yet another massive European war. But U.S. policy should not be based on fear of such an improbable event. There is no European power today or in the foreseeable future that has either the intention or the ability to replicate the campaigns for continental hegemony made by Nazi Germany or the Soviet Union—or even the more limited bid for preeminence made by Wilhelmine Germany in 1914.

From the standpoint of American interests, what matters in Europe is the conduct of the handful of major powers. As long as those states remain at peace with one another, and no menacing would-be hegemonic power emerges, there is no credible danger to America's security. Nor is there a danger to America's other important interest: keeping Europe relatively open to American trade and investment. Events involving small countries on Europe's periphery may create annoyances, but they do not affect European stability or the overall configuration of power on the Continent. Becoming obsessed with problems such as the three-sided squabble in Bosnia or the status of Kosovo confuses the need for macrostability in Europe—which is important to American interests—with the unnecessary and unattainable goal of microstability.

U.S. policymakers seem unable to distinguish between parochial squabbles and serious threats. The case for the new NATO embodies the flawed historical analysis made by former national security adviser Anthony Lake. According to Lake, "If there is one thing this century teaches us, it is that America cannot ignore conflicts in Europe."[24] President Clinton made a similar argument in favor of NATO's intervention in the Kosovo dispute, stating that after what we experienced in World War I and World War II, the United States had a "clear interest" in preventing similar episodes.[25]

Clinton, Lake, and other advocates of a U.S.-led proactive NATO ignore the crucial point that both of the armed conflicts in which the United States ultimately intervened were wars involving all of Europe's great powers. Such serious disruptions of the international system obviously had the potential to place important American interests at risk. But not every conflict that has erupted in Europe, or is likely to do so in the future, has wider strategic implications. Since America proclaimed its independence, Europe has seen more than a dozen significant armed conflicts that have not drawn in the United States.[26] The belief that limited struggles, especially those involving small countries in peripheral regions, are destined to escalate into continental conflagrations that will ultimately compel the United States to intervene is fallacious. Even Brandeis University professor Robert Art, a prominent advocate of continued U.S. leadership of NATO, concedes that "wars among the lesser powers" in Europe "(for example, a war between Hungary and Romania over Transylvania) would not require American involvement."[27]

The contrary proposition, that the United States must use NATO to take proactive measures in peripheral areas, lest the problems

escalate and produce more serious outbreaks of violence, was succinctly stated several years ago by Sen. Richard Lugar (R-Ind.), a
senior Republican on the Senate Foreign Relations Committee:

> The critical strategic change in the new Europe is that the
> locus of conflict has shifted from its center to the periphery,
> or the so-called twin arcs of crisis to the east and south.
> However, potential and real crises *on* the periphery are not
> periphe*ral* to the future of European stability. There can be
> no lasting security at the center without security at the
> periphery.[28]

Lugar's assumptions have now been incorporated into the alliance's new Strategic Concept. But as foreign policy scholar Benjamin
Schwarz pointed out in response to Lugar's arguments, it would be
difficult under such a formulation to establish *any* geographic limit
to NATO's security concerns:

> The logic that dictates an expansion of NATO's responsibili-
> ties eastward has extremely unsettling implications. . . . After
> all, if the United States, through NATO, must guard against
> internal instability and interstate security competition not
> only in Western Europe, but in areas that could infect West-
> ern Europe, where would NATO's responsibilities end? It is
> often argued, for instance, that the alliance must expand
> eastward because turmoil in East Central Europe could pro-
> voke mass immigration flows into Western Europe, threaten-
> ing political stability there. Of course, turmoil in, for example,
> Russia or North Africa could have the same effect, as could
> instability in Central Asia (which could spread to Turkey,
> spurring a new wave of immigration to the West). Must
> NATO, then, expand even further eastward and southward
> than is currently proposed?[29]

NATO's hint—or perhaps more than a hint—of interest in the
security problems of the Caucasus demonstrates that Schwarz's concerns are well-founded. Even more chilling is President Clinton's
comment that, in Africa as well as in Europe, "we will not allow"
people to be attacked because of their race, ethnicity, or religion.
"We will stop that," the president proclaimed.[30]

U.S. policymakers and the American people should firmly reject
proposals to transform NATO into an organization for performing
missions for which it was never designed. Instead, they must come

to recognize that the alliance has outlived its usefulness and that entirely new security arrangements are needed in post–Cold War Europe. Those arrangements ought to be directed by Europeans and tailored to European concerns and requirements. The campaign to transform NATO is an ill-advised attempt to resuscitate a moribund Cold War–era institution.

Creating a new security relationship with Europe requires new thinking on the part of an intellectually sclerotic American foreign policy establishment. It would mean overcoming the twin fallacies that NATO is an alliance for all seasons and that NATO is the sole effective mechanism for promoting and protecting U.S. political and economic interests in Europe. The post–Cold War era cries out for a more flexible and creative U.S. policy toward Europe.[31] It is time to stop treating NATO as an icon that must be preserved even if that means undertaking unrewarding and dangerous new missions in the Balkans and beyond.

## Notes

1. Steven Erlanger, "7 Checkpoints, 3 of Them Russian, Are Attacked in Kosovo," *New York Times,* August 7, 1998; Tom Cohen, "Violence Erupts as French Keep Albanians from Serbs," *Washington Post,* August 8, 1999, p. A27; "Briton Hints Kosovo Rebels May Be Out of Control," *New York Times,* August 9, 1999, p. A8; and "Troops Arrest 78 in Kosovo Clampdown," Reuters, August 11, 1999.

2. See the comments of analyst James Lyons of the International Crisis Group, one of the most consistent advocates of the NATO mission in Bosnia, quoted in Fredrik Dahl, "Dayton Has Failed, Balkan Expert Says," Reuters, July 22, 1999. Indeed, Jacques Klein, the second-ranking international civilian official in Bosnia, reportedly stated that NATO should be prepared to stay in the country "permanently." Quoted in Donald Devine, "Foreign Policy Fluxes, Miscues, and Misfires," *Washington Times,* February 12, 1999, p. A25.

3. That outcome was predictable even during the earliest stages of the Bosnia mission. See Ted Galen Carpenter and Amos Perlmutter, "Strategy Creep in the Balkans: Up to Our Knees and Advancing," *National Interest* 44 (Summer 1996): 53–59.

4. "Remarks by President Clinton, French President Chirac, Russian President Yeltsin, and NATO Secretary General Solana at NATO/Russia Founding Act Signing Ceremony, Elysee Palace, Paris, France, May 27, 1997," White House, Office of the Press Secretary, pp. 1–2.

5. Ibid., p. 6.

6. "The Alliance's Strategic Concept Approved by the Heads of State and Government Participating in the Meeting of the North Atlantic Council in Washington D.C. on 23rd and 24th April 1999," NATO press release NAC-S (99)65, April 24, 1999, p. 5, http://www.nato.int/docu/pr/1999/p99-065e.h.

7. Ibid.

8. Ibid., p. 12.

9. Quoted in Gregory F. Treverton, *America, Germany, and the Future of Europe* (Princeton, N.J.: Princeton University Press, 1992), p. 153.

10. Wolfram F. Hanreider, *Germany, America, Europe: Forty Years of German Foreign Policy* (New Haven, Conn.: Yale University Press, 1989), pp. 6–12, 142–43, 157; and Christopher Layne, "Toward German Reunification?" *Journal of Contemporary Studies* 3 (Fall 1984): 7–37.

11. James A. Baker III, "Drawing the Line at Macedonia," *Los Angeles Times*, May 2, 1995.

12. Henry Kissinger, "No U.S. Ground Forces for Kosovo," *Washington Post*, February 22, 1999, p. A15.

13. See, for example, David Buchan, "In the Line of Fire," *Financial Times*, March 26, 1999, p. 21; Anthony Lewis, "In Credibility Gulch," *New York Times*, March 20, 1999, p. A 27; and Helle Bering, "NATO Meets the Beast," *Washington Times*, March 31, 1999, p. A 21.

14. "Remarks by the President to AFSCME Biennial Convention," White House, Office of the Press Secretary, March 23, 1999, p. 7.

15. Anthony Blair, "Doctrine of the International Community," Speech to the Economic Club, Chicago, April 22, 1999, http://www.number-10.gov.uk/public/info/releases/speeches/index.html.

16. Warren Christopher and William J. Perry, "NATO's True Mission," *New York Times*, October 21, 1997, p. A27.

17. Quoted in William Drozdiak, "European Allies Balk at Expanded Role for NATO," *Washington Post*, February 22, 1998, p. A27.

18. Marc Rogers, "Will NATO Go Global?" *Jane's Defence Weekly*, April 14, 1999.

19. Quoted in Stephen Kinzer, "Azerbaijan Asks United States to Establish Military Base," *New York Times*, January 31, 1999, p. A1. See also Michael Lelyveld, "Caucasus: U.S. Military Presence in Caspian Appears Inevitable," Radio Free Europe/Radio Liberty commentary, February 4, 1999; Hafiz Pashayez, Azerbaijan's ambassador to the United States, "East Looks West for Security," *Washington Times*, April 21, 1999, p. A19; and James Kitfield, "Stars and Stripes on the Silk Route," *National Journal*, March 13, 1999, pp. 676–78.

20. Carol Giacomo, "NATO Urges Caucasus to Avoid Kosovo-Like Violence," Reuters, April 25, 1999. For a Russian perspective on the various Caucasus disputes and concern that the West, especially the United States, is meddling in those disputes, see Sergo A. Mikoyan, "Russia, the United States, and Regional Conflict in Eurasia," *Survival* 40, no. 3 (Autumn 1998): 112–26.

21. Blair, p. 5.

22. Ibid.

23. Ibid., p. 6.

24. Anthony Lake, "Bosnia: America's Interests and America's Role, Remarks at Johns Hopkins University, Baltimore, Maryland, April 7, 1994," State Department, Press Office, p. 1.

25. "Remarks by the President to AFSME Biennial Convention," p. 7.

26. For a discussion of some of those struggles, see Christopher Layne, "Why Die for Gdansk? NATO Enlargement and American Security Interests," in *NATO Enlargement: Illusions and Reality*, ed. Ted Galen Carpenter and Barbara Conry (Washington: Cato Institute, 1998), pp. 59–60.

27. Robert J. Art, "A Defensible Defense: America's Grand Strategy after the Cold War," *International Security* 15, no. 4 (Spring 1991): 45.

28. Richard Lugar, "NATO: Out of Area or Out of Business: A Call for U.S. Leadership to Revive and Redefine the Alliance," Remarks delivered to the Open Forum of the U.S. Department of State, August 2, 1993, p. 4. Lugar's emphasis.

29. Benjamin C. Schwarz, "NATO at the Crossroads: Reexamining America's Role in Europe," RAND Issue Paper, January 1994, p. 3.

30. "Clinton Says NATO Is Ready to Fight Repression in Europe, Africa," Agence France-Presse, June 22, 1999.

31. For some suggested alternatives, see Ted Galen Carpenter, *Beyond NATO: Staying Out of Europe's Wars* (Washington: Cato Institute, 1994), pp. 123–49.

# Contributors

**Doug Bandow** served in the Reagan administration as special assistant to the president. He is now a senior fellow at the Cato Institute, and his weekly opinion column appears in newspapers across the country. Bandow has written or edited several books, including *Tripwire: Korea and U.S. Foreign Policy in a Changed World* (Cato Institute, 1996) and *Perpetuating Poverty: The World Bank, the IMF, and the Developing World* (Cato Institute, 1993).

**Ted Galen Carpenter** is vice president for defense and foreign policy studies at the Cato Institute. He is the author or editor of 10 books, including *NATO Enlargement: Illusions and Reality* (Cato Institute, 1998) and *The Future of NATO* (Frank Cass, 1995). Carpenter's articles on international affairs have appeared in such journals as *Foreign Policy*, *Foreign Affairs*, and *Mediterranean Quarterly*.

**Jonathan G. Clarke** is a research fellow in foreign policy studies at the Cato Institute. He is a former career diplomat with the British Diplomatic Service and coauthor of *After the Crusade: American Foreign Policy for the Superpower Age* (Madison Books, 1995). Clarke writes a regular column for the *Los Angeles Times* and has contributed articles to *Foreign Policy*, *Foreign Affairs*, and several other journals.

**Gary Dempsey** is a foreign policy analyst with the Cato Institute. He is an expert on U.S. security issues, with an emphasis on the Balkans. Dempsey's articles have been published in numerous newspapers and journals, including the *Christian Science Monitor*, the *Journal of Commerce*, and *Mediterranean Quarterly*.

**James George Jatras** is a policy analyst with the U.S. Senate Republican Policy Committee. Prior to that, he served at the U.S. Department of State as a foreign service officer in Mexico and in Washington in the Office of Soviet Union Affairs.

**Stanley Kober** is a research fellow in foreign policy studies at the Cato Institute. Before joining Cato, he worked as an analyst for the Hudson Institute and the Center for Naval Analyses. He is an expert on U.S.-Russian relations and European security issues. Kober, who frequently lecturers for the U.S. Information Agency, is the author of several studies and journal articles.

**Christopher Layne** is a visiting scholar at the Center for International Studies at the University of Southern California and a MacArthur Foundation Fellow in Global Security. His articles on international affairs have appeared in *Foreign Policy, Foreign Affairs, International Security,* and many other journals.

**John J. Mearsheimer** is the R. Wendell Harrison Distinguished Service Professor at the University of Chicago and the codirector of the university's Program on International Security Policy. His books include *Liddell Hart and the Weight of History* (Cornell University Press, 1988) and *Conventional Deterrence* (Cornell University Press, 1983).

**Michael Radu** is a senior fellow at the Foreign Policy Research Institute, contributing editor to *ORBIS: A Journal of World Affairs,* and the author or editor of numerous books, including *Collapse or Decay? Cuba and the East European Transitions from Communism* (Endowment for Cuban American Studies, 1997) and *The New Insurgents: Anti-Communist Guerrillas in the Third World* (Transaction Books, 1990).

**Spiros Rizopoulos** is a senior associate at the Western Policy Center. His emphasis is on U.S. geostrategic interests and Western policies toward southeastern Europe. Rizopoulos is published widely in the Greek press on American foreign policy toward Greece and Turkey as well as toward Cyprus.

# Index

Abkhazia, 163
Adams, John Quincy, 43–44
Albania
  crisis (1997), 147
  economic losses, 60–63
  effect of partitioned Kosovo on, 131
  effects of NATO bombings in, 56, 59
  experience of Operation Alba in, 147–48
  impact of refugees in, 62
  as member of BSEC, 144
  as member of SECI, 145
  as member of SEEBRIG, 146
  as NATO protectorate, 172
  NATO's presence in, 8
  pan-Albanian nationalism in, 61–62
  potential for unification of Kosovo with, 129
  power of Gheghs in, 131
  requests for IMF financial assistance, 71
  *See also* Greater Albania
Albanian American Civic League, 26, 129
Albanian diaspora
  contributions to KLA, 126
  lobbying U.S. Congress, 38
  in Macedonia, 129, 136
Albanians in Kosovo
  ethnic cleansing by, 1, 39–40
  KLA seen as legitimate representative of, 25
  pre-1989 administrative control, 22
  pre-1989 demands for republic status, 22–23
  response to cease-fire agreement (1998), 13
  response to downgrading of Kosovo's autonomy, 23
  seeking independence from Serbia, 12–13, 22–23
  timing of expulsion from Kosovo, 51–53
  *See also* Kosovo Liberation Army (KLA)

Albright, Madeleine
  charting of U.S. policy at Rambouillet, 15, 24
  depiction of leaders of some countries, 28
  expectations of Rambouillet process, 17
  on improved European defense capabilities, 159
  on Kosovo crisis as precedent, 167
  mistaken perceptions, 11
  on NATO as force for peace, 7, 176
  on NATO's role in Yugoslavia, 164
  on OSCE operations, 163
  perception of Kosovo crisis, 11, 18
  recommends action to punish Belgrade, 13
  as Russophobe, 80
Algerian civil war, 2, 32
Aliyev, Heydar, 29n10
Al Shayab, Husni, 114
Arbatov, Alexi, 79
Armenia
  as member of BSEC, 144
  OSCE mediation of dispute with Azerbaijan, 163
Art, Robert, 179
Artemije (bishop), 26
Azerbaijan
  asks to join NATO, 177
  as member of BSEC, 144
  Nagorno-Karabakh problem, 29n10
  OSCE mediation of dispute with Armenia, 163

Bacon, Ken, 39
Baker, James, 175–76
Baker, Jamil Abu, 114
Balas, Peter, 67
Balkan countries
  continuing problems in, 5–8
  idea of promoting regional cooperation, 142
  impact of NATO campaign on, 3–4, 8
  NATO obligations in, 171–72

# Cato Institute

Founded in 1977, the Cato Institute is a public policy research foundation dedicated to broadening the parameters of policy debate to allow consideration of more options that are consistent with the traditional American principles of limited government, individual liberty, and peace. To that end, the Institute strives to achieve greater involvement of the intelligent, concerned lay public in questions of policy and the proper role of government.

The Institute is named for *Cato's Letters*, libertarian pamphlets that were widely read in the American Colonies in the early 18th century and played a major role in laying the philosophical foundation for the American Revolution.

Despite the achievement of the nation's Founders, today virtually no aspect of life is free from government encroachment. A pervasive intolerance for individual rights is shown by government's arbitrary intrusions into private economic transactions and its disregard for civil liberties.

To counter that trend, the Cato Institute undertakes an extensive publications program that addresses the complete spectrum of policy issues. Books, monographs, and shorter studies are commissioned to examine the federal budget, Social Security, regulation, military spending, international trade, and myriad other issues. Major policy conferences are held throughout the year, from which papers are published thrice yearly in the *Cato Journal*. The Institute also publishes the quarterly magazine *Regulation*.

In order to maintain its independence, the Cato Institute accepts no government funding. Contributions are received from foundations, corporations, and individuals, and other revenue is generated from the sale of publications. The Institute is a nonprofit, tax-exempt, educational foundation under Section 501(c)3 of the Internal Revenue Code.

CATO INSTITUTE
1000 Massachusetts Ave., N.W.
Washington, D.C. 20001

DISCARD